Leisure Travel
A Marketing Handbook

Stanley C. Plog, Ph.D.

PEARSON

Prentice
Hall

Upper Saddle River, New Jersey 07458

Library of Congress Cataloging-in-Publication Data

Plog, Stanley C.
  Leisure travel : a marketing handbook / Stanley C. Plog.
    p. cm.
Includes index.
  ISBN 0-13-049317-1
  1. Travel—Marketing. 2. Travelers—Psychology. 3.
Travel—Psychological aspects. I. Title.
  G155.A1 P58 2003
  910'.68'8—dc21

                              2003009830

Editor-in-Chief: Stephen Helba
Executive Assistant: Nancy Kesterson
Executive Editor: Vernon R. Anthony
Director of Manufacturing and Production:
  Bruce Johnson
Editorial Assistant: Ann Brunner
Managing Editor: Mary Carnis
Production Liaison: Adele M. Kupchik
Senior Marketing Manager: Ryan DeGrote
Production Management: Pine Tree
  Composition, Inc.

Production Editor: Jessica Balch, Pine Tree
  Composition, Inc.
Manufacturing Manager: Ilene Sanford
Manufacturing Buyer: Cathleen Petersen
Creative Director: Cheryl Asherman
Senior Design Coordinator: Miguel Ortiz
Printer/Binder: Phoenix Color Corp.
Cover Design: Christopher Weigand
Cover Illustration: Getty Images/PhotoDisc
Cover Printer: Phoenix Color Corp.

Pearson Education LTD.
Pearson Education Australia PTY, Limited
Pearson Education Singapore, Pte. Ltd
Pearson Education North Asia Ltd

Pearson Education Canada, Ltd.
Pearson Educación de Mexico, S.A. de C.V.
Pearson Education—Japan
Pearson Education Malaysia, Pte. Ltd

10 9 8 7 6 5 4 3 2 1
ISBN 0-13-049317-1

To my many clients, business associates, and academic friends with whom I have shared the process of discovery and from whom I have learned so much. Your friendship has enriched me immensely. Travel truly is a wonderful field of exploration that brings people closer together and leads to greater understanding.

Contents

Preface

This book provides a different perspective on travel, based on the more than 35 years that I served virtually all aspects of the industry as a consultant and researcher. Major airlines, hotel chains, cruise lines, tour operators, rental car companies, resorts and destinations, travel media, and large travel agency conglomerates have been clients. These experiences provide an overview of the industry that I could not get if I had worked only in one segment, such as the airlines, hotels, or as a director of a tourism bureau. The range of experiences has allowed me to see similarities and differences across the field that otherwise would not have been possible. It has been a wonderful life experience and, to use the term of the psychologist Carl Rogers, I have felt self-fulfilled. I count as personal friends many people I met over the years, including clients, academicians, people in the press, executives in advertising agencies, and others. They have taught me much while giving freely of their time and their ideas as we worked jointly to solve problems or work through issues.

My views may be different or unique, but they grow out of trying to understand how to attack each situation in the hundreds of studies that I have personally conducted. The focus has been on trying to learn why people travel, why they don't, and how to understand the psychology and subtleties of the travel experience. To handle the new challenges that clients provided almost weekly, flexibility and open-mindedness have been qualities that are essential to achieve success. You can't approach any situation assuming that you already know the answers. After the long period that I have been associated with the industry, I am still amazed at how much there is to learn. I cover a lot of topics in the pages that follow, but the subject matter could easily have filled a volume three to four times its current size.

Although this is a marketing book, it focuses primarily on the psychology of travel—why people travel and why they don't, and how to reach and motivate them more effectively. Anyone who wants to capture greater market share must have good knowledge about the motivations, thoughts, and lifestyles of important market segments. Otherwise, advertising and promotional dollars for programs supporting these efforts miss their intended targets. The media-intensive culture of today exposes consumers to thousands of advertising messages daily through television, radio, and print publications. Weak, unfocused messages easily get lost in the clutter.

Special thanks belong to a number of persons who have helped by reviewing certain sections of the book about events with which they had intimate knowledge and by offering suggestions. These include Tony Antin, Joe Buhler, Barbara Colwell, Bob Cozzi, Kim Greenspan, Al Keahi, Don Lum, Murray Markin, Renee Monforton, Allan Muten, John Pelletier, Lily Shum, and David Swierenga. Their names are referenced in the text in the sections referring to specific events or help provided. Appreciation is also due to former colleagues and still friends at Plog Research who have helped with various materials, including John Antonello (President), Ruth Sharp (Vice President), and Loretta Valdez (Manager of Production Services). Finally, Vernon Anthony of Prentice Hall has been great to work with. He is a gem in the world of book publishing.

Stanley C. Plog

CHAPTER ONE

A Personal View of the Travel Industry

Colleagues tell a story about Albert Einstein during the time that he directed the Institute for Advanced Study at Princeton. While proctoring a final exam for one of his advanced physics classes, a student approached and said, "Excuse me, Dr. Einstein, but there must be a mistake. The questions are the same as in last year's exam." Einstein answered, "That's all right. You see, all of the answers have changed."

And so it is with travel. During the time I have worked in the field, clients have asked mostly the same questions. Their most common queries center on a few topics. "How can I motivate more people to travel?" "How can my destination (or airline, cruise line or hotel company) reach a bigger audience?" "How do I make my marketing programs more effective?" "What are the best prospect groups for me to target with my promotional messages?" "What media are most effective to reach my audience?" "What message(s) should I give?" Like Einstein suggested, the questions may be the same, but the answers have changed radically. Many millions more travel today. They make more informed and better choices about where they want to go, how they want to get there, and what they want to do while there than most travel executives could have imagined even a decade ago. To achieve success, companies have had to modify and enlarge the products they offer, target their markets better, change advertising and promotional materials dramatically, learn new ways to distribute their offerings, cope with new competition that arises constantly, and adapt to the Internet and other new technologies. Various chap-

1

ters address these changes and their implications for those who want to be part of an exciting and constantly challenging field.

As pointed out in various chapters, leisure travel is a growth industry and will continue on that path for the foreseeable future. Its rate of growth could be more dramatic, if the industry mends some of its ways. But the important point is that people want to travel—to get away and recharge their psychic batteries. They seek to do something very different from their daily routines and the pressures and strains of jobs or interpersonal relationships. Recharging can come in two opposite ways: a very active, energetic, and involving vacation trip, or one that is completely relaxing and perhaps even meditative.

Travel differs considerably from the views held about it by outsiders. It is a much more complex and confusing field than the uninformed could ever imagine. It is also seductive—attracting capable individuals who could do better financially if they chose other careers. And it is dynamic, providing an ever-changing array of opportunities and problems to deal with daily. Unknown to most, the travel industry has changed the social fabric of the industrialized world. And it will alter the future course and direction of many developing countries that see tourism as a way to bootstrap their economies. Over the years, it has developed its own language, sometimes not very intelligible by outsiders. Though most may know the meaning of jet-age, only those more acquainted with the industry can define time-share, rack rates, FITs, incentive travel, commission overrides, electronic ticketing, inclusive packages, code-share, event marketing, and so on. The industry also brings forth lots of emotion from those employed in the field. In conversations, they are likely to describe it with words like *exciting, demanding, challenging, rewarding, frustrating, ever-changing, dynamic, financially rewarding, financially limiting, intellectually stimulating, personally broadening,* and on and on. Friendships run deep, even among competitors, and last for decades. Although I have often heard discussions between executives expressing their puzzlement about the crazy new ideas of someone they know, less backstabbing seems to occur than in most other fields where I have also conducted research. Someone who does well with a new concept seems to generate mostly feelings of respect, rather than jealousy. Insiders recognize that numerous difficult situations must be mastered between the creation of an idea, bringing it to reality, and ensuring its success after launch.

Gaining understanding about some of travel's unique characteristics can make the industry more intelligible to those who want to make their organizations grow more rapidly, or for anyone considering a career in the field. You can achieve greater success if you have perspective on an industry, including important and significant events in its history, than by approaching the field de novo. Although my views may differ from those of most insiders, they come from more than three and a half decades of consulting work. During these very dynamic and fast-changing times, I saw tourism grow from an underappreciated contributor to world economies to the point where most nations now include tourism as part of the national policy and some have established cabinet-level tourism agencies. It's worthwhile to review some of the unique characteristics of this fascinating and ever-changing field. Your marketing and development plans may even benefit by gaining a little more background knowledge.

A COMPLEX AND CONFUSING INDUSTRY

Carl Icahn, the corporate investor who took over Trans World Airlines in 1985 and directed its operations until late in 1991, when he unloaded it in bankruptcy, once commented, "TWA was the worst investment I ever made." By his standards, it truly did not provide the financial returns he expected. On the surface, he lost money. In fact, he probably came out ahead, but not in the way he planned. His usual strategy was to take control of a company, often through a hostile takeover, drastically slash costs, and sell assets to recover the initial investment. Then, he'd make a large profit by selling what remains to another company or through a public offering. For manufacturing companies, this approach usually works quite well. Cut costs by closing plants with excess capacity and lay off workers. If the parent company has subsidiaries, sell these for an amount greater than their current values on the parent company's books. If everything goes as planned, the full value of the original purchase price has been recouped at this point. The smaller remaining parent company is then sold for a handsome profit. Applying that formula to TWA, Icahn sold its PARS reservation system (to Delta and Northwest), reduced spending for food and other in-flight services, and delayed purchases of new airplanes. Most fateful, he sold the airline's Heathrow landing slots and moved operations to the older, lower-cost Gatwick Airport. With that move, TWA no longer could connect its schedules with other international carriers through the most important international hub, London's Heathrow Airport. TWA's international operations suffered greatly as a result. A central question grows out of what happened: How could a guy with Icahn's financial savvy misjudge the situation so badly that he had to put the airline into bankruptcy twice? Well, travel is a service business and operates with essentially different ground rules in order to be successful. Manufacturing companies often have no direct contact with their customers. Black & Decker, Sunbeam, Hoover, and others distribute through retailers. Consumers don't notice management turmoil at one of these businesses and don't care, unless quality of the product suffers. For an airline, however, reducing staff ratios, cutting meal budgets, and other actions that negatively impact employee morale immediately get noticed by consumers—the passengers. But takeover artists from other industries often assume that their formulas from the past will work in a new environment. They believe they can provide the product at lower cost and turn a losing company into a winner. They apply skills honed through pulling up other companies that have gotten into trouble, and then quickly move on to their next adventure. Dozens of outsiders have stubbed their toes following their naïve assumptions and have damaged venerable travel enterprises in the process. Like others who entered from the world of finance, Icahn simply didn't understand the travel business and TWA went into a downward spiral from which it never recovered.

During the years that I directed two market research companies that I formed, I served a variety of industry segments. Clients included automobile manufacturers, beverage companies, food processors, large retail chains, ad agencies, entertainment and music businesses, government agencies at local and national levels, and more. I find each of these to be a piece of cake compared to travel. Take automotive, for example. It's a huge industry that nearly rivals travel in size. Looking at the U.S., there are roughly 22,000 new car dealers. They sell the cars, service them, and take in trades when customers need a new model. Although most are independent dealerships and not owned by the factories, the manufacturers maintain strict control over how they operate. Dealers must sell a minimum number of cars to retain their franchises, have their service staffs trained by factory specialists, build facilities that meet standards, and promote and sell the brands in ways that please the manufacturers. Dealers that don't measure up face pressures from the manufacturers to conform or lose their dealers' licenses. Tight control of the distribution channel is a fundamental fact in the automotive world. Less than 20 manufacturers account for most of the market, although most offer multiples brands (like GM's Chevrolet, Pontiac, Buick, Cadillac, Saturn, and GMC trucks). And each brand offers several models. But it doesn't take a lot of effort to learn how the system works.

Travel, in contrast, presents a labyrinth of confusing, interrelated companies, products, and services that cut across the distribution channel. The 25,000 retail travel agencies in the U.S. have declined from 36,500 before commission caps and cuts and probably will ultimately drop to about 22,000, the same number as auto dealerships. But any comparison stops there. Buying a car seems like a piece of cake. The dealer controls just about everything a customer needs. It sells the vehicle, offers financing, handles vehicle servicing after the sale through the manufacturer's warranty, and even takes in the old car on trade. And the dealers do that day in and day out, with little variation in their business practices. In contrast, booking a trip usually involves contact with many different companies, a host of individuals, and a lot of coordination effort. The U.S. has about 60 hotel brands but a total of over 60,000 hotel properties. And around 12,000 individuals, partnerships, and investment groups own the individual hotels and operate under franchise agreements with the chains. There aren't many airlines of importance (about 60 major carriers out of a worldwide total of nearly 650), but they have somehow confused everyone in the distribution system by frequently offering 100 or more fares on a single, competitive route. Some of the factors influencing fares include the carrier selected, time of day and day of week for departure, advance booking discounts, whether sold through a Web site or travel agency, class of service, special discounts available to certain types of travelers (senior citizen fares), and seasonal specials. In an interesting article, the *Los Angeles Times* examined a single United Airlines flight (# 106, Los Angeles International to Chicago O'Hare departing at 8:50 A.M.) and found 26 fares for that flight.[1] These varied from a low of $218.25 to a high of $1,924.25 one way, depending on class of service, advance booking time, and other factors. Fliers can never be certain that they are getting the best deal, leading to a sense of frustration among many. Most important, unlike an auto dealer that stocks only a few models (in different colors and equipment choices), a typical travel agency offers thousands of products to its clients. Selling airline seats and hotel rooms is the easy part. But how can agents be certain about the quality and location of hotels in cities they haven't visited, even those flagged under well-known brand names? What assurance do they have that a small hotel in the Tuscany area of Italy lives up to the description in its brochure? It probably isn't even listed in a common hotel directory or online databases used by agents. If a cruise is part of the trip, which are the best lines and the best ships of those lines? And what itinerary should be recommended for that client's cruise—the Caribbean, Alaska waters, the Mediterranean, or Asia? Can anyone keep up with the fine points of difference between all of the new ships coming online each year as the cruise lines continue to increase their capacity? Selecting an appropriate tour operator presents an even more confusing array of choices. Bob Whitley, President of the U.S. Tour Operators Association (USTOA), estimates that more than 2,500 tour operators serve the American market, although only about 100 are of sufficient size and have the financial backing to qualify for membership in the USTOA. My estimates agree. These smaller and sometimes odd companies offer jaunts to familiar places and expeditions to spots that are difficult to locate on a map. The number of tour operators continues to multiply each year because it's an easy product to assemble. How can anyone be expected to stay on top of which packages are the best and which tour operators offer consistent quality across all of their programs?

Major and minor destinations around the world number in the tens of thousands, each of which has a different ambience, price level, variety of things to do, and varying levels of quality for its local hotels, restaurants, and entertainment. Can any agent be certain that the travel suppliers used last year will continue of offer the same high-quality service and attention to clients this year at these destinations? Travel agents take heat from their clients if something goes wrong on a trip. Most travelers assume that an agent is an expert on travel and should have complete knowledge of everything he or she offers to the public. The task is daunting and difficult. And its rewards sometimes seem few, as we will see later.

Even within a single segment of the industry, the complexities can seem overwhelming. Running an airline can offer incredible daily challenges. If weather problems shut down a major airport like Chicago's O'Hare or Lon-

---

[1]*Los Angeles Times,* September 24, 2002, p. S4.

don's Heathrow, it grounds airplanes throughout the system—those that can't get out and those that can't get in and then on to their next destinations. These carriers' traffic schedulers earn their money because they know how to make the system fully operational again, usually by the next morning. Similar problems occur with other parts of the industry. If a cruise ship runs aground or has an engine problem, passengers may have to be sent home from a small village that lacks air service. And other cruises must be canceled or rescheduled that would have used the same ship for the next sailing. Even rental car companies have problems not recognized by others. For 10 years (1980 to 1990), I ran a small rental car company that I had formed (locations at LAX and SFO airports) as a marketing service to some of my automotive clients (Saab, Audi, Alfa Romeo, Peugeot, and others). They wanted the opportunity to get people behind the wheel of their vehicles who normally wouldn't consider walking into dealer showrooms. I still shudder at the problems I encountered daily because I had to turn over luxury cars to people unknown to me after they presented a small piece of plastic (a credit card) to an employee. Cars were involved in accidents, stolen by drivers or from drivers, driven to Florida on drug runs, used for stunts in movies and totaled (a Fiat in the movie *Fletch*), left at airport curbside check-ins, and abandoned in strange places. I received dozens of parking tickets that proved impossible to charge back to the renters. Whatever segment of the industry you might look at, just assume that complexity rules. Investors without a depth of experience should be well advised. You enter the field at your own risk. Stick to manufacturing companies. Then you might come out ahead!

EXCITEMENT AND CHALLENGES!

In a world where too many people seem bored by their jobs, the travel industry stands apart. In spite of its numerous problems, it offers excitement, intellectual challenge, and a sense of personal fulfillment to its professional work force that those in many fields might never experience . . . if you can handle its pressures! To succeed in almost any segment of the industry requires the energy level and personal commitment of a long-distance runner. Its intricacies and subtle interrelationships can challenge the intellects of even those with the highest IQs. And managing multiple tasks concurrently can make some feel like a juggler who spins plates on poles while keeping several balls in the air at the same time. Frustrations also abound. Leisure travelers generally have a "door to door" mentality in which they hold a travel company responsible for events that are beyond the control of that company. If bad weather cancels all flights into a city, an airline is expected to provide hotels and meals for the night in cities where hotels currently may be sold out. And, the next day, it must find ways to get passengers out on flights that already have high load factors. If a destination that was included in the itinerary of a tour operator or cruise line suddenly faces political instability, all previous plans get thrown out the window. The tour operator must locate a new city with enough rooms to handle the group and arrange for transportation to that city. Next, the task is to develop a new temporary tour program to fill the time that would have been spent in the troubled city, and continue to make tour guests feel relaxed and cared for. The cruise line also faces the challenge of finding a new port to replace the one that now cannot be entered and restock food and other supplies at the new port from unknown suppliers. New day tours have to be found to replace the ones that had to be canceled. For the most part, these are the expected challenges of daily life. Acts of terrorism can cause weeks or months of long days and nights before things return to normal for executives and others at travel companies. And, when the stresses and strains of the job become too heavy because of long hours of work and job stress, what do travel executives do? Most take a busman's holiday—they visit a destination that they especially like, hoping to recover sufficiently to take on new challenges when they return.

Few people in management positions in the industry, however, complain that they are bored with their jobs or "burned out" by the long hours and constant pressure. And few ever leave the field. Some may opt out temporarily, accepting better-paying positions in other industries, but most return, even if they can't equal salaries they received elsewhere. The adrenaline rush provided by being part of an airline, cruise line, or even a travel agency creates a sense of daily excitement. When problems occur, it's time to rise to the occasion and provide solutions. And, when things go smoothly, there's time to handle the rewarding parts of a job for which they were hired—develop new marketing programs, plan new itineraries, or ensure that the products delivered to travelers measure up to company standards. *Boredom?* Never! *Challenges?* Regularly! *Excitement?* Often! *Satisfaction?* Usually! Those who work in the field sometimes get asked by friends or acquaintances as to how they could also locate an interesting job in travel. Their current positions don't offer the level of excitement they desire. To outsiders, the grass still looks greener on the travel side of the fence.

All of this wouldn't be possible unless people wanted to take trips and go to places different from where they live. Fortunately they do. For centuries, leisure travel has occupied a special place in the hearts and minds of citizens throughout the world. And that desire has continued to grow as more nations reach levels of affluence that allow their citizens the opportunity to fulfill their dreams and visit lands that they had previously only read about or had heard described from friends and relatives. The joke gets told that, if you want to feel safe on the streets at night, carry a slide projector and pictures of your last vacation. Well, perhaps some people talk too much about their travels but, for the most part, descriptions about past trips usually interest friends and colleagues. Even strangers want to hear where you have been and how you liked it. They want to take more exciting trips and believe that they can learn from your experiences. If you happen to be in the industry, people are likely to find your conversation more interesting than talking with an accountant, lawyer, or real estate salesperson about what they do at their jobs. Yes, travel is interesting, educational, exciting, and even glamorous.

Just about everyone knows that technology has changed how we work and adapt to life. But few recognize that travel has also transformed the psychology of the entire world, probably more so than the impact of technology over the last couple of decades. Not only does the world seem smaller and more intertwined, but those who travel have a greater understanding of strange and exotic cultures than they can get by reading books or articles. Many argue that leisure travel offers a way to world peace. Countries that depend on tourism don't want to go to war because it would cut off their major revenue source. And tourists and the natives they visit learn more about each other, hopefully leaving most encounters with mutual feelings of respect and understanding. The changes that have occurred in travel and in the world are so dramatic that I could not foresee most of them when I reported on my first travel-related project in 1967.

A SEDUCTIVE INDUSTRY

Travel is fun, which makes working in the industry enjoyable. Because so many like their jobs, travel probably attracts a better class of people than a lot of other industries. A large number of entrepreneurs who started tour companies, travel agencies, resorts, and airlines did so because they wanted travel to be a continuing part of their lives. Their enthusiasm for what they do is mirrored in the attention and care they give to handling their guests and clients. And they still hang around when they are long past retirement age. As was mentioned, competitors tend to respect each other, even while still trying to steal market share. Because the industry still has room for new ideas, a fresh group of entrepreneurs arises on a regular basis, thereby helping to change the products and services offered to the public. And these folks have some of the spirit, drive, and personal interest in travel of those who started companies after World War II. Few start companies because they believe this is the industry where they can make the most money. Other industries will often provide better rewards. Travel also has its share of those who are less than honest and take advantage of their guests and suppliers. Their actions tend to get known by others, however, which limits the degree of success they might have. It may be a large industry, but it's surprising how small it can seem at times. If you don't know about someone, call a few friends and you'll get the scoop on whether or not that person speaks the truth or with a forked tongue. In general, its complexity, variety, and ever-changing nature make travel a fascinating field in which to work or study. I seldom hear friends and associates complain about the routine nature of their daily activities. Rather, new challenges arise constantly that test one's ability to be inventive, flexible, and resourceful.

Travel has a seductive side. It attracts and keeps very capable people who could do better financially in other fields. Except for a few top executives who head up major corporations, pay scales generally fall behind most major industries, a point that is reviewed in the next chapter. Yet, people stay in their jobs. Why? They simply enjoy its excitement and daily challenges. Barbara Colwell, a long-time friend who worked at TWA, accepted a much higher-paying job at CBS television but returned to TWA because she found her new position too boring. Later she joined Cigna Insurance's property and casualty division in a senior marketing position. Ultimately she was promoted to Senior Vice President of Marketing, the only woman to hold that position in the company's history. But she continued to look for a way to return to travel. When asked by a reporter for *Money* magazine why she would give up unvested stock options worth a high six figures to return to travel (she was also featured on the cover), she replied, "Because I simply love travel." Most travel agents receive close to minimum wages for their efforts, but they stick to their jobs even in the face of pressures by airlines and other travel suppliers to cut them out of distribution channels and reduce their chances to make a living. Although airline pilots receive very high salaries because of their strong union contracts, and mechanics also do quite well, inflight attendants hardly make a living wage at most carriers. But they hold on to their jobs and seldom threaten to strike. They like what they do, even though they may have flown to the some places hundreds of times. Check-in personnel at airports fall near the bottom of pay scales across industries, but turnover is low. At the time of writing of this book, an airline had just granted a modest raise to its airport ground personnel, the first after eight years of no adjustments in salary. Directors of tourism offices and convention and visitors bureaus (CVBs) face special problems, a topic that is reviewed later in this book. Strong political pressures and public criticism can make their lives difficult. Yet they also usually hang around, refusing to look for better-paying or less controversial positions that they might find elsewhere. Travel is like a drug. Once exposed to the industry, it seems that people have a tough time kicking the habit. They get their daily fix by meeting new challenges and seeking out opportunities. Even when better opportunity knocks, they tend to stay where they are.

Airlines perhaps best demonstrate the degree to which people want to be part of what they perceive to be an exciting and challenging field. From the time of the founding of commercial aviation in the early 1930s through the mid-1990s, the airlines collectively broke even. Profits since then until the terrorist attacks on September 11, 2001 were obliterated by losses approaching $30 billion in the three-year period of 2001 through 2003. Yet the romance of the skies lures new money to its doorsteps on a regular basis. In 1978, the commercial aviation industry was deregulated, providing an opportunity for the birth of startup carriers. Although nearly 200 airlines either operated for a period of time or had active applications to the Federal Aviation Authority for licenses, only a handful of those startups exist today. A few, like People Express, gave the appearance that they might change the character of the industry with low fares and a non-union work force approach. But, in spite of its early success, People Express collapsed under the weight of intense competitive pricing by the major carriers, poor route and schedule planning, and inadequate accounting procedures. New carriers have begun elsewhere around the world as deregulation has taken hold—in Europe, Australia, Canada, and in Asia, to a slight degree. The results usually mirror those in the U.S.—a collapse after a promising start. If an industry can't show growth and profitability, it should have trouble attracting venture money. Yet, investors still take the gamble of starting new airlines in the face of huge odds. I have served as a consultant to several startup carriers. In each case, optimism abounds, based on statistics the founders dig up to justify assumptions that a market exists and that they have found a new formula for success. In the din of their overwhelming enthusiasm, it's difficult for me to get management to understand what they should do to maximize their chances for success. Their frenetic energy too often blinds them to the realities of the mountains they must climb before they can achieve success. They simply want to be part of the excitement that surrounds aviation. The only winners are the Wall Street investment firms that get a percentage of the money raised for each new venture, and the high-priced specialty lawyers who help put the packages together.

A bizarre incident reveals how strong the attraction to travel can be. I was called to meet with the president and majority owner of an airline who had just put up more than a million dollars more of his own money to save it from bankruptcy. The carrier had been around for a few years but had a succession of top-level management changes and was still losing money. The money guy (and president) was a very successful surgeon. Like too many others, he was drawn by the allure of being part of the aviation industry. He finally took control when he recognized that he could lose his early investment because of the downward course over the past year. At the time I met with him, he was so nervous and distracted that he could not focus on what I tried to tell him that he must do to save his airline. He had a financial guillotine hanging over his head. He ultimately lost it all when the airline finally shut down. Throughout the time, he continued his surgical practice because he needed the income, but I wondered how he could maintain his operating room skills facing those pressures. I knew I would not want him opening me up. I still wonder what made him think that he could understand the airline business or why he would be willing to risk so much of his personal fortune on a high-risk venture.

Travel continues to attract people to lower-paying jobs and keeps them in place in the face of crisis after crisis. In the end, perhaps that's the correct attitude. Why not work at something you enjoy, in spite of the difficult challenges and potential meager monetary rewards, rather than pursue a career in an industry that seems less exciting and offers little feeling of romance? Travel is seductive. But that's why it also can offer a life-long feeling of enjoyment, excitement, and a reason to get up every morning eager to get to work.

CHAPTER TWO

An Industry that Changed the World

How people travel and the importance they place on travel in their lives has changed dramatically over time, especially since the end of World War II. Travel has become a more central part of their lives and is viewed as a right, rather than a privilege. In fact, someone who doesn't take pleasure trips seems odd to most of us. We think they are too serious about life. Getting away from it all for a period of time, most of us believe, recharges our psychic batteries so we can handle the pressures and strains that we experience daily. It also exposes us to new ideas, providing perspective that can make us wiser. We gain understanding of how people in other countries differ from us or are similar. But travel didn't always occupy this lofty position. It has had to compete with many other ways that people can spend their discretionary income. It's useful to understand some of the changes that have happened to place travel in proper perspective. Such understanding can help in developing more effective marketing programs.

A BRIEF HISTORY OF LEISURE TRAVEL

If we want to understand leisure travel, we need to know something about the conditions that make it possible. Although travel's history goes back for centuries, most of its phenomenal growth has happened after World War II, and in large part since the mid-1970s. Why? It relates to what each society considers to be the proper relationship between work and play. People are the offspring of their cultures, and lingering images from generations past encourage or discourage their interest in venturing to distant lands. Living in an age when it seems natural to get away on a vacation, we can fail to recognize that leisure travel for the masses is a very recent happening. Even for the majority of the twentieth century, most people had neither the means nor the desire to take expensive trips. A 1971 article in *The Cornell Hotel & Restaurant Administration Quarterly* summarized presentations at various conferences on travel during the year and points to the dismal view about the prospects for growth.[1] Walter Mathews, a friend and highly respected travel marketing consultant, speaking at the annual conference of the Travel & Tourism Research Association, stated that

> there is no travel industry as such but merely interested economic participants. . . . We people in the travel industry make the mistake of thinking everyone is like us, that they like to travel and all we need to do is to let them know about what we have to offer. . . . (But) in our industry, we provide travel as a fringe benefit which results in travel oriented people taking our jobs. It's like hiring alcoholics to sell whiskey. Our promotion may instill a desire for travel but not get people to plunk down their dollars and get over the insecurities. We must make travel part of people's life style. (p. 8)

William S. Blair, publisher of *Harper's* magazine, speaking at the same conference, gave a similar theme and pointed out that "more people with more money simply doesn't add up" (to more trip taking). He went on to suggest that a blue-collar family earning $15,000 or more (adequate to go by air at that time) has a different lifestyle than a middle manager with a similar income. The blue-collar person, he believed, would probably buy a television or camper, rather than take a trip (p. 8). These dismal assessments of the state of personal travel reflect the spirit of the times. These speakers may not have recognized important changes that were underway, but they expressed some dominant concerns in the industry. *Travel did not always measure high as a priority in people's lives!*

Leisure travel depends on four conditions: (1) sufficient time away from work, (2) good travel infrastructure (roads, airports, and/or public transportation), (3) adequate income or financial reserves to afford travel, and (4) a high level of desire to travel. On the first point, little personal travel occurred during most of the world's history because work didn't allow time for vacations and companies didn't have retirement plans. In agrarian societies, most couples wanted large families to work the lands, and a bigger family meant that more children could support the parents when they could no longer work. In the industrial age, however, children were a financial burden because they couldn't help support the family until they reached their teenage years. At that time, workers usually left their jobs only when they had grown too old to per-

---

[1]*The Cornell Hotel & Restaurant Administration Quarterly*, February, 1971, pp. 8–12.

form the strenuous duties demanded or management decided to replace them with younger, stronger workers. When that happened, role reversal occurred. The elderly became a financial burden to their still active children, who now had to support them. As recently as the mid-nineteenth century, few people in Europe, the U.S., or elsewhere in the world expressed much interest in personal travel. Generations grew up, raised families, and died in the communities where they were born. Since most friends and relatives were close at hand, little need existed to venture out to see others. The old folks who no longer worked but had the free time to travel lacked the money to get away and were too old and feeble to venture out.

The concept of retirement with guaranteed income, fulfilling the first necessary condition to make travel possible for the masses, came about slowly and depended on a set of mostly fortuitous circumstances. Author Mary-Lou Weisman summarized the history of how planned retirement occurred.[2] "In the beginning," she points out, "there was no retirement. There were no old people. In the Stone Age, everyone was fully employed until age 20, by which time nearly everyone was dead, usually of unnatural causes. . . . As the centuries passed, the elderly population increased. By early medieval times, their numbers had reached critical mass." Patricide became all too common in post Medieval Europe, she adds, as some sons sought to either get rid of the burden of their parents or get their inheritance early. The big change came from a surprising source. "In 1883, Chancellor Otto Von Bismarck of Germany . . . to help his countrymen resist [the] blandishments [of Marxists] . . . announced that he would pay a pension to any non-working German over age 65. Bismarck was no dummy. Hardly anyone lived to be 65 at the time." Bismarck doesn't appear on anyone's scale of the most benevolent leaders of the ages, but he established the concept of paid retirement and how long we should work—until the age of 65.

The Industrial Revolution changed family structure dramatically. As mentioned, people who work in factories view children as a liability, not an asset. Kids can't help out in the fields if the family doesn't farm. Instead, children must be supported financially until they are old enough to go out and earn their own living. As a result, average family size decreased dramatically, beginning in the nineteenth century. Some factories began offering modest retirement stipends in Western countries before the beginning of the twentieth century, but the big push came from another source—the Great Depression of the 1930s. The New Deal of President Franklin Delano Roosevelt recognized that, without enough work for everybody, you could handle the problem better by creating jobs for young people and putting the old folks out to pasture. Thus, the concept of Social Security came into full flower. The concepts of

---

[2]Mary-Lou Weisman, "The History of Retirement, From Early Man to A.A.R.P.," *New York Times*, March 21, 1999, p. 19.

pensions and retirement plans, whether through businesses or the government, are now firmly embedded into the psyches of all modern civilizations.

Taking a two- to three-week vacation, which provides an opportunity for personal travel by average persons before the age of retirement, is also a relatively recent idea. The concept began in the mid-nineteenth century but did not reach its fruition until the decades following World War II. Ruling classes and the idle rich may have always traveled to new and exotic places to alleviate boredom in their lives, but most people continued to follow the biblical directive of a day of rest after six days of work. The Bible itself does not talk about taking vacations or holidays. If it did, we would undoubtedly have made it a part of our lives centuries ago. Rather, the seventh day had the purpose of rest and relaxation to recover from a strenuous week and, most important, to meditate and show our reverence to God. No mention is made of the need for longer periods of rest. Those who traveled in ancient times, like St. Paul, usually had a purpose—for commerce or to proselytize, in St. Paul's case.

The Henry Ford Museum in Dearborn chronicles the birth of the modern American vacation in a book it produced:

> The modern vacation originated in the mid-nineteenth century when [some] business executives and loyal office employees received time off with pay— usually one or two weeks—in order to recover from the strenuousness of their "brain work." . . . As early as 1855, a *New York Times* editorial suggested "Vacations for businessmen" as a way to refresh the body and mind, while *Demorest's* in 1866 urged that "It is women above all others who need this annual holiday . . . as a release from the pressures of incessant household care."[3]

The Ford guidebook also points out that a consistent push toward annual vacations began in the early twentieth century when more than a third of manufacturing employees received paid vacations as early as 1910. But most industries still had no policy for annual leave, feeling that the work performed was not sufficiently stressful to require release from jobs on a yearly basis. The big change came after World War II, when unions began demanding paid vacations as a standard part of every employment agreement. Europeans place a higher value on time away from their jobs than their American cousins, who have followed a more Puritan ethic to define the proper balance between work and play. Residents of the Continent and the U.K. have more vacation days (holidays, as these often are called) than their American counterparts. Asia generally lagged behind both regions, but unions in various countries have fought for and have won significant paid leave concessions for workers in most of the region since the 1960s.

In part, the slow growth of leisure travel in most industrial societies also relates to the second condition. Inadequate methods of transportation made

---

[3]*Americans on Vacation,* published by Henry Ford Museum and Greenfield Village, 1990, p. 8.

getting anywhere quite difficult until the nineteenth century was well underway. Whether by horseback or buggy, poorly developed roads and pathways limited the distance covered on most journeys to a range of 15 to 30 miles each day. This distance is too short to get to most places that people might want to visit, and even one day of bouncing around in a buggy could be arduous and tiring, diminishing the value of getting away. A day's travel didn't produce much change in the landscape or scenery, so why travel unless you had to? A nationwide railroad network was expanding by 1840, and relatively cheap ticket prices made it the common person's mode of travel whenever greater distances were involved. But these journeys could also be long with uncomfortable conditions, particularly before the more common use of Pullman sleeping cars in the 1860s. Sleepers still failed to remove major discomforts. Steam heat didn't appear until 1861, and electric lighting only came around by 1887. Large passenger steamboats developed concurrently with trains but were slower and more expensive. Both forms of transportation required extended periods of confinement with strangers, often a poor beginning or ending to a planned vacation.

Railroads reached their peak mileage by 1916, after which the automobile began its steady climb to dominance as the transportation mode of choice for personal travel, including leisure trips. It offers unprecedented freedom of movement at low cost and allows weekends to become getaways without the necessity of an overnight stay. From 1915 on, a system of roads was developing in the U.S., particularly in the Northeast, that ultimately would become the backbone for nationwide motoring. By the 1920s, all major transportation systems were in place to support broad-scale leisure travel—railroads, steamships, and an extensive road network for business and pleasure driving. Europe followed a somewhat similar path, but the development of a vastly superior railroad network allowed people on the Continent and in the U.K. to experience the joys of longer getaways earlier than in America.

Rising affluence among industrialized nations during the latter half of the twentieth century provided the basis for the third condition, financial reserves that make personal travel possible. Social Security, combined with expanded retirement plans built into union contracts, provides workers with a sense of personal security. They now feel comfortable about taking trips because they have just about all of the material goods they feel they need—a well-furnished home, a car or two, and even adequate money to support expensive hobbies. Some call this the age of "affluenza." Many people own so much that they don't know what to buy next. Even trips can lose a sense of excitement because the vacationers come away with a sense they have been there and done that before. But, make no mistake, people throughout the world now have the income and financial stability to take the kinds of trips that kings and queens a century ago could only dream about.

Two golden ages of travel occurred during the twentieth century that helped create the fourth and final condition—a desire to take leisure trips. These two time periods, although brief, helped fuel the need to escape from our relatively routine and often boring lives to experience the glamour and excitement that comes when we explore the world in which we live. Each period grew out of unplanned social changes. In the mid-1920s, the first golden travel age was about to happen, at least for the Western world. World War I, ending in 1917, jolted America out of its sense of isolation. Returning GIs, many of whom had never ventured further than 50 miles from their farm homes, now had a sense of how other people lived, loved, and played. A number of them wanted to reach out and explore more of the world they had not seen. Everything was in place to make it happen. Stately ocean liners provided comfort and a party atmosphere on board for the five-day cruise across the Atlantic, a lifestyle also popularized in movies in the 1930s. A great railroad system had developed in Europe, some with storied histories that offered convenient connections between large and small cities. Grand hotels also sprang up in Europe and the U.S. to complement an elegant lifestyle. The spirit and feeling of the Roaring Twenties also added to the sense that these were exciting times. Though few could live out their travel dreams because of the cost and the time required for a trip, this age of elegance and adventure created a desire to visit other lands—someday in the future. Some soldiers from the Great War, as it was called, didn't return home, at least immediately. They lived bohemian lives in the great cities of Europe as they honed their skills to become some of the best known novelists of the twentieth century. With vivid descriptions of foreign lands as a backdrop for their novels, they stirred the imaginations of their readers with their storytelling and created a sense of adventure and excitement that comes from travel. They found an eager audience for their writings among soldiers who had seen some of the same unique and historic places and wished they could return. Paris particularly became a favorite refuge for intellectuals and those with new ideas. Only a few average Americans could afford to take leisurely trips to the Continent or England, but it became a mark of social prestige and status among upper-class society to take grand European vacations. Wealthy industrialists created many of the grand hotels and luxury resorts that sprang up in places that had dramatic settings and vista views. Steamship lines and railroads competed to provide memorable levels of service, and motor car touring became popular as roads improved throughout Europe. Most destinations retained their unique character and charm because tourism didn't overwhelm local cultures and lifestyles. A traveler could visit places that truly were different from where he or she lived. The images created by popular authors survive today beyond their books and short stories. Travel writers continue to use descriptive phases penned by Ernest Hemingway, T. S. Eliot, F. Scott Fitzgerald, Marcel Proust, Ezra Pound, and others of the era in their articles for magazines and newspaper travel sections. Their impact shows up in airline destination advertising that tries to create a desire to visit the spots that they serve. This was an age of elegance in travel that didn't last long, only about 15 years between the mid-1920s and the beginning of World War II. However, it helped stimulate an intense desire to travel for pleasure among people throughout the world and shaped many of the images we still hold of these destinations.

World War II interrupted travel growth for up to two decades, but it ultimately had the same impact as the Great War and set the stage for more tourism and the next golden age of travel. American GIs, who generally came from small towns across America, brought back a new sophistication about the world and a desire to see more of it. But the pickup in travel was not immediate. Rebuilding had to be done in most Western nations, and these temporary soldiers and sailors were serious about getting an education through the GI bill and finding good jobs. In fact, the common view about the dim prospects for leisure travel's future led American Airlines to make one of the classic blunders in judgement of the times. It sold its North Atlantic airline routes (called American Overseas Airways, at that time) to Pan Am in September 1950 because it thought there would never be sufficient demand to support the operation. Not until decades later was American able to reestablish its presence in Europe, belatedly trying to make up for its earlier mistake.

The second golden age of travel lasted slightly over two decades, from the late 1950s to just before the dawn of the 1980s. If the first served society's upper crust, the second belonged to its middle class. Longer vacations, guaranteed by an increasing number of union contracts that also became part of white-collar workers' rights, along with rapidly rising wealth in the United States and Canada, provided the necessary conditions to allow mass travel. Although great novelists no longer congregated in Paris or the old, familiar romantic spots of the world, a growing group of travel writers churned out endless reams of copy to describe the wonders of foreign lands. But two other events were needed to propel that growth.

The first was the rise of a viable commercial aviation sector that made a reliable, safe, and generally affordable transportation system possible. Although good air transport really began in the late 1930s with the introduction of the twin-engine Douglas DC3, commercial airplanes that were under design at the start of the war were hurried into production by the War Department and converted to transport use. The four-engine DC4s and the bigger and better DC6s provided a new level of inflight comfort with wider aisles, more headroom, and pressurized cabins. Europe could now be reached within a day's travel rather than a five-day cruise. Many more destinations opened up to the traveling public, including some in more remote parts of the globe. A big contributor to travel growth was the rise of ABCs (advance booking charters). These *non-scheds* (non-scheduled airlines) did not serve regular routes with fixed schedules. They fit in a loophole of government regulations that allowed "affinity" groups to book flights for their members. Thus, German-American clubs were able to go to Germany, Italian-American clubs to Italy, camera clubs to almost anywhere, and so on. People joined clubs whether or not they qualified for membership to get the cheap fares. The charter carriers, such as World Airways (no longer around), didn't organize the clubs. They simply served them. Fares were often a third to half of the cost of flying on a major carrier because non-scheds had much lower operating costs (non-union crews and no advertising expenses). Tens of thousands took advantage of this low-cost travel. But members also paid a price in lack of convenience. Trips had a definite length (usually 10 days to two weeks), each flight dropped off and picked up at a specific location, and you had to take your trip at a time the affinity group selected. And, if a mechanical problem grounded the aircraft assigned to your trip, you might have to wait several days until it was fixed or another airplane could be diverted to pick you up because non-scheds did not have backup aircraft available. Nevertheless, group travel blossomed by filling a need in the mass market.

But it was the introduction of commercial jets that changed the face of the world more than any other factor, along with the willingness of governments throughout the globe to build the infrastructure to support the expansion of both business and leisure travel. New airplanes require years for development, from concept to takeoff. This delay provided governmental agencies with time to plan and build airports for an eventual reality. It may be difficult to believe today, but airports were originally planned to provide maximum passenger comfort and convenience. A new romance and language became associated with air travel. Our vocabulary now includes "jet set," and the travel patterns and habits of this group established styles and trends that have been emulated by the less wealthy wanabes.

The British De Havilland Comet initiated commercial jet service when BOAC (now British Airways) carried the first passengers on April 12, 1952. The true workhorses of the era were the Boeing 707 (first flight on October 26, 1958—Pan Am, New York–Paris) and the Douglas DC8 (both United and Delta initiating service on September 18, 1959). These planes have set the standards for commercial aviation since that time and are still in service throughout the world. Flight times were cut in half from the older piston-powered airplanes, with a London–New York schedule under six hours. The capitals and villages of even the most distant countries around the world became accessible because of shortened travel times and lowered commercial air fares that resulted from the greater operating efficiencies of the jets. They simply didn't have to be serviced as often as propeller aircraft. A leisure travel boom began on a scale previously unknown. The outer islands of Hawaii, until then just sleepy sugar and pineapple plantations, blossomed as prime destinations when major resorts were built, made possible by inter-island air travel. Small villages in Europe refurbished castles to serve as historic attractions or small hotels. Even remote Pacific islands showcased their relaxed lifestyles after they built airports. It truly was a golden age for mass travel. Airports were new, with facilities designed for passenger ease, and generally close to city centers. In most places, automobile parking was within walking distance of departure gates. Rental cars at the other end of a trip were on airport grounds. No shuttle bus to an off-airport location was required. And, obviously, there were no security lines to check through. You simply presented yourself at the ticket counter or gate and were welcomed aboard. Airlines, operating under government regulations that determined route structures and controlled ticket prices, competed on the basis of service. Constant battles to gain market share led to numerous improvements in on-board meals and amenities. If a flight lasted an hour and 15 minutes or more, a meal was served. Now, to reduce expenses, food typically isn't served until flight time approaches three hours and sometimes not at all. In today's market, fares for business class and first class are several times higher across the North Atlantic than for a coach seat. The airlines simply charge what the market will bear to maximize their revenue. But throughout the 1950s and 1960s (really, until deregulation in 1978), first class was never self-supporting. The premium for a first-class seat over coach between New York and Los Angeles for much of the time was only $15.00. For that difference, a passenger not only had more room, but free drinks and more attention from the inflight crew. TWA also offered chateaubriands cooked on board, not precooked and just warmed inflight. Airlines even promoted their affiliations with Club 21 in New York or that they had hired world-class chefs to prepare their menus. In coach, seat pitch standard was 34 inches and occasionally 36 inches (as in a Western Airlines campaign). Now it comes in at 32 inches, and sometimes even 31.

Travel had comfort, convenience, and affordability—all at the same time. And those who took advantage of the opportunity still could discover a world that had retained its uniqueness and charm. Although growth rates for international travel were compounding, travel abroad began from a relatively small base of travelers. Tourists didn't dominate any city. Small villages and towns welcomed visitors with a friendship not typically experienced today because few outsiders had ever come calling prior to that time. Crowds of tourists may have been just around the corner, in a time sense, but all was leisurely then. A visitor could savor the history and glories of the past that famous authors had written about while still enjoying the comforts of the present. In time, tourists would overwhelm small villages, especially as escorted tours became more popular among the less savvy, less venturesome travelers. In the late 1940s, a cruise ship arrived once a week in Hawaii, carrying about 400 passengers. Today more than 60 twin-aisle jets built by Boeing and Airbus land there daily, each carrying about as many passengers as a cruise ship of that more leisurely era.

For a couple of brief moments in time, travel could stir the imaginations and emotions of people in a way that cannot be repeated. It offered more contrasts to our daily lives than currently are possible. As the world becomes more homogeneous, travelers expect to sleep every night in three- or four-star hotels in all major cities and be served by a staff that speaks English. Even gourmet restaurants offer meals that replicate eateries back home, and a McDonald's is probably just around the corner for those who desire traditional American fast food. Fewer unpleasant surprises greet unsuspecting travelers. But they also have less opportunity to experience the sense of discovery that comes from visiting places that differ in dramatic ways from where they live. Now even small villages in the English countryside can seem overrun with tourists, and the natives not engaged in the travel business would just as soon stay out of their way. Much has changed since the 1970s. The biggest and most successful travel providers focus on mass markets but may lose a sense of personal touch with their clients in the process. And large segments of the travel industry offer a commodity product in which they compete mostly on price rather than on service. Travel is more available for a broad range of income levels throughout the world, but it also is less unique and educational. Shed a tear for times past that will return nevermore. For several decades now, the world has met the four criteria that allow most people to travel, specifically time availability, excellent infrastructure, personal wealth, and a desire to take leisure trips. But some events also occurred in more recent history that kicked along the travel bug even more, a topic covered in the next section.

TRAVEL: THE NEW NECESSITY

An unknown author penned a ditty that fits what has happened to travel in developed nations:

> *Little luxury, don't you cry;*
> *You'll be a necessity, by and by.*

How true for travel. What was once considered a very expensive luxury is now viewed as a necessary antidote to the difficulties of modern living. The travel mobility of populations in today's world may make it difficult for many to realize that it wasn't always that way. As recently as the mid-1960s, according to Gallup surveys released by the Air Transport Association, only 42 percent of the U.S. adult population had ever been up in a commercial airliner. Today that ratio has reversed completely, with 80 percent having flown and up to a third taking to the skies each year. Unrecognized by most social historians, the basic psychology of the nation has changed dramatically. People who lived most of their adult years as cautious, conservative, stay-at-homes have become more venturesome, relaxed, personally expansive, globe-trotting sophisticates.

Most projects for my clients in the mid-1960s to the early 1970s centered on how to get more people to consider taking a vacation trip—especially by commercial airline. A large multiclient-sponsored study completed by my first company (Behavior Science Corporation/BASICO) provided the opportunity to probe the psychology of why some people travel and others do not (reviewed in depth in Chapter 3). Two-hour in-depth interviews probed deep into the personal backgrounds and history of why some people traveled less and especially why they avoided air travel. The study provided a clear understanding of how the culture of the nation changed after World War II and into the 1960s. At the time, a philosophy of hard work and saving for the future reigned supreme. Most adults had experienced the Great Depression of the 1930s, followed by the war. They worried that such man-made catastrophes could repeat. The work ethic that built the nation was reinforced by these events. Long-distance pleasure travel seemed to be a relatively expensive and somewhat frivolous activity. It could not compete with the perceived need to save for a rainy day, for retirement, or setting aside dollars to purchase household furnishings or home improvement projects. People generally spent most of their disposable income on practical use items even when they reached retirement age and had the freedom to pursue long-time dreams. Travel was considered a luxury that was expensive and short lived. As recently as the early 1960s, people performed a mental equation that compared the cost of a vacation to the material goods they could buy instead, such as a new dining room set, a washer and dryer, or a down payment on a new car. Vacation trips often lost out in this comparison. A purchase of something for use at home, they reasoned, would last 10 to 15 years. But the same money put into a vacation trip was over and done with in two weeks with no lasting benefits.

A new psychology began developing in the late 1960s and came to fruition in the 1970s. It arose with the sons and daughters of this hard-working and very productive group, the "greatest generation," as Tom Brokaw has called them. Unlike their Depression-scarred parents, young people had an anti-materialistic attitude that suggested that *experiences in life and relationships with people are more important than owning things*. The trips you share with someone you care about, they believed, create cherished memories that last a lifetime. In contrast, the goods you buy have a limited life. These will wear out in 10 to 15 years, long before the important memories of your experiences in life have faded from your mind. Their culture also focused on doing what you want to do—now, not later. The baby boom generation had never known the tough times of a depression or the horrors of war. Relative prosperity had always been their lot in life since their parents tended to indulge them in material goods and shield them from the tough times of their own generation. This younger group assumed that the comfortable life they had always known would not change in the future. Aided by the new low leisure air fares that came with the arrival of jets and the impact of charter flights on non-sched airlines, enormous numbers of teens and young adults took to the skies to venture far and wide. They left with little money in their pockets and little thought about when they might return. They covered the world, visiting strange and exotic places, many of which their parents had not even read about. Arthur Frommer made his fortune and established a lasting travel company with a series of books that followed a successful format that began with *Europe on Five Dollars a Day*. Young people learned to survive while spending very little on their trips but enjoying a sense of discovery and adventure. They believed that the special moments and experiences of their travels created memories that would last a lifetime. They enjoyed meeting and sharing their lives with citizens in other cultures and learning that, after all, most people are pretty much alike. Appreciating important moments on those trips and remembering those experiences to share later with others helped form their personal psychology that continues with them today. In visiting foreign lands, the boomers seemed oblivious to the need to settle down, work hard, and build up a comfortable nest egg since they anticipated that the future would always be as comfortable as the present. A job could always wait until later. Instead, an international trip upon graduation became the rite of passage for many high school students, to be repeated during summer college breaks. A generation became hooked on travel and considered it to be a part of everyday life. And they now pass on their "traveling feet" to their offspring as part of a value system they assume is common to people of all ages.

The pleasures of travel enjoyed by the young not only affected their lifestyles but changed their parents' views of life as well. While their offspring hopped from country to country with no thought for tomorrow, older generations came more and more to feel that they were leading rather deprived lives. Their children were enjoying life, while the parents continued to work hard and build equity. Perhaps, the old folks reasoned, they had needlessly held back on enjoying the fun things in life, especially considering their current level of financial security. They became convinced that the golden tomorrow they had dreamed about and planned for might never happen because of a sudden illness or accident. They might as well enjoy today and the pleasures it can bring while there still is a today. Ultimately, large numbers of the parents of boomers expressed the view that, "If I'm ever going to have fun, it better be now while I still have my health and am able to travel." And, having seen that their children truly had little concern about money and financial security, they questioned why they should leave such a sizeable inheritance. If the kids truly didn't want the money and might also spend it unwisely, then perhaps it's best to enjoy the fruits of their own labors—now. The desire for travel moved to a higher place on their list of priorities. The older folks took to the roads and the skies like no other similar aged generation had done previously. Even for them, leisure travel came to be perceived as a psychological necessity. Younger folks tend to see it as a necessary relief from the perceived stresses and strains that today's world places on you daily. At least one trip a year helps keep the mind and soul together, and two or more are better. Their parents came to the conclusion that travel is a welcome reward for years of hard work, self-denial, and delay of gratification while trying to guarantee a financially secure future.

This dramatic 180-degree turnabout can be summarized in the following simple equations:

Changed Views about Leisure Travel
1965

    Travel = A luxury offering only short-term benefits

    Material goods = A necessity with long-term benefits

1980 and beyond

    Travel = A psychological necessity with long-term benefits

    Material goods = Not as necessary and offers only short-term benefits

These patterns continue today. Boomers, now entering middle age and the empty-nest stage, continue to have the travel spirit they possessed when they were young. Their parents, now in their mid-sixties and seventies, and even older, continue to travel like no generation before them. Leisure travel truly falls into the cultural category of a psychological necessity rather than an expensive luxury. And it will continue to remain so. The need for regular getaways is now part of the core values of citizens in most developed nations.

TRAVEL: THE NEW 800-POUND GORILLA ON THE BLOCK

In case you hadn't noticed some important changes during the last few decades, travel has grown to become the largest industry in the U.S. and the world. What was once a relatively small part of the economies of most nations as late as the 1960s has bolted ahead of industries that you might think are much larger. According to the World Tourism Organization (WTO),[4] the travel industry now accounts for 12 percent of the world's economy. Its size exceeds annual sales of other big competitors like technology, health care, agriculture, or automotive. With favorable demographic changes still unfolding for the next couple of decades, including the post–World War II baby boom population entering its most travel-prone years with the highest incomes and equity of any generation ever, the travel industry will continue on an upward path. Annual increases will slow down from the torrid pace in the 1990s in most nations because of some inherent problems it faces (see Chapter 6). But overall, the general trend is favorable. Mostly it relates to the fact that aging baby boomers have reached the most travel-prone years (45 and up, after the kids have left home). Unlike similar-aged people in the generations that preceded them, boomers have both the income and the equity that permits travel, along with the desire. Some countries that hardly had a visitor at one time, like the Bahamas and other Caribbean islands, now find that tourists contribute 80 percent of their annual gross domestic product. Tax collections can be even higher because tourists get taxed more through high hotel and airport fees than the natives. Since tourists don't vote in local elections, they can't complain. They can only protest with their feet by not coming, and few select that path. Developing nations often choose tourism as a way to pull themselves up by their bootstraps to economic growth. Tourism provides more jobs for unskilled workers at better pay than conventional smokestack industries. It also requires less governmental investment on infrastructure development and can offer more rapid growth than other large industries, such as agriculture, manufacturing, or textiles.

---

[4]Reported in *Travel Industry World Yearbook, The Big Picture, 2000*, p. 7.

Figure 2.1   Growth in World Tourism Arrivals and Receipts
(By Decades)

	Percentage Increase In	
	Arrivals	**Receipts**
1950–1960	174%	227%
1960–1970	139%	158%
1970–1980	73%	488%
1980–1990	60%	155%
1990–2000	50%	67%
2000–2010 (est.)	56%	150%
50-Year Change (1950–2000)	2,617%	21,244%

Source: World Tourism Organization, 2001.

A couple of examples will help place these dramatic changes in perspective. The WTO, based in Madrid, collects data on international travel. Figure 2.1 recasts WTO's numbers on arrivals and receipts (revenues)[5] into percentage increases. The 1950s serves as a good starting point since that represents the time when travel began its steady climb into prominence and dominance. Several points stand out in the chart:

- The growth in tourism arrivals has been phenomenal by any standard. Overall, it represents a market that has increased by 2167 percent. The decline in the rate of growth during the latter part of this period relates to the fact that the travel industry's base is so large it can no longer maintain the same torrid pace as when it was smaller.

- Revenues have grown even faster—overall about eight times above the growth rate in the number of tourists during this 50-year period. Why? Inflation obviously contributes its part, but people now take better trips. More go by air than was true in 1950, which costs more money per person than traveling by car or train to a destination. Also, travelers generally demand a better class of hotels than previously. The cost for lodging has increased faster than the rate of inflation, especially in Europe and Asia. And, finally, since travel occupies a more central place in the lives of most people, they set aside a larger portion of their budgets to take trips. But, basically, countries that at one time offered cheap vacations no longer do.

- The sheer number of tourists traveling the globe today, along with the fact that travelers continue to upgrade the type and quality of their trips, offers assurance that even small increases in numbers of tourists

---

[5]*Travel Industry Yearbook, The Big Picture, 2001,* p. 4.

will result in larger percentage contributions to the economies of nations around the world.

Another demonstration of tourism's increasing importance comes from Dr. Charles R. Goeldner, director of the tourism program for decades at the University of Colorado (Boulder) and former Editor in Chief of the *Journal of Travel Research*. He compared the academic status of travel during the period of 1965 to 2000, roughly the time that he was most active in the field. He examined the number of professional associations dedicated to travel and counted the number of journals available for review during this period of time. Figure 2.2 contains those results. In 1965, only the Western Conference of Travel Research (WCTR) and the Travel Research Association (TRA) represented the travel field. These were combined into a single organization, the Travel & Tourism Research Association (TTRA), in 1972. By the turn of the century, probably more than a dozen such groups sponsor or encourage research of some type. No academic journals existed in the late 1960s to report the results of studies conducted either by academics or other researchers. Goeldner now counts more than 60 journals. Travel research wasn't even reported in other journals during that earlier period. Today it's impossible to get an accurate count of the thousands of articles available, with hundreds appearing each year in journals throughout the world. During the 1970s and 1980s, Melinda Bush—the dynamic group publisher of the quarterly *Hotel & Travel Index*—built it from less than 400 pages to over 1500. It had only 64 *Readers' Digest*–sized pages when it began in May of 1939. When she left the organization, the publication weighed in at over 15 pounds, and was printed in an oversized format.

An industry this large with demographic trends pushing it toward growth will continue to provide more jobs in the future. Its large infrastructure of hotels, airlines, resorts, and destinations will advertise and promote their products to ensure that they grow and remain profitable. As a mature industry, it has the marketing know-how to pull itself out of economic downturns. But it could double its rate of growth, except for some significant problems it faces, as will be seen in Chapter 6.

Figure 2.2   Professional and Academic Status of Tourism Research: 1965 vs. 2000

	1965	2000
Research by Travel Associations	WCTR & TRA (Combined into TTRA in 1972)	TTRA, TIA, CHRIE, ATME, ISTTE, AH&MA, IAST ASTA, ACTE, NTA, CLIA, USTOA, NBTA, more
Number of Research Journals	None (*Journal of Travel Research* launched in 1972)	About 60 English language, many more in foreign languages
Academic Body of Research Literature	None (A few bibliographies, but no basic research)	Thousands of articles available

Source: Dr. Charles R. Goeldner.

TRENDS THAT CHANGED LEISURE TRAVEL

The dramatic growth of travel from the 1950s to the present, as reviewed previously, results from both technological and social changes. Technology changed travel in many ways. As was reviewed, commercial jets opened up the world by allowing travelers to venture further, even to fly several hundred miles away on weekend jaunts. And, because of their lower operating costs compared to piston planes, the cost of an air trip dropped. Flying to distant lands became possible even for working classes. But the greatest impact has come from changes in the psychology of people in most developed nations, first in the U.S. and then spreading elsewhere. Nations that previously held isolationist views now have a broader perspective because so many of their citizens have traveled abroad and have a greater understanding of the uniqueness and similarities between peoples around the world. The changes that I have tracked during the 35-plus years that I have been associated with the industry are more dramatic than many futurists of the 1960s and 1970s predicted. And few social scientists at the time believed that people could alter their lives to this degree without facing psychological disruption. They operated under the assumption that human nature required daily stability in order to function normally.

The New Philosophy: Take a Trip While You Can

Practically everyone knows that boomers didn't turn out quite the way that social analysts had predicted. They ultimately settled down, got good jobs, and became very productive. As a group, they married later than generations before them and also began their families later. But they maintained a philosophy of enjoying life for the moment. After they got jobs, they continued to travel the globe, following a pattern they had established when they were younger. They also bought things—lots of things, like SUVs, RVs, and fancy items for their new homes. But, unlike their parents, who always saved for a rainy day and used whatever they purchased for a long time, boomers often bought what pleased them for the moment and got rid of it when it no longer met their needs. The generation also produced more dual-career working couples than ever. Two incomes allowed boomers to satisfy their interests in travel and to buy whatever they wanted when they wanted. Their savings rate plunged to the lowest level recorded in U.S. history. However, they either were given some stock in companies where they worked or bought some on their own and enjoyed the fruits of the best rise in the market ever during the 1980s and 1990s. And, combined with the rising values in their homes, their equity increased even faster than had been true for their hard-working parents. Boomers had it all. They demonstrated that you could enjoy life to the fullest without having to worry too much about the future.

But a recession hit in the late 1980s for which they were unprepared. The companies where they worked began making changes—restructuring operations to reduce expenses and make money even in leaner times. The process became so widespread that it even had cute names, like *rationalizing a company*, *reengineering*, and *downsizing*. But whatever euphemism was used to describe it, hundreds of thousands of workers lost their jobs. In the early 1990s, leisure travel took a nosedive. Those who were out of work could not afford to take vacations. And those who still had jobs stayed home for fear that they might soon join the ranks of the unemployed and they needed to save for that event. Even those who had put away a comfortable nest egg worried that if they left town for a pleasure trip, their jobs might not be waiting for them when they returned. The company, they reasoned, might make decisions about their future when they weren't around to protect their rights when the next downsizing was announced. Their superiors might assume that they really didn't care much about their jobs if they left town on a vacation while the company faced financial pressures. Even in two-career households, if one spouse lost a job or was uncertain about the future, leisure travel got postponed. The recession from the late 1980s to the early 1990s impacted travel to a greater degree than many other industries because leisure travel is a discretionary purchase.

A couple of interesting things gradually took place that I measured in some of our continuing surveys. First, several years of staying home led to strong feelings of cabin fever. Boomer couples especially came to the conclusion that can be summarized as, "We haven't had much fun for a long time. If we don't take a vacation trip soon, we might never get one because who knows what tomorrow may bring. One of us could die, get sick, or lose our jobs even if we do everything right. So, it's time to get away and have some fun before life passes us by." Second, workers also noticed that loyalty to a company doesn't necessarily mean that the company returns the favor. Those who had been in their positions for 20 years often were the first ones kicked out the door in a downsizing because, with their seniority, they had higher salaries. CEOs knew that getting rid of older employees and keeping younger ones lowered payroll costs the most. So the conclusion by many boomers was, "The company doesn't care for me anymore, so why should I care for the company?" It was another reason to consider taking a vacation regardless of what might be going on at the office. An outgrowth of this weakened loyalty is that workers change jobs and careers more frequently now than ever before, in part because they feel less loyal to their employers. The point of this discussion is that the importance that people place on leisure travel in their lives received a further boost from the recession of the late 1980s and early 1990s. The change in attitude boils down to a feeling that many now have. Specifically, *I need to look out for my own best interests because no one else will. I'll take time away from the job whenever I feel like it, even if the possibility exists that my job won't be there when I return. I'll always find work someplace else. It's my life to live, and I've got to enjoy it now.*

Based on measuring the build up of this feeling, I predicted that leisure travel would start a new boom in 1994, and it did—in March, to be exact.

Domestic U.S. travel increased in high single-digit numbers and international-ly it jumped by double digits. That pace has since cooled down for reasons explained later in this book. But the spirit of doing what you want to do when you want to because of the perceived impermanence of life continues today. It justifies taking leisure trips even during times of economic uncertainty. The new beliefs of "Why scrimp and save for an unknown future?" and "Don't give too much loyalty to your company because it may not return the favor" will continue in the future. It will help to sustain the travel market even during dif-ficult times. Travel providers have things going their way, if they take advan-tage of the opportunities.

The Flattening of the Travel Season Curve

Another change has helped many travel suppliers. When I started my research company in the mid-1960s, a number of clients had a similar request: how could they extend the travel season? At the time, the three primary months of the summer—June, July, and August—consumed about half of all travel demand for the year. People traveled when school was out, with the result that most places were crowded and expensive during that time. During the rest of the year, these spots died on the vine. Low numbers of visitors in the off season meant that many places could not support their staffs and had to close down. Ski resorts have long faced this problem: crowded in the winter, especially if they have a good snow pack, and ghost towns in the summer. Surprisingly, even those who could travel at off times, couples without children and retirees, also usually did most of their travel during the limited summer sea-son. This was the best time to get away, they reasoned, because others did the same thing. They also believed that weather is more comfortable and pre-dictable, and that resorts and destinations gear up to handle tourists appro-priately for their busiest times. Off seasons had the image of providing second-class vacations. Perhaps not enough staff remained to serve guests adequately, and those who stayed might lack interest in their jobs. Travelers also believed that some of the best restaurants and tourist attractions would be closed, limiting the amount of enjoyment that could be experienced at the place.

My clients wanted to extend their seasons and get more visitors to their places during the shoulder months that immediately precede or follow the popular summer period. Research pointed out the misconceptions of travelers outlined previously, and a straightforward answer was rather simple: educate them about the advantages of shoulder month travel. Through advertising and promotion, make it clear that most places still have great weather (sometimes even better) in the preseason of April, May, and early June, or the postseason of September, October, and early November. Also, educate the public about the fact that resorts and destinations maintain sufficient staff to handle demand, and it can even be a more enjoyable time with all the crowds gone. And, popu-lar restaurants and attractions remain open. This seems like a no-brainer today, but it was an issue at the time. As a result of good marketing campaigns, the huge bump in the travel demand curve that always appeared in the summer has flattened considerably. The shoulder months now do quite well compared to several decades ago. This fact can be seen in Figure 2.3, which summarizes the amount of travel by month of the year for the U.S. population. It represents a comparison to an average month. Specifically, if all months had an equal amount of travel, the index score would always be 100. A month that

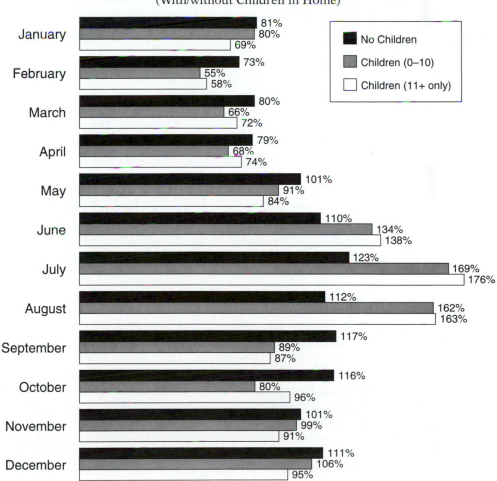

Figure 2.3 Average Percent of Leisure Travelers by Month (With/without Children in Home)

■ No Children

▨ Children (0–10)

☐ Children (11+ only)

Month	No Children	Children (0–10)	Children (11+ only)
January	81%	80%	69%
February	73%	55%	58%
March	80%	66%	72%
April	79%	68%	74%
May	101%	91%	84%
June	110%	134%	138%
July	123%	169%	176%
August	112%	162%	163%
September	117%	89%	87%
October	116%	80%	96%
November	101%	99%	91%
December	111%	106%	95%

Indexed: 100% represents the average

Source: NFO/PLOG Research, American Traveler Survey

is above average by 20 percent would read 120, and a month that has 15 percent fewer travelers would read 85. The chart still shows that the summer months have a higher than average number of travelers because of the impact of family travel, but September, October, and November now fare rather well. And April and May have started to catch up. December's above-average reading reflects the high incidence of people going home for the holidays. At one time, summer travel would peak at 160 to 170 percent above average and winter fall back to 50 to 60 percent. This curve will continue to flatten in time because an aging population of empty nesters and retirees will take more of their trips during the shoulder months.

Client requests now turn to the more difficult task of attracting a greater number of visitors during the true off-season months. How can you get tourists to Austria in the winter? Or entice people to Palm Springs, California in the summer? Or attract crowds to theme parks when school is in session? The task requires more creativity, but it's not impossible. Although this is not the place to cover marketing strategies (see Section III), some simple solutions provide examples. Ski resorts can generate summer crowds by scheduling evening jazz or chamber music concerts and renting out horses for trail rides or ATVs for use on the ski slopes during the daytime. Popular summer destinations can partially fill their off seasons by creating festivals that focus on special interests, such as art shows, opera, or drama and theatre. Those who have hobbies or particular interests demonstrate a strong willingness to travel at any time of the year and to almost any place to be with others of like interests. The true off seasons will become more popular over time as more destinations learn that they can control their destinies to a greater degree than they thought possible. Again, this change in direction comes more often in a mature industry. For various reasons, shoulder month travel and true off-season travel will grow over time. The travel demand curve will flatten even more.

Travel—the New Economic Forecaster?

As was mentioned earlier, the upturn in leisure travel in March of 1994 in the U.S. occurred prior to an upturn in the economy later that year. The same scenario happened in 2001 and continuing into 2002. The mild recession of 2001–2002, caused by a collapse of the technology sector and corporate accounting scandals, had a ripple effect throughout most of the economy. The September 11, 2001 terrorist attacks compounded these problems dramatically. But, contrary to popular opinion, leisure travel did not drop. Travelers simply substituted the mode of transportation used for many of their trips. Travel in the family car increased, especially among more frequent leisure travelers. Data from the American Traveler Survey (ATS) of NFO/Plog Research indicate that travel was relatively strong until the terrorist attacks. After a brief downturn in late September and early October, it picked up significantly. ATS pointed out that those who take less than four leisure trips a year increased their auto trips by 5 percent post 9-11, while more frequent travelers (five or more trips a year) picked up by 10 percent. Corroborating evidence comes from U.S.

government data: Vehicle miles driven during 2001, an indirect measure the government uses to estimate leisure travel, increased above the previous year. More important, future travel plans also began to show improvement. And retail sales continued to increase over the previous year for almost every month.

Economic forecasters have been puzzled as to why consumers continued to spend freely when the two most commonly quoted consumer confidence indexes showed a steady decline during the U.S. recession that began in 2001 and continued into 2003. During the rather steady drop in the indexes, consumer spending continued to show year over year increases. What accounts for this discrepancy? Well, the indexes use inappropriate measures to gauge potential changes in their behavior. Consumer spending accounts for approximately two-thirds of gross domestic product in developed countries. Therefore, studies that measure consumer confidence receive considerable attention. The monthly surveys of the New York Conference Board are even included as part of U.S. government forecasting data. And the University of Michigan index also gets widespread press coverage. Two types of consumer sentiment measures get reported from the studies (i.e., consumers' views of the *current state of the economy* and an index of consumer sentiment about the *future of the economy*). But these indexes have an inherent problem. The average person surveyed knows very little about something as complex as the economy, either currently or how it will do in the future. Their awareness comes from the media reporting about the predictions of Wall Street analysts and financial gurus who examine various sets of governmental, industry inventories, and consumer spending. Each analyst offers a personal interpretation of the data. The press dutifully makes headlines out of what most analysts currently believe. Consumers read or hear this information and, when asked about how they feel about the economy, tend to parrot back what they remember from newspaper stories or nightly TV news. But travel plans aren't linked to what financial analysts say. People take trips when they feel at least moderately comfortable about their own financial futures. And, if they are willing to travel, it also means that they will make other consumer purchases. The University of Michigan actually asks a better question (the perceived financial position of consumers now vs. a year ago), but this information does not get reported in the press. As a result, Wall Street and the financial research community seem amazed when consumers continue to spend at a time when a number of economic indicators look relatively weak and the consumer confidence indexes haven't bounced back to previous strong levels. Writers for *The Wall Street Journal, Fortune, Forbes, BusinessWeek,* and major newspapers around the country tried to explain why consumer confidence continued to fall during 2001 and 2002 but consumer spending and home sales grew month after month. An article in CNN/Money demonstrates their confusion:

> Economists are spending a lot of time fretting about how American consumers are feeling. . . . Those consumers are giving them mixed signals. On

the one hand, they express growing pessimism in confidence surveys. On the other, they continue to spend money anyway. . . . Showing astonishing re-silience, consumers spent money during a recession that began in March 2001. They spent money after the terror attacks of Sept. 11, 2001. They spent money after learning of scandals at Enron, WorldCom and elsewhere. They spent money after stock prices plunged this summer.

And they often did that spending even while they were telling the Con-ference Board and the University of Michigan—compilers of the two most closely watched U.S. consumer sentiment surveys—how unhappy they were.[6]

In contrast, travel demand is sensitive to personal financial fortunes. It can fall more quickly and more deeply than other sectors of the economy. As a discretionary purchase, people can easily delay plans for upcoming trips and wait awhile before they feel comfortable about leaving home. But, because of the change in attitudes about doing what you want to do when you want to, fewer people are willing to put off getting away from home. Long-term delay of gratification belongs to generations past. If they are willing to travel, they also will spend on other consumer items. The new mantra is do it now. Younger generations have more of that spirit, a social trend that will continue.

The indicators that travel provide about a potential slowdown in the economy and early indications of a turnaround will continue to happen in the future. Leisure travel has become so ingrained into the psyche of people in the Western world that more analysts and government officials should pay attention to what these signs mean. After all, the largest industry in the world deserves closer scrutiny than it receives at present. But any measure of travel plans as an economic indicator must include all forms of travel. Air travel may rise or fall for a number of reasons, but auto use for trips (85% of total travel) provides a more stable measure. Simply count the number of people leaving home for leisure trips to get a better feel for whether or not consumers will continue to spend on other items.

Leisure Travel—It's Now a Mature Industry

Considering the fact that leisure travel's infancy stretches for several thousand years, it's surprising how quickly it grew up. The most dramatic changes hap-pened in a short period of time—since the end of World War II (see Chapter 4). It is now a mature industry (i.e., one marked by significant competition and a higher bar for new entrants coming into the field). Maturity has changed the industry in several ways. And these changes also can be expected to last well into the future.

Travel as a Commodity Product   One mark of a mature industry is the presence of commodity pricing. In economic terms, it occurs when supply is plentiful and the offerings of competitors seem very similar with the result

[6]Mark Gongloff, *CNN/Money* Online, September 27, 2002.

that consumers show little preference for one brand over another. They buy primarily on the basis of price, not brand loyalty. Competitors in a mature industry typically must slug it out with each other and try to capture each other's clients in order to grow their companies since few untapped markets exist. For example, consumers usually select a bank that's close to where they live or work, or because it offers more free services. They seldom believe advertising claims suggesting that one bank offers superior service or is safer than its competitors. But free checking or higher interest rates on savings accounts draw new depositors. In insuring a home or a car, people readily change companies when they find a better deal. Few believe that one company pays off sooner or more freely than another when filing claims. Companies that distinguish their products or services from the pack can command a premium in their pricing and profits rise. The automobile industry shows clearly the benefits of creating brand loyalty to avoid commodity pricing. American cars, many of which now represent excellent engineering and good value for the money, suffer from past reputations. Far too often U.S. manufacturers must move cars by offering deep discounts or very low financing packages. In contrast, selected European manufacturers (BMW, Mercedes) and Japanese companies (Honda, Toyota) have created images that suggest they offer better engineering and are better built. As a result, they need fewer special promotions to move their products, especially because used car prices for their models hold up better. But some realities don't necessarily match their images. In looking at Plog Research data on Japanese models, I was amazed at the low quality scores of one well-known popular Japanese manufacturer. Yet the company continued to score high marks among consumers, who, if they had problems with their cars, assumed that they just happened to buy one of the few cars coming off the production line that had problems. They didn't recognize that many others had experienced similar problems. If that happened to American cars, owners would have damned the manufacturer even more.

New industries, in contrast, usually do not confront commodity pricing pressures. Rather, entrepreneurs expect high rates of growth, compounded each year for a period of time. Profits can be high and revenue growth rapid. During the early development phase of modern technology (computers, software, cell phones), many companies increased their annual revenues at 200 to 300 percent a year. Later growth rates were still extraordinary, at 30 to 40 percent annually. Now, much of technology has become a commodity (i.e., a similar product offered by multiple qualified companies and subject to discount pricing). In buying a personal computer, less brand loyalty exists than previously. The number of buyers purchasing on the basis of price, rather than brand preference, continues to increase. As a result, many hi-tech companies now face the dual problems of lowered expectations for growth of both revenue and profitability in the future.

The travel industry confronts these problems. Travel demand will continue to grow moderately over the next decade or two, but it has become a buyer's market throughout much of the industry. Too many competitors offer too many similar products. Some examples prove the point. Among airlines, the carrier with the cheapest fare on a route will get the business. But, in this case, many of their problems are of their own making. During the long period that airlines operated in a regulated environment, governments around the world determined which routes that airlines could fly and established prices to charge passengers. It was almost impossible to start a new airline (established carriers petitioned against new competition), and existing high fares ensured that no airline went bankrupt, regardless of its inefficiencies or high cost structure. Airlines competed primarily on the basis of service, each advertising that it offered better meals, more comfort, or a more helpful and friendly inflight crew (*Fly the friendly skies of United*). Deregulation in the U.S., however, changed the ground rules. New airlines were allowed to begin service from any airport where they could secure gates, serve routes of their choice, and offer lower fares. And a plethora of startups happened around the world. But the major carriers fought back, matching fares and, usually, adding more flights. Lacking deep pockets, most startups failed. The majors also went on an acquisition spree, acquiring other carriers with the goal of creating a size that could not be challenged by other large competitors. Today, some venerable names have disappeared, along with some not so famous, either through bankruptcy filings or acquisitions by competitors. In the U.S. alone, the ghosts include Pan Am, TWA, Republic, Braniff, MGM, Morris Air, People Express, Kiwi, Air Cal, PSA, Allegheny, ValuJet (renamed after a mid-1990s fatal crash), Reno Air, Legend, ProAir, Regent, Tower Air, Midway, Northeast, Pacific, Western, Eastern, Ozark, Texas International, Midway, Big Apple, National, Frontier, and Piedmont. Periodically, someone attempts to revive an older name (as Pan Am and National), but the panache associated with these brands has long since disappeared. In the U.S. alone, about 80 airlines have failed. That pattern has been repeated to a lesser degree in Europe, the Pacific, and Asia as these areas also deregulated airlines, even their national carriers.

Today, after diminishing the quality of the product offered to the public, little differentiation exists between airlines. In general, they fly the same airplanes, configure them with the same number of seats across, and usually with the same seat pitch. The decline in on-board and on-the-ground service has occurred over a couple of decades and adds to the problem. In the days of industry regulation, I conducted studies for some carriers on flight length and passenger demand for meals. The conclusion? When a flight approaches one hour in length, passengers expected a carrier to provide a snack. At two hours, they anticipated a full meal. Today, few carriers offer snacks or meals in coach on flights of three hours or less, and cut off all meal service for flights departing after 7:00 P.M. Low-cost carriers don't even serve snacks on transcontinental flights of five or more hours. Staff cutbacks now contribute to extended times on the phone to reach a reservations agent and longer check-in lines at airports. And airlines face extra delays caused by the additional screening procedures put in place after 9-11. Some old-style competition exists on international long-haul routes for business class passengers because of the high fare structure and little discounting of the price. But few airlines express concern about satisfying low-paying coach passengers. The undisputed exception among major carriers is Singapore. Its consistent high level of customer care and attention to detail result in a passenger base that will pay more for tickets and change flight schedules to enjoy their on-board service.

Frequent flier programs became a weapon to create loyalty. Addicted program members will fly at odd times, include unnecessary stopovers on their trips, or pay more for a ticket in order to earn extra mileage points or maintain their premium status and its privileges. But these do not create true brand preference. Fliers simply stick with a carrier on which they have accumulated the most miles. But in spite of these efforts, the number of travelers buying tickets on the basis of cheapest price continues to rise each year. Airlines hoped that their efforts to bypass travel agencies by reducing or eliminating commissions would drive more customers to their Web sites where they could create loyalty by maintaining direct contact with them. But this plan has backfired. Encouraging use of the Internet, carriers helped make some of their best customers Web smart by driving them to check out other discount sites that may offer better deals (see Section IV). The carriers now face an even bigger challenge. The high cost structure of established major carriers and their inability to get away from commodity pricing bodes ill for their prospects of ensuring a healthy financial future. If your stock broker suggests buying airline stocks, consider these to be a short-term investment (see Chapter 13).

The problem pervades the industry. Hotels largely escaped some of the difficulties faced by the airlines, except for a period in the 1980s, when a number of hotel chains overleveraged themselves and went bankrupt or were acquired by larger, healthier chains. Each time the airlines had price wars to fill empty seats, hotels were the beneficiaries. More travelers came to town without requiring advertising by hotel groups. Leisure travelers bought cheap tickets but, with hotel occupancy still high, they had to pay close to rack rates to get rooms. That too has changed. Travel Web sites like Expedia, Travelocity, and Hotels.com have created a new ball game. Offering deep discounts on major brands, consumers increasingly check out several sites for the best deal. In the process, brand loyalty gets watered down significantly. Consumers can specify that they want a three- or four-star hotel and its approximate location in a city and immediately get an array of choices through the Internet. A mild form of brand preference only comes into play when competitors have rooms available at approximately the same price. In an effort to protect their brand names, four hotel chains (Hilton, Marriott, Six Continents, and Starwood) and Pegasus (electronic reservations company) started the Hotel Distribution Network to protect brand equity of members and control the depth of discounts for their members. Jake Fuller, an analyst at Thomas Weisel partners in New York, commented on HDN's venture, "You want consumers to view Marriott differently than, say, Hyatt. These companies have spent billions to build their brands."[7] But this effort cannot accomplish its goal. Whichever site offers the best deals and the largest selection will be visited most often. And each time a traveler selects a hotel from a Web site on the basis of price, the roots of commodity pricing grow a bit deeper.

Other travel segments experience similar problems to varying degrees. Rental car companies sometimes let their cars out on daily rates that won't support the costs of depreciation and interest. They also live by the mantra that they must keep as much of their fleet on the road as possible or their fixed costs will bury any chance they have to make a profit. So they offer deep discounts to attract a larger group of renters, but competitors usually match those discounts. Packaged vacations show similar vulnerabilities. Supplier pricing on packaged trips to sun destinations, such as Hawaii, Myrtle Beach, and Caribbean islands, often includes hotels at half of rack rates and air fares well below what is available to the public since this space is committed months in advance by the packagers. Sometimes trips to Europe, Asia, and the South Pacific include several elements with bargain prices that don't cover operating costs of the companies providing the services. When this occurs in a market on a regular basis, consumers begin to expect steep discounts and often won't travel until they find them available again. This situation can create problems for companies trying to get their pricing up to rational levels (i.e., a point at which they can at least make a profit).

With growing competition among travel providers and an increasingly sophisticated group of buyers, expect commodity pricing to continue its upward climb in the marketplace.

New Products Must Target Smaller Niches   Looking again at the technology industry, don't expect a startup company to capture a large market share. Established players offer such deep discounts that new entrants can't get the profit margins needed to sustain a good business model. And the deep pockets of major players allow them to offer temporary discounts to drive new competition out of business. Only niche products have a chance—offering a new concept to a smaller but well targeted group of potential customers.

Travel follows the same model. For the most part, small market segments must be targeted in order to have any chance for survival. The greatest chance for success comes if the new company can identify a segment that competitors had overlooked or chose not to serve. The history of startup airlines since deregulation of the industry in the U.S. in 1978 has been one of dismal failure, for the most part. Most new carriers hope to "fly under the radar" of large competitors. They select routes that major airlines underserve or have overlooked, offer a first- or business-class level of service at coach prices, and frequently fly out of smaller and less expensive airports located away from those used by the majors. But, lacking interline connections and having weak fre-

---

[7]*Los Angeles Times,* April 8, 2002, p. C8. Associated Press article by Brad Foss.

quent flier programs, the new guys on the block are almost always forced to take a discount approach to the marketplace. That image brands them as a discount airline from that point on. They aren't saddled with the high cost structure of a long-term unionized work force and work rules that stifle flexibility. But they also don't have the financial backing to survive a protracted economic downturn or a concerted onslaught of discounted pricing from a major competitor.

As a segment, tours and packages have probably proliferated more than any other part of the industry. But, interestingly, tour companies still maintain some true brand identity and loyalty among consumers. Although packages and tour products are relatively easy to assemble, no competitor has attempted to challenge a major company by providing tours to Europe or other destinations that seem similar to what already exists. Large tour companies have locked up the best hotels in major cities at the most favorable rates, signed deals with quality coach operators, and developed strong reputations for providing quality products. A new competitor must target small market segments. The greatest numbers of new offerings focus on adventure travel of some kind. The variety is endless: fishing trips to Alaska, bicycle trips through the wine country of France or New England in the fall, excursions down the Amazon in Brazil, treks up the Himalayas led by local guides, excursions across the Antarctica, learning falconry in Mongolia, or similar very active vacations. These operators hope to grow and someday challenge their much larger competitors but usually have trouble accomplishing their goals. With a limited prospect base and high marketing costs to reach small niche segments, profits elude most new tour operators. They either barely hang on or quietly go out of business. Most adventure travel companies can't even sell out to a larger tour provider. Their balance sheets and prospects for growth don't support an attractive business plan.

Travelers benefit from a mature industry. They get discount prices and have more choices about the kinds of trips they want, when they will take them, and the quality level among various companies providing the products. Cruising provides a good example. So much capacity has come online during the last couple of decades that many cruises offer pricing equal to or sometimes less than buying a comparable land-based vacation, including hotels, meals, and transportation. More significantly, the range of choices is exponentially larger than what was offered in the 1980s, when cruising began its dramatic growth. Choose an adventure cruise, a luxury sailing, a leisurely week or two in the warm and sunny Caribbean or Mediterranean, a cooler Alaska glacier trip, an around-the-world excursion, or a themed cruise featuring jazz combos, big bands, or Broadway musicals. Some travelers go on a cruise each year without feeling they have repeated a previous trip. A broad array of choices will continue in the future, but it becomes more difficult each year for small competitors to enter the market. In a mature industry, many ideas have already been tried with success or have demonstrated their lack of viability and the companies have gone out of business.

A clear message grows out of this review. The growing maturity of travel as an industry means that a new entrant faces a difficult market unless it has a dramatic new idea or has discovered a largely untapped market. Satisfying either condition usually proves difficult. The final result can often be a failed business model or an operator that hangs on for years in the hope that conditions will become more positive soon. Too often an owner can't figure out what else he or she would do for a living after closing the doors.

The Lessening Impact of Industry Disasters   On July 17, 1996, TWA Flight 800 bound for Paris exploded shortly after takeoff from New York's JFK airport, killing all 230 people on board. Although speculation at first suggested that a terrorist missile brought it down, an extensive investigation by the National Transportation Safety Board concluded that the Boeing 747-100's fuel tank probably exploded from a spark caused by frayed electrical wires that run through the tank. TWA had a weak image from two previous bankruptcy filings, an aging fleet, and cutbacks in on-board service levels in prior years. It never recovered financially from the disaster. It could not make money even during the travel boom years of the mid to late 1990s. Its assets were acquired by American Airlines in 2001 during TWA's final bankruptcy application. On May 25, 2002, a similar accident occurred to a China Airlines Boeing 747-200 bound for Hong Kong. It exploded over the Taiwan Strait only 170 miles after it had lifted off from Taipei's Chiang Kai-shek airport. All 225 onboard were killed. China Airlines also had a very weak image from a series of crashes in the 1990s during which 470 lives were lost. Both 747s were among the earliest models of the venerable airplane that went into service in 1971. Like TWA, China Airlines suffered a further drop in public confidence, and large cancellations in bookings and revenue followed. But these two carriers represent an anomaly in the industry. *Other airlines did not experience a downturn in bookings, and few fliers changed schedules to avoid trips on 747s.* Confidence in the operating procedures of major airlines and in Boeing engineering protected the industry from a drop in confidence about the safety of air travel.

By the 1980s, public confidence in the safety of air travel provided a halo effect for most airlines that protected their markets even in times of disasters. If an accident happened and lives were lost, the public did not avoid air travel, the airline that had the accident, or the airplane model that had been involved in the accidents. Rather, ordinary citizens typically explained away the events to themselves and continued their daily routines, including taking to the skies for both leisure and business trips. In focus groups I conducted, they parroted back themes from airline ads in the 1970s and early 1980s: "Flying is a lot safer than driving, so my chances of getting there and back safely by air are still a lot better than if I drive." And they added their own personal philosophies: "If it's your turn to go, it's going to happen no matter what you're doing." And, "At least if you go down in an airplane, it'll all be over quickly. In a car accident, you could live on in agony for a long time."

It wasn't always this way. At the time of my first study for the airlines in 1967, focus groups and quantitative studies I conducted revealed considerable fear of flying, even among frequent business fliers. Some of the often repeated statements coming from group participants include, "If God meant for man to fly, he'd have given him wings!" "The more you fly, the more that the odds will catch up and it'll be your turn." "Why don't the airlines give passengers parachutes to jump out when there's trouble, like the military does?" And, "At least in a car accident, you have a chance to make it out. When an airplane goes down, no one gets out alive." Superstitions also abounded. A common belief was that accidents happened in threes. If an airliner crashed, another would happen shortly. Don't take to the skies until after the third accident, which could also be expected because that's what usually happens. And it even included the view that a major airline with a very good safety record should probably be avoided. They reasoned that it was just a matter of time until the laws of probability would catch up and it would also suffer a disaster. At least the companies that had accidents had figured out what was wrong with their airplanes, they reasoned. When Boeing or Douglas introduced a new model, a sizeable number of people would avoid it until "all of the bugs were worked out." What did that mean? Usually it had to experience two or three air disasters to discover design flaws overlooked during early engineering and testing stages. In the 1960s, and to some degree throughout the 1970s, every commercial airliner crash dampened air travel demand by 15 to 20 percent for up to nine months. For this reason, American Airlines and several other large carriers launched educational campaigns with the theme that air travel is very safe, and especially safer than traveling by car. Fear of Flying (FOF) groups also sprouted up. Led by psychologists and counselors, the object was gradually to work through the overt fears of the cowardly to the point that they could eventually take air trips, first in the company of someone else and ultimately on their own. Books on how to overcome these fears became semi-best-sellers. Over the years, the impact of accidents gradually declined to six months, then three, and now very little fallout is evident. Air travel has matured to the point that few people are like John Madden, the football broadcaster who avoids air travel by using his motor home to get between game sites each week.

The cruise industry had to go through a similar maturation in the reaction of the public to events that bring headlines. Unfortunate happenings could still impact cruise bookings until the mid-1990s because it was a much younger industry. Ted Arison and Knut Kloster started Norwegian Caribbean Lines in 1966 to serve just that corner of the world with leisurely sailings between islands, rather than using ocean liners to cross the Atlantic. Good year-'round weather and beautiful islands enticed a number of people to try a cruise for the pleasures it offers rather than a land-based vacation. But the vast majority of the population wouldn't even consider a cruise. Murray Markin, then Vice President of Holland America Cruises and today a leading industry consultant, called for a study shortly after joining the line in 1977 to determine why this was the case and what could be done to change existing attitudes. Results were somewhat surprising, especially in light of today's attitudes about life and travel. Some avoided it because of the carryover of images about the kind of people that traveled on transatlantic voyages (old, rich, stuffy, slept in deck chairs most of the way, wore tuxedos every evening, and played shuffle board for entertainment). Advertising depicting younger people onboard participating in lots of fun and exciting activities solved that problem. Others avoided cruising because they heard about the lavish dinners and were concerned about how much weight they might gain. That image has been addressed today by providing more activity onboard, incorporating spas and exercise rooms, and offering lighter cuisine. Some even worried that they might be tempted to have a romantic affair that could make them feel guilty later. The *Love Boat* series on television helped change that. Now few worry about losing self-control, and the thought of a short-term romantic interlude sounds enticing to some. But lingering fears about personal safety continued much longer. These include concerns about sea sickness, getting ill at sea without medical specialists onboard (although all ships have physicians along), food poisoning, and the possibility of a fire or other disaster that would result in abandoning ship. Images of the fate of the *Titanic* linger in the minds of some. Cruise lines added to their image woes by shooting themselves in the foot during the 1980s and into the mid-1990s with some well-publicized problems. Several food poisoning incidents, a couple of ship fires (one captured by television crews because it occurred close to the Florida Keys), and a couple of minor ship accidents (a grounding, running into a telephone cable in a harbor) received wide press coverage. These incidents hurt cruise bookings. At that time, any one of these events could cause trip cancellations and lower bookings by 10 to 15 percent for three to six months. Now, the tide has changed and barely a ripple can be seen after incidents like these. Attitudes have matured. Cruise prospects, in effect, say to themselves, "Well, you could get sick at a restaurant on land and the standards for cruise lines are higher than at the places where I usually eat." And, "Fires don't happen on ships very often but, if they do, cruise lines know how to handle them." Stories of cruise problems, unless out of the ordinary, do not get front page coverage as in the past and don't impact the industry to any great degree. Even when happenings result in headlines in newspapers and lead stories on television, few people cancel upcoming cruises. Holland America's *Amsterdam* experienced problems on four consecutive cruises in 2002, when over 500 people contracted the flulike Norwalk virus. It finally canceled a ten-day cruise in November of that year to allow professionals to decontaminate all passenger cabins, crew quarters, and common areas. And it pulled the *Ryndam* temporarily from its Alaska run in August of that year after 400 passengers and crew on previous voyages contracted the virus. Also in November, 275 passengers and crew on the Disney ship *Magic* came down with the Norwalk virus. When a similar outbreak occurred on the next sailing, Disney canceled a cruise to thoroughly disinfect the ship. In spite of the fact that over 1200 passengers had gotten sick on cruise ships within a four-month period (the worst outbreak in six years, according to the Centers for Disease Control and Prevention), cancellations were few and new bookings held up. Cruising, like air travel, has grown up. One woman ready to board the next sailing of Disney's *Magic* summarized the new feeling when she stated, "Well, you can get sick anyplace, even at home. I'll just try to be careful."

Terrorism and political instability are a different matter. Wherever people travel, their first thought is about personal safety. Travelers vote with their feet. If one part of the world faces disruption, they'll go elsewhere. The long conflict in the Mideast stopped most tourism to that part of the world. Surprisingly, the Palestinians have lost more than double the tourism revenues of the Israelis because Bethlehem and the Church of the Nativity are located in Palestinian territory.[8] Egypt, once a growing destination because of continued interests in the pyramids and its historic culture, has suffered a long-term drop in visitors as a result of reported anti-American feelings and the fact that some American tourists were killed by terrorists in 1996. The Chernobyl nuclear explosion in July of 1986 set back tourist revenues for three to four years, not only to Russia but to much of central Europe because of the widespread reports that nuclear clouds had drifted over Europe and had irradiated food crops and dairy herds. In 1985, the cruise ship *Achille Lauro* was taken over by armed terrorists and an American Jewish passenger was executed. That hurt cruise bookings for a couple of years because people recognized how easy it would be for armed gunmen to board a ship in most foreign ports. The biggest event of all, obviously, was the attack on the twin towers of the World Trade Center in New York City and the Pentagon in Washington, D.C. on September 11, 2001, using airplanes as weapons. For the first time, foreigners intent on indiscriminate killing of people had violated U.S. soil. Of all industries, traditional travel suffered the most. The trade press reported that nearly 10 million tourism industry workers lost their jobs worldwide, about 2 million of that number in the U.S. Las Vegas alone saw cancellations for 40 percent of its conference and meetings in October of that year, and 30 percent in November. The impact of this event will linger for years as people consider more carefully where they want to travel, how they want to travel (by car or by air), and whether they even really want to take a trip. The implications of September 11 are of greater magnitude than most other events. People will still travel, as was discussed, but will change their mode of transportation.

Most industries face only one kind of problem not under their own control—a depressed economy. Four types of events, however, can impact travel strongly, contributing to its up and down nature. These include a softening economy, disasters (air crashes, cruise line problems), disease outbreaks, and terrorism. When the economy drops in any nation, travel demand will also decline at some point. But the relationship is not immediate. Travel's down-

---

[8]*Travel Industry Yearbook: The Big Picture, 2001*, p. 4.

turn usually is delayed at least six to twelve months. An air crash or cruise line problem, unless very dramatic, has far less impact today. But terrorism's impact is immediate, unpredictable, uncontrollable, and relatively long term. The industry may be exciting and seductive, but its future is also tied to unforeseen world events. However, overall, the industry has matured. Travelers don't react to events the way they did at one time.

A Growing Group of Sophisticated Travelers   A important trend has been overlooked by many in the travel industry. It is the tremendous growth and increase in the number of smart, sophisticated travelers. With 80 percent of adults having traveled by air, and up to a third of the population in any 12-month period, the result is a group of trip takers who essentially "know the score." Their personal savvy means that they select destinations that meet more of their needs than previous generations and obtain more and better information about these places (or cruise lines or tour operators). They also look for travel bargains on the Web and are more willing to try new types of trips and travel arrangements. Travel agencies have had trouble adapting to this new group. A couple of decades ago, most agents had visited more parts of the world than their clients. That no longer is true. People with money leave town regularly and go to more places than lowly paid agents. The Web provides a lot of travel information, especially for leisure travelers, making it easier to bypass traditional channels of distribution, like travel agencies.

Other segments of the industry also feel the impact. If something goes wrong with a flight, more passengers know their rights. Tour operators have to be concerned about attaining ever higher standards for all of their operations because fewer of their guests are first-timers. Hotels need to refurbish more often or guests will begin to avoid certain properties. To have the desired impact, a large percent of advertising must change its approach. Too much copy seems to talk down to the intended audience as though it knew very little about travel, rather than addressing the high level of sophistication of today's travelers. The important point is that most travelers have a wealth of knowledge and experience about what to expect from a supplier. Failure to recognize that quality products have become the norm hurts the growth potential of companies that don't maintain high standards. Travelers know more today, and they make better choices than their counterparts did a few decades ago.

Tourists: Saviors or Villains?[9]   As destinations gradually decline in the quality of experience provided to visitors through overdevelopment and excess commercialism, attitudes about the benefits of tourism for local com-

---

[9]Some of the material in this section has been presented in previous speeches and in the article by Stanley C. Plog, "Leisure Travel: An Extraordinary Industry Faces Super-ordinary Problems," in *Global Tourism: The Next Decade*, edited by William Theobold; Butterworth-Heinemann Ltd., Oxford, 1994, pp. 40–54.

munities also begin to change. At one time, most travel professionals, government officials, and local residents believed that tourism was and always would be the best economic contributor to a local community ever conceived. Its positive contributions seemed limitless and negative impacts almost unnoticeable. Very little must be spent on infrastructure development to get ready for increasing numbers of visitors, and unemployment rolls drop as relatively unskilled workers get hired in the service sector. Over time, developers and investors increasingly pump millions of dollars into local economies, and tax coffers swell as tourists bring their hard cash and spend freely. The formula seems magical. Who can lose? Local officials continually state that they want more and more tourists. They take nothing but pictures and leave nothing but footprints. Tourists seem to wear halos around their heads. Everyone loves them. But the impact of footsteps, billions upon billions of them, grows with the passage of time. Increasing numbers of citizens gradually recognize the negative consequences, such as the following:

- *Deterioration of destination facilities:* Unplanned and uncontrolled growth almost inevitably leads to excessive commercial development. What was once quaint, unique, and unspoiled now can appear a bit rundown and seedy around the edges. Because the process is gradual, local citizens and government officials wake up to slowly to what has been happening for years and take effective action too late to accomplish what is needed.

- *Destruction of the environment:* Too many tourists visiting the same place at the same time can create environmental havoc. New hotel development tears up scenic spots, sewer systems get overwhelmed because little forethought went into determining future needs, inadequately treated waste water enters local streams or oceans, and native plants and animals disappear. Road development can't keep up with demand, and too much traffic creates smog and congestion.

- *Destruction of local cultures:* Tourism companies, often outsiders, increasingly receive bad press for exploiting the resources of developing nations, especially for contributing to the loss of many unique cultures throughout the world. In their effort to ensure uniform standards and have an efficient work force, they obliterate local beliefs and customs. The goal of setting standards for how guests are treated results in a Western, homogenized, and uniform view of work and how people should relate to each other.

The chorus of criticism and complaints continues to grow louder each year. Hawaii gets mentioned frequently as the place where hundreds of local species of plants and animals have disappeared as a result of tourism growth. And the complaints about the negative impacts of tourists have increased in recent years. In the U.S., CBS's popular *60 Minutes* has aired three stories in the past decade on the impact of too many tourists on Venice, including the city's inadequate sewerage system. ABC's *20/20* and several of NBC's news magazine formats have presented the negative side of tourism. *National Geographic* has produced TV specials and coffee table books about how we have destroyed and continue to destroy our precious heritage throughout the world, some of which is based on the impact of tourism. Numerous magazines and daily newspapers in the U.S., also write on the same theme. Even *The Wall Street Journal,* a supporter of capitalist ideas, has recounted how acid rain caused by visitors' cars traveling to alpine slopes in Switzerland is killing off forests. Athens, Greece faces well-known problems of heavy, continual smog causing destruction of historic sites and buildings. Uncaring local tour operators have dumped raw waste into the Amazon for decades. Alaska has fined several cruise lines millions of dollars for dumping both oil and waste in pristine waterways. The state has instituted capacity limits on cruise ship visits—not only to control dumping, but to protect small villages from being overrun with tourists. Bermuda also controls cruise lines to protect the island nation from uncontrolled growth. The Great Barrier Reef in Australia faces well-documented problems of decline in precious coral beds because these have not been adequately protected.

The list goes on and on. As a result, tourism no longer enjoys the unbridled support it once had. Fewer places will be willing to approve plans for further growth and development because of the negative impact that too many visitors can cause on local cultures. A change to more controlled development may occur slowly because those who make their livings from tourism fear loss of jobs if controls are adopted. But, as criticism continues to mount, the anger of local citizens may result in some severe restrictions for the industry. These consequences need not happen, and a plan for how to control development appears in Chapter 14.

This review has covered a large amount of territory. It has one purpose—to summarize the amazing changes that have taken place in travel throughout the world and how travel has changed the lives of so many people. It will continue to impact individuals and nations in the future, although less dramatically than in the past. But the largest industry in the world cannot be ignored. It deserves more attention to its benefits and drawbacks by governments and travel suppliers. Greater understanding is needed about why people travel and how to motivate them to take more trips, especially the right kind of trips. These topics are covered in the next section.

CHAPTER THREE

Why Destinations Rise and Fall in Popularity

Destinations form the core of travel experiences and usually contribute most to whether or not travelers enjoy their trips or wish they hadn't left home. Obviously, they differ in many qualities, and what pleases one traveler won't satisfy another. But some general rules apply that determine why a destination is likely to be successful today and into the future, and why others fail. These rules relate to the kinds of people that a destination attracts. Some groups of visitors are better than others. The desired types travel more, spend more and, most important, influence others to follow in their footsteps and visit where they have gone. Psychographics (i.e., a study of the personality characteristics of individuals) defines these characteristics and how these influence travel patterns. This chapter reviews the personality dimension of *venturesomeness* and how it relates to the growth or decline of destination, and the personality characteristics of different types of travelers.

Tourist destinations, like humans, have life cycles, including a birth, early stages of growth, the teenage years, maturity, and decline. The process can happen in less than a human lifetime or take much longer, depending on a number of factors. Without good planning and controls, destinations tend to decline over time in the quality of experience they provide to visitors. The process often happens at such a slow rate that tourism and local government officials don't recognize the events taking place and fail to take steps to halt the decline. Or, by luck and good fortune, the place has matured gracefully in spite of the absence of good planning and foresight. But any exceptions confirm the rule. Destinations seldom die completely, in human terms. However, in their old age, so little may be left of interest to tourists that nearby residents contribute the bulk of the visitor count as they dine at restaurants or enjoy a movie. Former grand hotels now display "Rooms For Rent" signs at prices only a fraction of the rack rates in their heyday. Or the hotels may become condos or get converted to other purposes, like the once glamorous Shamrock Hotel in Houston, which now is a training center for nurses. With decay, picturesque and quaint streets of a previous day now have an abundance of empty stores and abandoned buildings. And what remains may feature garishly festooned discount stores, souvenir shops, or pornographic booksellers. This picture may sound extreme, but it happens all too regularly. Most important, though, these changes need not occur since it's usually possible to recognize the signs of decline and take steps to reverse the direction back to growth and a healthy local economy.

Destinations have personalities, as reflected in the types of travelers they attract. Some exude a feeling of self-confidence and vigor—a youthfulness that suggests these places will continue to grow unobstructed in the future. Others seem old and tired—not much left of interest to anyone seeking an active vacation. Whatever their spirit and ambience, however, destinations tend to change character over time as a result of unplanned growth. In the process, they no longer attract the audience or market segments that made them popular and now typically appeal to a less desirable group of travelers. This chapter explains how this happens and provides a framework to stop or reverse what otherwise might seem to be a path toward a feeble old age. The concept was first reported in the *Cornell Hospitality & Restaurant Administration Quarterly*[1] (1974) with updates presented in various speeches and in that same journal.[2]

To understand the dynamics of the process, we need to review some history and supporting data. The conceptual framework that describes the rise and fall of destinations grows out of my earliest foray into travel research in 1966 with a large study funded by the air travel industry. Since that time, the two research companies I founded, Plog Research (acquired by NFO World-Group) and, previously, Behavior Science Corporation/BASICO (acquired by Planning Research Corporation), have completed more than 200 projects using the concept. In addition, a number of academic researchers have tested the ideas in their own research projects. And I have given multiple speeches at tourism conferences around the world. Thus, a very large experience base supports those early conclusions about destination development and life-cycle stages. More important, the concept has been used extensively to reposition or initiate needed changes at destinations around the world and to change the

---

[1]Stanley C. Plog, "Why Destination Areas Rise and Fall in Popularity," *Cornell Hotel & Restaurant Administration Quarterly,* Vol. 14, No.4, February 1974, pp. 55–58.
[2]Ibid, "Why Destination Areas Rise and Fall in Popularity: An Update of a Cornell Quarterly Classic," Vol. 42, No. 3, June 2001, pp. 13–24.

personalities or types of products offered by travel suppliers, a topic covered extensively in Chapter 10.

Since destinations have personalities that attract or repel certain types of travelers, the appropriate basis for measuring these changes is psychographics. Similar to demographics, which use standard measures of income, age, sex, and other life segment categories to segment groups of people in meaningful ways, psychographics does the job with personality descriptions. Each psychographic segment has a unique lifestyle that leads to different choices about the kinds of products they buy, the personal interests or avocations they pursue, and the destinations they choose for their trips, including what they like to do when they get there. Though exceptions exist that are described in Section III, destinations that appeal to certain psychographic segments will grow, while those that attract the wrong segments will decline, as measured by tourism arrivals and tourism spending. This chapter defines the paths to continued success or mounting difficulties for destinations.

THE CONCEPT OF VENTURESOMENESS

To understand the process, it's necessary to review the foundations of the psychographic concept I call *venturesomeness*. It began when *Reader's Digest* assembled a group of 16 air travel industry clients at their offices in the Pan Am building (now Met Life building) in New York City in 1966 to determine how to get more people to take to the skies. It ultimately led to a call for research, a project that my young company, Behavior Science Corporation (BASICO), conducted. The need for the research arose from the fact that only 42 percent of the population had flown in a commercial airplane, according to data released by Gallup. And, since only 53 percent of airline seats were occupied at the time,[3] it was obvious something needed to be done. Worse yet, with the jet age just beginning, seat capacity was growing at more than 20 percent a year, versus an 8 percent growth in passengers. By 1969, the airline load factor remained at only 52 percent, with the Boeing 747 doing much better at 70 percent.[4] Airlines were desperate to get more people into the skies. Their basic questions centered on who does not fly, why not, and what could be done to get them to fly? Today, those ratios have reversed as a result of some of the programs initiated from the research and other events in travel. Now, over 80 percent of the population has been up in a commercial airliner, and about a third take to the skies every year. What a change in a relatively short period of time! As was stated earlier, travel has become a huge business, growing from

---

[3]Reported in *Reader's Digest* marketing presentation to advertisers on its successful 1970–1971 ad campaign designed to get more people to fly. *Reader's Digest* was one of the sponsors of the "New Markets for Air Travel" study of Behavior Science Corporation (BASICO).

[4]*Cornell Hotel & Restaurant Administration Quarterly*, February, 1971, p. 4.

about the 12th largest industry at the time of the original research to the largest in the U.S. and the world, according to the World Travel Organization.[5]

The original study allowed several research luxuries that don't happen in today's fast-paced, skinnied-down research environment. It began with an extensive literature review on what was known about why people don't fly (not much) and investigated a number of psychological theories to determine their applicability to the research needs. More important, over 60 in-depth, two-hour interviews were conducted by my business partner at the time, Dr. Kenneth B. Holden, with people who didn't fly but had sufficient income to travel whenever and however they might choose. These interviews explored their life histories, from childhood to the present, to determine developmental patterns or psychological characteristics that might be common among this group of nontravelers. The extensive qualitative research proved invaluable in determining the psychology of nonflyers. Our staff also monitored more than 1200 telephone calls at airline reservations centers from naïve travelers to learn about the kinds of questions these novices asked of reservations agents. Some queries from first-time flyers proved to be quite humorous and showed their lack of understanding of the dynamics of air travel ("If I feel sick, can I open the window?" "Are there bathrooms onboard?" "Do I tip the stewardess?"). A psychological conceptualization grew out of the exploratory research, along with a psychographic scale. These concepts were tested in a nationwide quantitative study based on a random sample of 1600 households using in-home, intensive interviews.

That project identified a constellation of three primary personality characteristics of the nonflyer personality:

1. *Generalized anxieties:* Those who suffer from a phobia have a specific fear, a condition that is relatively easy to treat. Behavioral therapies gradually expose them to the avoided objects or situations until the fear diminishes. But those with generalized anxieties daily face non-specific self-doubts and a continual low-level feeling of dread that can consume much of their psychic energy. These anxieties inhibit these persons from reaching out to explore the world around them with comfort and self-confidence.

2. *Sense of powerlessness:* Often these individuals believe that what happens to them in daily life is largely out of their control. The good that comes to them and the misfortunes encountered result mostly from chance happenings and events. Individuals cannot control their own destinies, they believe.

3. *Territory boundness:* These folks don't travel much as adults, by any means of transportation, and they did less traveling as children.

---

[5]Reported in *World Travel Yearbook: The Big Picture*, 2000.

Their lives have been restricted for decades in a number of ways, and they make no attempt to expand their horizons.

Originally labeled as *psychocentrics* to reflect the fact that so much of their personal energy focuses on the small events in their lives and restricts their psychic functioning, I later changed the term in a consumer book[6] I wrote to *dependables*, a term that is used throughout this volume. Mild levels of daily anxiety leave little time to face up to and effectively manage the larger problems most people encounter. Their preference for unvarying routine in their lives protects them from having to face unexpected or unplanned events. Thus, they can excel at jobs that others might find boring or too repetitive. Most employers like the dependable nature of their personalities. They usually are good reliable employees who seldom complain about work, seldom are sick, and can be counted on to help out in times of emergency. They simply want to keep their regular routine and not face the anxiety of looking for work, even if they could increase their incomes.

Through a series of follow-on studies, it was possible to define the personality at the opposite end of the spectrum. These individuals reach out and explore the world in all of its diversity. Self-confident and intellectually exploring, they measure low on all measures of personal anxiety. They make decisions rather quickly and easily, without worrying as to whether each choice is correct since life involves taking small risks every day. They have varied interests and a strong intellectual curiosity that leads to a desire to explore the world of ideas and places. Originally called *allocentrics* to reflect their varied interest patterns, I relabeled them as *venturers* because of their tendency to venture forth and seek new experiences with eagerness and enthusiasm. A more complete definition of the personality profile of each is useful since travel patterns flow directly from these characteristics.

Those labeled as *dependables,* the non-traveling type, have a constellation of personality characteristics they hold in common. They

- *Are somewhat intellectually restricted* and do not seek out new ideas or new experiences. They read less, watch TV more, and restrict the variety of contacts they might have with the world around them. In a word, they are less venturesome and less exploring than average.

- *Are more cautious and conservative in their daily lives*, preferring to avoid making important decisions and face the consequences of their choices on a daily basis.

- *Are more restrictive in spending discretionary income.* Uncertain about the future, they don't want to over commit and become financially stretched. Although frugality is a good habit, they choose it from a basis of fear, rather than from good planning.

---

[6]Stanley C. Plog, *Vacation Places Rated,* Fielding, Redondo Beach, California, 1995.

- *Prefer popular, well-known brands of consumer products* because the popularity of these items means that these are safe choices (everyone likes these, or they wouldn't be so popular).

- *Face daily life with less self-confidence and lower activity levels.* Some might call them more lethargic.

- *Often look to authority figures for guidance and direction in their lives.* Because of uncertainties about their own decision-making abilities, they may follow the advice or imitate the behaviors of public personalities. Thus, using well-known movie or television stars and sports celebrities in advertising and promotional materials is more likely to be influential with this audience than other groups.

- *Are more passive and non-demanding in their daily lives.* They often retreat when encountering problem situations, rather than aggressively taking charge to handle the difficulties.

- *Like structure and routine in their relatively non-varying lifestyles.* As mentioned, they make wonderful, trusted supervisors in many companies because of the predictability and routine nature of the lifestyles they lead. They serve as the flywheels of society, making certain that things run according to plan wherever they work, a good reason to label them as *dependables*.

- *Prefer to be surrounded by friends and family,* rather than establishing new friendships, because the warmth and comfort provided in long-established intimate circles make them feel more comfortable and secure.

With this description in mind, it's easy to picture those at the opposite end of the spectrum, the *venturers*. As their name implies, they

- *Are intellectually curious and exploring* of the world around them in all of its diversity. They seek new experiences on a continuing basis and like activity. They watch TV less and prefer what is novel and unique.

- *Make decisions quickly and easily* since they recognize that life involves risks, regardless of choices made, and you learn to live with those choices.

- *Spend discretionary income more readily.* They believe that the future will be better than the past, and they want to enjoy the fruits of their labors now.

- *Like to choose new products shortly after introduction into the marketplace,* rather than sticking with the most popular brands. The thrill of discovery overrides disappointments that can come from a new product that doesn't live up to its promise.

- *Face everyday life full of self-confidence and personal energy.* They eagerly venture out to investigate what might be new and interesting to learn more about the latest technologies, or explore exciting concepts and ideas with others.

- *Look to themselves, rather than authority figures, for guidance and direction* in their lives. In other words, they are more inner-directed and believe they can make the best choices for themselves, rather than relying on the opinions of experts.

- *Are very active and relatively aggressive* in their daily lives. If something does not go their way (a flight is canceled at an airport, a product they bought has flaws), they will actively and forcefully attempt to get the wrong corrected.

- *Prefer a day filled with varying activities and challenges,* rather than routine tasks. Although they can have great new ideas in business or cultural life, they may not be good at implementation since they don't like the day-to-day boredom and struggle that comes with bringing these ideas to fruition.

- *Often prefer to be alone and somewhat meditative,* even though they may appear to be friendly and outgoing to others. Trusting their own ideas, and sometimes feeling that people around them are somewhat dull and slow thinking, they may avoid social situations and parties.

In national samples, based on the questions developed from the original research, the dimension of Venturesomeness distributes rather uniformly on a normal curve, with a very slight skew (Figure 3.1). About 2½ percent can be classified as dependables and slightly over 4 percent as venturers. The remainder falls into the groups in between, such as near-dependables, near-venturers, or the largest group (centrics) with personality characteristics that lean to one

Figure 3.1   Psychographic Personality Types: Current versus (Previous)

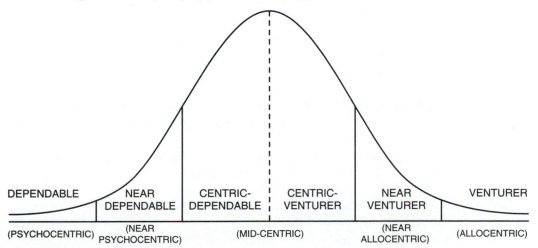

side or the other. The implications of this are considerable since it helps to explain why destinations rise and fall in popularity, as will be seen.

These personality characteristics determine travel patterns and preferences. Examining the two groups at the opposite ends of the normal curve once more allows an easier explanation of the concept. For *dependables*, research over several decades points out that they:

- Travel less frequently.
- Stay for shorter periods of time when they do.
- Spend less per capita on a daily basis at a destination.
- Prefer to go by the family car/camper/sport utility, rather than by air, because they can take more things with them to make it seem like home, making travel less anxiety producing.
- Like to use their mobile homes, stay with friends and relatives, or select the lowest-cost hotels and motels, rather than more premium-priced properties.
- Prefer highly developed, "touristy" spots since their popularity means these must be great places to visit or so many people wouldn't go there. Also, overdevelopment leads to fast food restaurants and convience stores, offering the comfort and familiar feeling of what they experience back home.
- Tend to select recreational activities at these destinations that also are familiar—video games for teenagers, movies and miniature golf for the family, and lots of discount shopping.
- Prefer sun 'n' fun spots, which offer the chance to relax and soak up the warmth on a beach or around a pool, consistent with their lower activity levels.
- Like escorted tours more than independent travel arrangements to places they haven't visited before.
- Buy trinkets and souvenirs, decals, and patches that identify a country or destination. Their purchases on these trips concentrate heavily on the strong visual reminders of where they have been.
- Are likely to return to a place they like again and again because it was a good choice. They don't have to worry about selecting a new destination that may not be as good as what they have recently experienced.

Having reviewed what pleases the dependable personality type, picturing the preferences of *venturers* follows easily. They:

- Travel more frequently because travel is an important part of exploring the world around them.
- Take longer trips.

- Spend more per capita on a daily basis.

- Take to the skies more than other groups because the convenience of getting there sooner reduces the tiresome part of travel (driving) and allows them to enjoy a destination longer.

- Strongly prefer unique, underdeveloped destinations that have retained their native charm. More importantly, they try to avoid crowded, touristy places.

- Gladly accept inadequate or unconventional kinds of accommodations that, to them, become an integral part of a unique vacation experience.

- Prefer to participate in local customs and habits and tend to avoid those activities that seem too common or familiar, or specially staged for tourists.

- Prefer to be on their own (FIT travel) on international trips, even when they don't speak the language, rather than be part of an escorted tour. Give them a car and they'll get around. Their self-confidence and venturesome nature make them feel comfortable in a wide variety of situations.

- Are very active when traveling, spending most of their waking hours exploring and learning about the places they visit, rather than soaking up the sun.

- Purchase mostly authentic local arts and crafts, instead of souvenirs. They avoid traditional tourist traps that sell replicas of local culture.

- Tend to seek new destinations each year, rather than return to previously visited places, to add to their treasure of rich experiences. Their travels enhance their feelings of self-confidence and self-worth, leading them to take even more unique trips in future years.

Now it's time to see how personality determines travel preferences and apply these concepts to the topic of destination development and decline.

THE RISE AND FALL OF DESTINATIONS

Most destinations follow a predictable pattern, from birth to maturity and finally to old age and decline. At each stage, the destination appeals to a different psychographic group of travelers that determine the character and success of that destination. An ideal "age" exists for most destinations, typically what might be called *young adulthood*. It is possible to control development or progress along the curve and to maintain an ideal positioning, but few places do. Why? Local authorities don't understand the dynamics of what contributes to success and failure and, even if they do, they usually lack the will to tackle difficult problems in order to enforce desirable changes.

Venturers, as will be remembered, are most interested in trying new products and services. In a similar vein, they like to visit new places each year, especially the forgotten, the undiscovered, the passed over, and the unknown. Requiring less in support services, such as hotels and restaurants, or organized sightseeing activities and "things to do," they like to go out on their own and discover the range of experiences that each place can offer. Whether the destination is primitive or refined doesn't matter. It simply becomes a new experience for them. They return home with cherished memories and talk about these with friends and relatives. Their enthusiastic descriptions of their recent trips convince their near-venturer acquaintances that they also should visit these wondrous places that sound so intriguing. Their more venturesome friends also provide tips on how to get there, what to do while there, and generally how to make the trip less difficult and more comfortable.

When these near-venturers visit, they initiate the development cycle for that destination because they also tell their friends, relatives, and associates about the joy of their discoveries. Venturers influence near-venturers, who, in turn, influence other near-venturer friends and others around them to take the same kind of a vacation. Since near-venturers outnumber venturers about four to one, the destination has now started on a growth path. Near-venturers don't like to "rough it" in the manner that venturers do, and hotels, restaurants, and shops that sell local crafts begin to appear. In the middle of this growth cycle, when near-venturers now constitute the majority of tourist arrivals, the travel press will likely discover the place. They note where the jet set is traveling as the search for something new to cover in their newspaper columns. Finding it to be truly unique, they write ecstatically about their new finds. The destination has now been "discovered" and it will soon confront the many pressures that arise from rapid growth and development. Not only has the press started to put out the good message, but near-venturers also talk about their exciting vacations with their mid-centric friends, who have some venturer leanings. They, in turn, want to go, especially because the destination now has developed a rather good infrastructure. Growth rates can be very high during this period. And, looking at the curve again in Figure 3.1, more centrics with venturer leanings exist by far than the near-venturer group.

Up to this point, everyone seems happy at the destination. Tourism growth continues unabated, property values rise as hotels continue to pop up, more local residents have jobs, tax coffers have increased over time, some run-down areas may have been cleaned up with newly collected tax dollars, and most residents believe that they have discovered the perfect industry (i.e., tourism). No ugly, smoke-belching factories need to be built. Unskilled workers find good-paying jobs in the new hotels and restaurants. And few tax concessions have to be given to attract more developers, unlike the situation for manufacturing industries. Local politicians and tourism officials congratulate themselves on their brain power because they think they have discovered a never-ending source of expanding wealth—getting more and more tourists to visit their corner of the world. It seems like nirvana for all. Growth, however, rests on the fact that the *tourism prospect base* has had a larger and larger population from which to draw. Near-venturers outnumber venturers; and centrics with venturer leanings comprise a much larger group than near-venturers. That fact holds true until the midpoint of the curve. The influence direction always moves from right to left (i.e., venturers influence people psychologically close to them [the near-venturers] and the near-venturers influence friends and associates who are psychologically close to them [mid-centrics with some venturer leanings]). The curve of influence does not go the other way (i.e., from left to right on the curve) (see Figure 3.2). Centrics, whatever their leanings, seldom sway the opinions of those who have venturer blood in their veins, and dependables have very little impact on the opinions or choices of those who have more exploring minds.

Early stages of growth at a destination usually enhance its existing qualities. The first hotels choose the most scenic spots, buy lots of land to add to their sense of beauty and isolation, and typically build only low-rise structures to fit in with the environment because construction costs are less than for high rises when land prices are low. Few tourist shops appear since there aren't enough tourists to support them. Nightclubs and other entertainment facilities don't interest those who seek escape from common, everyday experiences. And local residents exude friendship and warmth. They want to please their travel guests, who provide jobs and stimulate the economy. Some blighted areas get makeovers. New wealth improves the living conditions of a broad range of the population, especially because tourism causes ancillary businesses to sprout that serve tourism workers. All in all, it's a better place to live. And that contributes to why most people never suspect that tourism growth should be planned and controlled. It has been good so far, so why wouldn't it be even better in the future?

Figure 3.2   Psychographic Direction of Influence

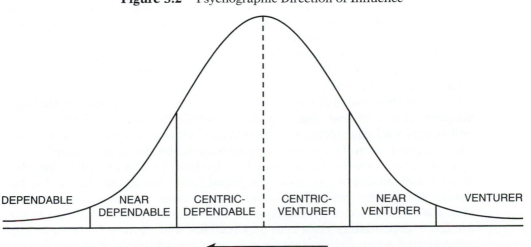

During this formative period, development is likely to continue almost unabated. Elected officials, who recognize the contributions of tourists to their area and their constituencies, happily proclaim their support of tourism and its multiple benefits for their community. They gladly approve plans for bigger hotels that add to the tax base. In time, these new properties in the most desirable locations fall into the first-class or luxury categories because land prices have risen to the point that only more expensive properties will pencil out. Politicians quickly discover that tourists don't vote, so they add tax upon tax to the lodging, airline, and rental car industries. Tourist shops, some representing large chains, sprout around town. Fast food restaurants appear and help to make the place seem more like the hometown that visitors just left. Video arcades, movie theaters, and other entertainment facilities sprout up to keep the new group of tourists from getting bored with the diminishing scenery. Gradually the place takes on a more touristy look. High-rise hotels now dominate the more attractive two- and three-story low-profile lodgings that came originally because only smaller parcels of land remain for development and these provide a better return on investment than low-rise properties, which "waste" costly land. Adequate local planning to control the spread of tourist sprawl has been woefully inadequate. Elected officials have no experience overseeing what they feel is a great benefit to their community. They allow small businesses of all types to spring up around town in an uncontrolled manner (drug stores that also sell trinkets, T-shirt shops, beach or ski shops, pseudonative stores, bars, etc.). The place begins to look like many other overdeveloped destinations, losing its unique character along the way.

Throughout this entire process, the seeds of a destination's inevitable decline and destruction lie within the grounds of its success. Just when most people at the destination seem happiest about the success of their efforts to grow tourism year after year, unseen forces have started to move against them that will spell trouble in the future. At some point, the type of visitor it attracts has moved from venturer to near-venturer to centric with venturer leanings and past the midpoint of the chart in Figure 3.1, ultimately passing over to the dependable side of the curve. With continued favorable publicity and ever-increasing popularity, dependables now also learn about it and they want to take a trip to this much-talked-about place. The greater its popularity, the more likely they will visit since they prefer to make safe choices. If that many people visit it each year, then it must be a good spot. Now the problems truly will mount and the decline of the destination is probably only a matter of time. As psychographic movement continues on the curve, several unfortunate consequences come to the surface. The destination now can only draw from smaller and smaller segments of the population after its psychographic positioning passes the magical mid-point on the chart. Fewer near-dependables exist than mid-centrics who have some dependable characteristics, and there are fewer dependables than near-dependables. The pattern is the opposite of what existed when the destination was on a growth curve. Not only have the numbers of visitors shown a decline but, it will be remembered, dependables travel less than their venturer counterparts. And dependables prefer the family vehicle (car, camper, or sport utility) over air travel. Thus, destinations that require an air trip will suffer the most. Dependables stay for shorter periods of time and spend less while they are there. All of these factors add to the misery now felt at the destination. Nothing has changed, local officials believe, so they can't understand why fewer and fewer visitors come each year and spend less while they're there.

The perfect psychographic positioning for most destinations lies in the *near-venturer* space on the psychographic curve. Why? Since the influence curve only moves from right to left, influence always comes from those who are more venturesome. That influence can extend to about 40 percent of the remaining portion of the curve. Thus, a destination positioned to appeal to a core audience somewhere in the middle of the near-venturer segment has the broadest positioning appeal possible because it can attract the largest number of people on the curve.

It's easy to point to destinations that face a declining future because of uncontrolled growth that results in attracting the wrong market segments. Deep discount travel packages abound, usually that include air and hotel (often with some meals or golf privileges thrown in). When 30 percent or more of travel bookings come from deep discount vacation packages, that destination probably will continue to go downhill over the next couple of decades! Confirmation of problems can come from a simple walk around town. The greater the number of fast food restaurants, video rental stores, bargain shopping outlets, and common forms of night-time entertainment, the greater the probability that these will never go away and will continue to contribute to the decline of the area. Storeowners pay taxes and vote (and support) those local politicians who promise to continue policies of the past. Almost no one recognizes that the future will become cloudier as fewer and fewer high-spending tourists will come their way. High-end resorts and luxury hotels often feel the negative impact the most. They paid top dollar for land to build their properties and now struggle to stay afloat as the quality of the tourism base declines. New arrivals don't want to pay high prices for their rooms. These are budget-minded folks, forcing luxury properties to do more deep discounting than the budget/economy hotels that already offer competitive rates. The dominant psychographic types that visit a destination determine its positioning. In most situations, this predicts the future of a destination and whether it can grow and prosper or will face difficulties brought on by fewer tourists, who spend less on a per diem basis and stay for fewer days. A place that appeals to those with more venturesome spirits feels more alive and active. One that attracts those with dependable psyches usually casts an aura of old age and decline. Figure 3.3 shows the direction of the decline that occurs when local planners don't recognize the harm that comes from overdevelopment and lack of foresight. Good planning is required to slow down or stop the natural aging process.

Proper positioning rests on two pillars—the inherent qualities of a destination and its image in the eyes of the traveling public. Maximum success usu-

Figure 3.3   Birth and Decline of Destinations as Related to Psychographic Positioning

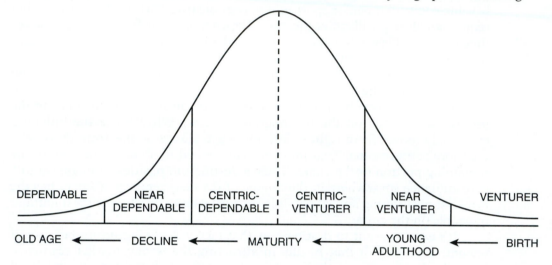

| DEPENDABLE | NEAR DEPENDABLE | CENTRIC-DEPENDABLE | CENTRIC-VENTURER | NEAR VENTURER | VENTURER |

OLD AGE ◄——— DECLINE ◄——— MATURITY ◄——— YOUNG ADULTHOOD ◄——— BIRTH

ally occurs when local planners recognize they should protect what originally attracted people to their community. Those qualities should be emphasized repeatedly in marketing and promotional programs. In a few places around the world, some smart local planners and politicians forbid the development of high-rise hotels and control the types of businesses allowed and their location. They protect and preserve open areas and ensure that local residents participate equally in the success of the destination and not just large outside developers. The natives also don't want to lose what they like about where they were born and grew up. Crowds, traffic congestion, increasing smog, high prices for just about everything, and a vanishing friendliness between neighbors who now seem to hustle constantly for tourist dollars make many locals long for the simpler life they once enjoyed. Lifestyles have changed in unwanted ways, but returning to the past is impossible given the huge infrastructure costs already sunk into the ground. Tourism and its ill effects on a local culture now become a controversial topic of discussion, not a friendly one as was true in the past.

With this in mind, destinations can be placed on the psychographic curve, based on the types of people who visit the most. Figure 3.4 presents an earlier positioning of some destinations, based on the original speech I gave in 1972 and later reported in the *Cornell Hotel and Restaurant Administration Quarterly.*[7] In contrast, Figure 3.5 summarizes where various destinations fit today. Placement on the psychographic curve comes from the American Trav-

---

[7]Stanley C. Plog, "Why Destination Areas Rise and Fall in Popularity," *Cornell Hotel and Restaurant Administration Quarterly,* Vol. 14, No. 4 (February 1974), pp. 55–58.

Figure 3.4 Psychographic Positions of Destinations (1972)

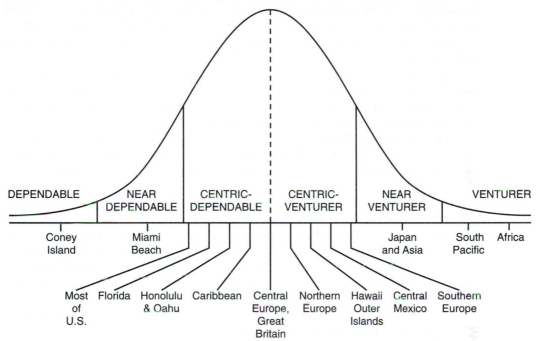

Figure 3.5 Psychographic Positions of Destinations (2003)

DEPENDABLE	NEAR DEPENDABLE	CENTRIC-DEPENDABLE	CENTRIC-VENTURER	NEAR VENTURER	VENTURER
			• New Mexico		
			• Arizona		
		• Alaska Cruises	• New England		
		• U.S. Parks	• Hawaii (outer is.)		
		• Illinois	• Washington State		
		• Washington D.C.	• Oregon	• Russia	
		• The Carolinas	• Colorado	• Tahiti	
	• Hollywood	• Michigan	• Wyoming	• New Zealand	
	• Las Vegas	• Chicago	• Montana	• China (big cities)	• Alaskan
	• Theme Parks	• Georgia	• San Francisco	• Poland	Wilderness
	• Honolulu	• Kentucky	• New York City	• Costa Rica	• Guam
	• Florida	• Hilton Head	• Quebec	• Egypt	• Fiji
	• The Dakotas	• Philadelphia	• Bermuda	• Jordan	• Hard Adventure
	• Ohio	• Los Angeles	• Brazil	• Thailand	Travel
• Branson	• Kansas	• Caribbean (most)	• Mexico (interior)	• Australia	• Vietnam
• Atlantic City	• Mexico (border)	• Ontario	• Hong Kong	• Ireland	• Antarctica
• Myrtle Beach	• Caribbean	• London	• England	• Scotland	• Amazon
• Orlando	Cruises	• Rome	(countryside)	• Kenya	• China (interior)
• Beach Resorts	• Escorted Tours	• Israel	• Scandinavia	• Africa	• Tibet
• Indian Casinos	(U.S. and Europe)	• Italy	• Paris	• Expedition Travel	• Nepal

eler Survey of NFO/Plog Research, the annual study of travel habits of 10,000 households, but the actual location is meant to be conceptual, not exact. And, although this chart is more inclusive than the original graph, it serves only as a representative list since it is impossible to cover all destinations in a chapter of this length.

In comparing Figures 3.4 and 3.5, it is obvious that a number of destinations have moved to the left on the chart, from the venturesome side of the scale toward a dependable positioning. The amount of movement typically relates to the degree that the destination has become more touristy in character. Not apparent in Figure 3.5 is the fact that fewer destinations today can be classified as venturesome in character because the earlier chart presented in a 1972 speech (Figure 3.4) included only a limited number of destinations for illustrative purposes only.

A few destinations actually appeal broadly across the spectrum, attracting near-venturers to near-dependables. Two criteria determine this. First, these places offer a lot to do, from adventurous activities to sitting on a warm sunny beach, thus pleasing various segments. And, second, they have maintained their original character over a long period of time, even though they have been around for decades as popular places. Hawaii, Colorado, Ireland, and Scotland, for example, fall into this desirable category. Placement for each destination on the chart, however, is based on its dominant characteristic. What cannot be forgotten is that some places can draw huge tourism crowds, even though they have a dependable character. Branson, Missouri confirms that fact. The State Director of Economic Planning at the time Branson was conceived, William Boyd, purposely positioned it from the beginning to have a dependable (psychocentric) appeal. He was familiar with the Plog psychographic system from a Hawaii development project we worked on together to position Waikoloa at the opposite end of the spectrum (i.e., as more venturesome than its image among travelers at that time). He recognized that Branson had dependable characteristics because of its focus on country music and that it would be a drive-to destination, both of which are more dependable in character. Las Vegas draws a broad spectrum of people who want to see the latest hotel marvels. But gambling as an activity generally appeals to dependable personalities. The general rule still remains that most destinations enjoy greater success when positioned for near-venturers because they influence others to follow in their vacation footsteps.

Since psychographics describe the personality characteristics of different types of travelers, highly focused marketing campaigns can be developed to target specific segments. Thus, destinations can make advertising and promotional campaigns more effective and efficient by creating marketing messages of interest each group. And, a destination can take the larger step and reposition itself by changing an inappropriate image into a set of expectations that attract the desired psychographic groups. Demographics, currently the most widely used tool of marketing to target desired audiences of travel prospects, doesn't allow this possibility. How to employ the concept of venturesomeness for more effective marketing or to reposition destinations and travel products is covered in Section III.

As mentioned, the dominant psychographic type of traveler that visits a destination determines its positioning. This, in turn, predicts the kind of future a destination will likely encounter, whether it can grow and prosper or is likely to face difficulties brought on by fewer tourists who spend less on a per diem basis and stay for fewer days. Each destination must decide what it wants to be. And its positioning and branding strategies should be consistent with its planned psychographic image to ensure success. Finally, it must deliver on its promise (i.e., that visitor experiences match their expectations so that they don't go home disappointed). How to achieve these goals is covered in upcoming chapters.

DOES THE CONCEPT OF VENTURESOMENESS REALLY WORK?

Venturesomeness as a concept may be an interesting idea that helps to stimulate thinking on how to develop more creative travel advertising, but ultimately it must pass the test of demonstrating its utility in order to be taken seriously by travel professionals. So, the question of the day is, *Does it work?* The answer is a strong yes. Solid evidence exists to support this statement.

Household income serves as the test case for comparison purposes because most travel suppliers use it to target their markets. In general, they want to reach households with annual incomes of $60,000 and above, believing that these groups travel more and take longer and more expensive trips. Many luxury travel providers focus on households above $85,000 or $100,000, or even above $150,000, as is the case with top-end cruise lines and resorts. Income is also utilized because it is easy to select media for marketing campaigns on the basis of readers' or viewers' household incomes. Travel marketers less frequently use other demographic characteristics such as age, sex, and marital status, while education is excluded as a variable in many travel industry studies as unimportant.

Two primary questions dominate this review. First, which characteristic does the better job of predicting the amount of leisure travel (i.e., household income or venturesomeness)? And, second, which dimension more accurately predicts the activities that people pursue when they are on vacation? Data for this analysis also come from the American Traveler Survey (ATS) of NFO/Plog Research, Inc. It gathers a complete set of demographics and includes my psychographic questions that divide people into different segments. A simplified review of the data analysis is presented here for easy understanding. A more technical and statistical presentation that includes cross tabulations, correlations, and multiples regressions can be found in an article I prepared for the

Figure 3.6   Number of Trips in 12 Months (Psychographics vs. Income)

	Household Income				
	<$40,000	$40,000–$60,000	$60,000–$85,000	$85,000–$100,000	$100,000+
Air	0.4	1.1	1.8	2.4	4.2
Car/camper	1.8	3.0	3.8	4.1	4.4
Business	0.5	1.4	2.2	2.6	4.1
Leisure	1.8	2.8	3.5	4.0	4.5
Total	2.3	4.2	5.6	6.6	8.7

	Venturesomeness				
	Dependable	Near-Dependable	Centric	Near-Venturer	Venturer
Air	0.5	0.7	1.2	1.7	2.5
Car/camper	1.4	2.2	3.0	3.2	4.6
Business	0.5	0.7	1.5	1.8	3.0
Leisure	1.4	2.2	2.7	3.2	4.2
Total	1.9	2.9	4.2	4.9	7.2

Source: NFO/PLOG Research, American Traveler Survey.

Journal of Travel Research.[8] Portions of this section have been taken from that article.

Figure 3.6 presents data on the amount of leisure travel by air vs. car/camper, related to income and psychographics. For these purposes, the important column is the total leisure trips. Note that both income and venturesomeness show a straight-line relationship to travel. Specifically, the higher the income, the greater the amount of travel, whether by air or the family automobile. Air travel records the steepest increase, as would be expected, since auto trips generally cost less for persons who have more marginal incomes. Venturesomeness also demonstrates the same straight-line increase. Venturers travel the most, followed by near-venturers, centrics, near-dependables, and dependables, in that order. Venturers don't travel quite as much as persons with the highest incomes in this analysis, primarily because of a necessary adjustment made in the data analysis. The small number of pure venturers available for comparison (about 4% of the sample) would make the analysis unstable. Thus, some less than pure venturer types were added to the venturer group for stability in data analysis, but this reduces the strength of the findings. On the other side of the coin, the dependable group

---

[8]Stanley C. Plog, "The Power of Psychographics and the Concept of Venturesomeness," *Journal of Travel Research*, February, 2002, pp. 244–251.

travels less than those with the lowest incomes in this study. The primary conclusion? Household income and venturesomeness both predict the *amount of leisure travel* about equally well.

If venturesomeness only predicts the amount of travel, it has limited utility for travel marketing and as a theoretic concept to stimulate research and inquiry. Income currently serves that role quite well since all media regularly survey their audiences on demographic characteristics and report the results to advertisers. The true test comes in determining which dimension does a better job in predicting the kinds of activities pursued while on vacation. The American Traveler Survey also helps out. Respondents indicate which activities they pursued on their last vacation from a 38-item list. Figure 3.7 summarizes the results for 16 of the 38 ATS items, broken out by income and psychographics. Not included in this list, for brevity's sake, are some items not useful for purposes of this analysis (use of air travel for trips, and international travel) and items with very low participation overall. The data indicate that venturesomeness provides greater predictive power than income. Overall, venturers participated in more activities on their last leisure trip than those with the highest incomes (over $100,000 a year). On the other side of the coin, dependables took part in fewer activities than households with the lowest incomes (under $40,000). More specifically, the table points out the following:

- On 11 of the 16 items, income basically *does not* show a relationship to participation in the activity; that is, as household income increases, involvement in an activity does not increase (or decrease). For only four items does income show a clear relationship. These include *shopping, fine dining, visits to museums/art galleries,* and *attendance at night clubs/stage shows. Use of health club/exercise facilities* potentially also falls into this category.
- In contrast, venturesomeness demonstrates a relationship on 11 items. In this case, the more venturesome the individual, the greater the participation. Those activities for which venturesomeness relates to the activity (the more venturous the individual, the greater the participation) include
  - fine dining
  - visits to historic churches/sites
  - visits to art galleries
  - visits to old homes/mansions
  - nature travel/ecotouring
  - hiking/backpacking/camping
  - attending theatre/drama events
  - attending musicals

Figure 3.7 Percent Participating in Activity on Last Leisure Trip
(Income vs. Psychographics)

	Household Income				
	< $40,000	**$40,000-$60,000**	**$60,000-$85,000**	**$85,000-$100,000**	**< $100,000**
Shopping	61	64	69	70	70
Fine Dining	35	34	43	47	54
Visit Historic Churches/ Sites	32	33	36	34	36
Visit Museums/ Art Galleries	23	24	25	26	29
Visit Old Homes/Mansions	20	18	19	21	22
Nature Travel/Ecotouring	14	15	13	13	14
Nightclubs/Stage Shows	13	13	14	16	16
Hiking/Backpacking	10	16	12	9	9
Theatre/Drama	9	9	8	10	11
Musicals	9	6	5	6	7
Use Health Club/Exercise	6	5	7	9	10
Wine Tasting/Winery Tours	5	6	7	6	7
Jazz Concerts	4	1	1	2	2
Bicycle Touring	3	2	2	3	3
Symphony/Opera	2	2	2	3	3
Scuba Diving	2	1	2	2	3

	Venturesomeness				
	Dependable	**Near-Dependable**	**Centric**	**Near-Venturer**	**Venturer**
Shopping	66	64	63	64	70
Fine Dining	32	33	34	43	51
Visit Historic Churches/ Sites	22	31	32	36	41
Visit Museums/ Art Galleries	11	22	22	30	34
Visit Old Homes/Mansions	9	17	18	24	26
Nature Travel/Ecotouring	6	12	13	17	19
Nightclubs/Stage Shows	10	12	12	13	24
Hiking/Backpacking	6	9	13	14	17
Theatre/Drama	6	9	8	9	9
Musicals	3	8	6	7	9
Use Health Club/Exercise	2	3	6	7	14
Wine Tasting/Winery Tours	2	3	5	9	12
Jazz Concerts	2	1	2	3	6
Bicycle Touring	1	1	3	3	6
Symphony/Opera	1	1	2	2	3
Scuba Diving	2	1	2	3	5

- wine tasting/winery tours
- attending jazz concerts
- bicycle touring
- attending symphony/opera concerts

The case can be made that a relationship also exists for *scuba diving* since only one segment category does not fall in a straight-line relationship (participation level for dependables is slightly higher than for near-dependables). Note an important consistency in this list of items. Venturers actively and aggressively explore both *the physical and cultural worlds* around them. Their aggressive, self-confident nature is quite evident in these results. Also note the following:

- On three items in the scale, both income and venturesomeness follow the pattern of showing an increase in the activity as either income or venturesomeness increases. However, *venturesomeness demonstrates a stronger relationship* (i.e., the differences apparent between participation by dependables versus venturers are greater than the differences between the lowest and highest income groups). These items include *fine dining, museum/art gallery visits,* and *attendance* at *night clubs/stage shows.* Thus, both variables predict participation, but venturesomeness does a better job and is about equal in predicting enjoyment of *fine dining.* Participation by the highest income group (over $100,000) is stronger than among venturers but, on the other side of the coin, dependables do less shopping than those with incomes below $40,000.
- On only one dimension, *shopping,* does income do a slightly better job of predicting participation. But differences between top and bottom groups within the dimension are only marginal. In this case, 61 percent of those from households with income below $40,000 shop while on a leisure trip, a figure that increases gradually to 70 percent as income rises to above $100,000, a difference of nine percentage points. In the case of psychographics, that difference is only four points, with 66 percent involvement by dependables, increasing to 70 percent for venturers.

This chart demonstrates that income has limited utility in determining the types of activities people pursue on leisure trips. Higher-income travelers may travel more and spend more wherever they go, but it is difficult to determine their specific pursuits. For the world of travel marketing, this finding has important implications because travel executives almost uniformly assume that participation levels increase for most leisure-time activities as income goes up. As this analysis points out, that assumption often is not true. Rather, the psychographic dimension of venturesomeness has greater utility for travel marketers who want to position their products or target specific market segments to reach high potential prospects.

A fundamental and obvious point in Figure 3.7, mentioned earlier, is that the more venturesome the individual, the more that the person reaches out to explore the world. These differences include both physical activities and pursuits of the mind. Thus, venturer types do more nature travel and ecotouring, hiking and backpacking, bicycle touring, and scuba diving. But they also are more likely to visit old churches and historic sites, go to museums and art galleries, take in theatre and plays, and attend symphony and opera concerts. Their exploring minds take them almost everywhere, even to enjoying fine dining experiences when traveling and nightclubs and stage shows. This broad range of activities pursued makes them a high potential target group for destinations and ground suppliers at those destinations.

In spite of these conclusions, venturesomeness and other psychographic systems are not likely to replace income and other demographic variables (age, sex, education, and marital status) in the everyday worlds of sales and marketing. Demographics are embedded strongly in the psyche of the media and advertising agencies. No magazine, TV series, or radio program currently promotes the characteristics of its audience on the basis of its favorable psychographics. However, both variables can work in concert to develop more effective promotional campaigns. Income provides the means to target travel-prone neighborhoods through zip code analysis, while venturesomeness can be used to formulate more effective marketing messages, modify travel products, or develop new ones. Some clients, both travel suppliers and their advertising agencies, want to attract specific audiences, such as venturers, and they support studies that determine their media habits, specific interests in sports, and other lifestyle characteristics so that their entire marketing programs will provide a better return on their investment. Consistent with what has been pointed out thus far, most clients want to target near-venturers since this is a relatively large group of people (about 17%). And, very important, their habits will influence the even larger middle portion of the psychographic curve (the centrics), approximately another third or more of the market.

The venturesomeness concept has consistently served three interrelated purposes: repositioning existing products to make them more acceptable to desired psychographic groups, developing new ones for various segments, and creating better marketing messages that meet the needs of these groups. Destinations around the world have been repositioned to increase interest among more venturesome kinds of people, with the marketing campaigns designed to appeal more effectively to these groups. Airlines, cruise lines, and other travel providers have also changed the ways they present themselves to the traveling public, again based on a new understanding of the wants and needs of different psychographic types. Resorts and tour operators have also developed products designed to capture a more venturesome kind of audience.

Although venturesomeness has primarily been applied to the field of travel, these concepts have relevance to other products and services. Technology, beverages, automobiles, and fashion have all benefited from past positioning efforts. Since venturers are the first to try out new products and services, addressing their needs and interests can help to achieve early acceptance in the marketplace. They buy and try, and then influence friends and associates, a true demonstration of the power of word of mouth advertising. Section III provides explanations and case examples of how to target the various psychographic groups for more effective marketing.

The concept is also applicable in other countries, based on research that has been conducted around the world by my company and academics that have tested it in various geographic areas. The distribution curve may vary somewhat from one country to another, as related to the dominant personality character of the nation. Canada, for example, leans a little more to the dependable side of the scale as related to its ethnic heritage. English Canadians distribute on the curve very similar to Americans. French Canadians tilt toward the dependable side of the scale. More often they choose warm, sun 'n' fun vacation spots, have a heavier preference for family vacations, and tend to engage in more activities on holiday that are similar to what they do back home on a regular basis. Australians lean more to the venturer side, with their New Zealand neighbors weighing in a bit more dependable in character. The English also match U.S. profiles closely, while people from Scotland and Ireland gravitate somewhat toward dependable characteristics. That fact is also true for most of central and southern Europe (i.e., the French, Germans, and Italians lean somewhat more to the dependable character). Asians even more so fall into that category, particularly the Japanese, whose preference for escorted tours and being surrounded by people they know on trips is well known. However, that tendency is changing gradually. More Japanese now are reaching out to become more exploring in their character. Many more now choose FIT (independent travel) than previously, and they are selecting places popular with tourists from other nations, such as various European locales and the western U.S.

Clients from different industries have used the concept to segment markets around the world. Molson's Brewery of Canada, for example, positioned all of its products in Canada to ensure that they covered the marketplace, from venturers to dependables. For each new brand they developed, they typically introduced it to the venturer group first, and gradually worked it across the spectrum until they stopped its movement at the desired psychographic group through effective positioning strategies. They did this by developing appropriate advertising campaigns that target each group and selecting the kinds of media used most by these segments. They also examined differences between beer drinkers in England and Scotland, again categorizing ale and lager drinkers into psychographic groups on the basis of quantitative studies. This occurred prior to discussions with major breweries in these countries about partnerships and joint development efforts. Major European auto companies, such as BMW and Saab, have positioned their products with the help of this psychographic system. Various destinations have created marketing campaigns for worldwide use, with a similar theme that targets more venturous people in their primary target markets. And, research has been conducted by academics around the world, especially by graduate students working on their master's or doctoral dissertations in countries in Europe, Asia, and the Pacific region. Approaches to effective marketing, using these concepts, are covered in Section III.

THE DESTINATION POSITIONING MATRIX (DPM)

From the descriptions presented thus far, it might appear that destinations must have a lot in common to appeal to a specific group of travelers, whether venturers or dependables. Yes and no! Venturers like uniqueness and unspoiled beauty, and they prefer places that have retained their original charm. Travel would quickly become very boring to them (less so to dependables) if all places had similar characteristics. They object to excessive commercialism. Variety not only is the spice of life, it's also what makes destinations attractive to a wider group of travelers. In contrast, dependables like to have many of the comforts and amenities available that they experience back home. But destinations differ on a number of characteristics that determine the kinds of tourists they attract. Some have broad appeal, cutting across most of the psychographic spectrum. Those with a more limited focus tend to attract smaller, more defined groups of travelers. The obvious point is that both psychographic extremes have a large number of places to visit that satisfy their needs. On the face of it, the diversity of types of places enjoyed by each group might seem to run counter to the theory. How could venturers enjoy visiting such a diverse set of destinations, from new developing areas around the world to big cities with all of their hustle and bustle? Even more fundamental, why do dependables sometimes go to places that have lots of action? Understanding the basics of how destinations differ in their appeal helps to explain why they appeal to certain groups of travelers.

Destinations differ not only on the degree of unique experiences they offer to visitors, but also on the number of activities that can be pursued. At many places, a visitor can't cover all there is to see and do in the time available. At others, one day of sightseeing is adequate. But both types of places can attract large crowds and place high on a growth curve. And both can appeal to a dependable or a venturer audience. But, overall, a destination must still measure up on certain fundamental characteristics in order to interest either segment. The psychographic dimension of venturesomeness not only describes and segments types of travelers, it also can categorize destinations. If it attracts mostly venturers, then it obviously fits on that side of the psychographic curve. If it primarily appeals to dependables, then it places on the other opposite side of the curve.

Although venturers tend to be more active while traveling, their energy level does not define their personality. Some vacations they choose can be very relaxing. And, as they age, they may not be able to pursue many of the more active interests they had when they were younger. Yet they would still be classified as venturers on the psychographic scale. More than any other characteristic, *intellectual curiosity* defines the differences between the two ends of the psychographic spectrum. Venturers simply have more of it. And, active minds more often choose active pursuits when traveling. Their high energy levels, which also are apparent at their jobs, can make them feel stressed out at times. Like most of us, they need a chance to kick back, relax, and periodically recharge their psychic batteries. At these times, they seek out places that create an aura of calmness and retreat. But even while taking it easy, their minds are working—catching up on their reading, pondering what they are accomplishing with their lives, or even leisurely exploring the historic countryside around where they are staying. Dependables too show differences on trips. Although they may occupy more chairs in the sand at sunny beaches than any other group, they also take active vacations. In fact, many dependables have higher activity levels than some venturers. Dependables own more RVs than average. They haul these behind campers and SUVs and drive to places where they can jet ski, ride their all-terrain vehicles, fish, or just camp out. But when they slow down, it's more from their usual sense of inertia or that they are physically exhausted, rather than mentally fatigued. Intellectual curiosity, to repeat, most distinguishes the differences between these two groups.

Destinations can also be described in a way that accounts for the breadth or narrowness of their appeal to different psychographic groups using two dimensions. Figure 3.8 provides the first of these characteristics (i.e., the dimension of *unique* vs. *familiar*), which flows directly from the discussion about what venturers and dependables prefer in a destination. The asterisks on the chart indicate the primary placement of each psychographic group on the dimension. The length of the bars extending out from the asterisk points to the degree to which a psychographic group can enjoy destinations that vary from its ideal type. As stated previously, venturers seek more unique experiences wherever they go; dependables like their surroundings to seem more familiar. But a place need not be newly discovered or totally natural for venturers to appreciate its qualities. More than most, they seek experiences that differ from what they encounter daily in their lives, especially those spots that have retained a strong sense of native charm. Thus a quaint village in almost any European country could be exciting to them because the local population seems unaffected by tourists. Either few visitors come by or, like the Pennsylvania Quakers, they don't allow the outside world to alter their daily activities. Conversely, a major historic city can

Figure 3.8   Degree of Overlap among Pyschographic
Types for Kinds of Vacation Experience Enjoyed

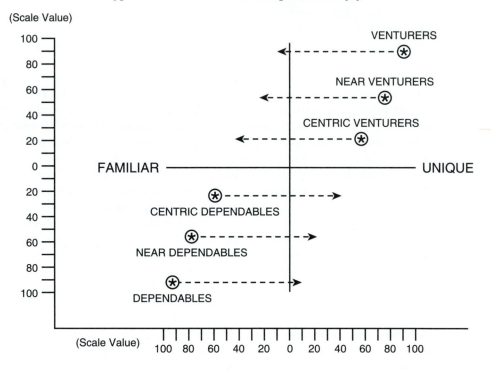

become so overly commercial in character that its appeal is primarily to those with dependable personalities. And some places, like London and Paris, have broad appeal because they offer many choices and options for travelers. The perception of uniqueness differs, therefore, depending on the country and local area where people live. Much of the U.S. is unique to first-time visitors from Europe. Dependables, in contrast, can like many places that offer out of the ordinary experiences, provided these also offer much that also has a familiar feel.

The second dimension, *relaxing* vs. *involving* (see Figure 3.9), describes the range of things available to do at a destination. The greater the number of choices at a place, the more that it can be described as involving. Arrows on the other axis of the chart indicate the degree to which each psychographic type can vary from its ideal destination experience and still enjoy the trip. To emphasize once more, involvement does not imply physical activity. Rather, it relates to the degree to which a person feels immersed in the destination experience. Thus, the presence of a number of quality museums and art galleries can place a destination high on the involving side of the scale. The two dimen-

Figure 3.9 Degree of Overlap among Pyschographic
Types for Kinds of Vacation Experience Enjoyed

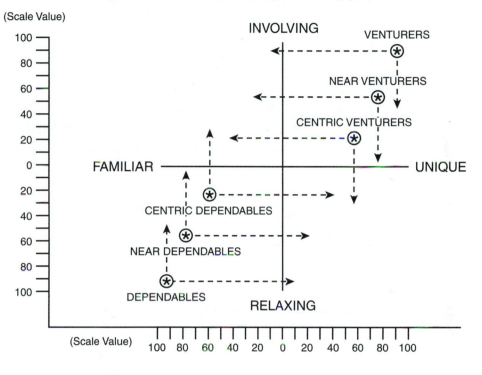

sions are independent of each other, or what researchers call orthogonal. That means that the two don't correlate with each other. One destination can be high on *unique* and *involving,* another might be *unique* and *relaxing,* a third *familiar* and *involving,* and a fourth *familiar* and *relaxing.* A proper positioning of a destination in terms of whether it is a relaxing or involving place helps to ensure that it attracts visitors who will come back from their trips with their expectations met. They return as goodwill ambassadors for those places that provide the destination experiences that they had anticipated. An improper positioning reduces the opportunities to ensure a successful future for a destination. And, critically important, an image must be based on reality. In other words, does the destination measure up to what is being said about it? If not, it should be repositioned to match its true reality.

Together, the two dimensions make up the Destination Positioning Matrix. It has the purpose of helping tourism planners determine the breadth of appeal for their destination. Understanding this fact can help to focus marketing strategies and make them more effective. Figure 3.10 places a small number of destinations on the same chart for illustration purposes.

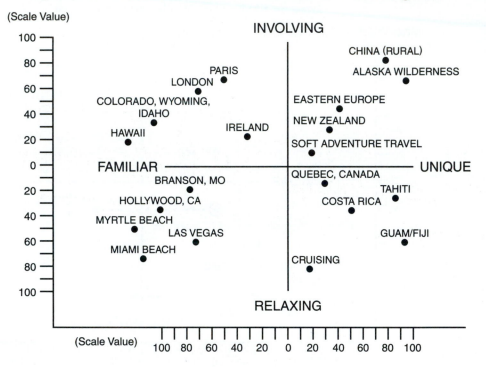

Figure 3.10 Placement of Destinations on Destination Positioning Matrix

As has been indicated, destinations also spread across the spectrum in terms of their appeal to various personalities. Hawaii, for example, has the broadest appeal possible. All psychographic groups enjoy what it offers. Venturers can back pack in remote areas on various islands and enjoy solitude and a sense of isolation from civilization. Pure dependables love Waikiki and even feel at home at places like Kaanpali, which now hosts crowds of people but as recently as the early 1980s was still relatively quiet and private. The greater the number of activities and things to do, the more that a place will attract a diverse audience. But it still holds true that the higher the placement of a destination on the uniqueness dimension, whether or not it is viewed as relaxing or involving, the greater its chances for achieving growth and success in the future.

CHAPTER FOUR

The Psychographics of Travel Segments

Psychographics also relates to lifestyle choices of leisure travelers. This chapter looks at some of those differences and how these influence the kinds of vacations travelers take. Those who concentrate on specific personal sports (golfers, tennis players, and skiers) tend to have different personalities and lifestyles. And those who prefer escorted tours or travel packages usually differ from cruisers and especially those who love adventure travel. Understanding the differences in the psychographics of these groups can help in knowing the types of products to develop, the messages that will be most effective in reaching travelers, and, ultimately, how to target travelers by selecting the appropriate media (covered in Section III). A discussion on the family travel market is also included in this chapter. Since most couples have children, psychographics do not play a strong role in identifying their travel characteristics because children often determine the type of vacation they will take. But family travel is a useful segment to examine because of its importance to some travel providers.

SPORTS PARTICIPANTS

Sports and travel go together. Packagers send golfers around the world to play some of the most beautiful, historic, and famous courses available. Even if you don't play golf, the settings of some famous golf courses like Pebble Beach Golf Club in Monterey, California add a breathtaking backdrop to a vacation with blue ocean, white sand, green fairways, and white clouds in an azure sky. Skiers jaunt off to the great mountains of the western states or the Alps in Europe to enjoy a few days on the slopes. Scuba divers seek out hidden corners of the world to experience the wonders of underwater worlds. Many travel providers target sports enthusiasts. This section focuses on participant sports (i.e., where a traveler actively engages in a personal sport) as contrasted with spectator sports, such as following your favorite college or pro sports team as it plays in other cities. Two points need clarification. First, crossover behavior is common. Some golfers play tennis, and some tennis players also golf. But most persons in either group strongly prefer one sport to the other and concentrate on that sport. Second, since venturers are much more active than their more dependable counterparts, they do more of just about everything. At times, they may even participate regularly in an activity that would seem to be more dependable in character because of the diversity of their interests. They stay involved, intellectually and physically. But these exceptions confirm the descriptions presented so far.

Figure 4.1 summarizes the percent of each psychographic type that played golf or tennis or skied on their last vacation. Typically tables do not include tenths of a percent, as in this case. However, with low participation on a specific (last) vacation, tenths of a percent become necessary in order to show differences since many of the numbers would round to 1 percent. The large sample size of the American Traveler Survey, from which the data are taken, helps to make the results more stable. Several points stand out in reviewing the data:

- Venturers participate more in each of these sports than those who are less venturous. Again, a straight-line relationship is evident for each of the sports (i.e., the more venturesome the person, the more that he or she participates in the activity).

- Tennis and downhill skiing fit the psychology of venturers more so than golf. Although more venturers play golf while on vacation than dependables, the ratio of differences points to a pattern. About twice as many venturers played golf on their last vacation trip as did dependables. However, *five times as many venturers played tennis as dependables and five and a half times as many venturers enjoyed downhill*

Figure 4.1   Participation in Personal Sports on Last Leisure
Trip (by Psychographic Types)

	Venturers	Near-Venturers	Near-Dependables	Dependables
Golf	7.0%	6.9%	4.4%	3.2%
Tennis	2.5	1.0	0.7	0.5
Downhill skiing	3.3	2.1	1.6	0.6

Source: NFO/PLOG Research, American Traveler Survey.

skiing on their last vacation. These two sports don't fit the psychology of dependable types very well.

A number of consulting projects for various clients that I have completed provide a portrait of the personalities of these sports participants. The profiles represent dominant tendencies, not necessarily what is found in every partici-pant. Crossover exists, as was mentioned, and there can be a variety of reasons for non-participation in a sport that fits an individual's personality. The person may never have been introduced to a sport that fits his or her psychology, physical limitations may prevent participation, or constraints of time or money dictate how free time is spent.

Golfers

An avid golfer typically falls on the dependable side of the scale. As a game, golf includes heavy doses of friendship. Foursomes of buddies who have known each other for a long time and who kibitz throughout the game add a strong sense of camaraderie and oneness to the group. Although the activity takes place outdoors and is only about a three-mile walk, golfers generally pre-fer to ride in carts. Convinced that they are getting healthy exercise neverthe-less, they tell others that the game improves how they feel physically and mentally. Friendship continues afterward on the "19th hole," the clubhouse bar, where stories and backslapping can continue for another hour or more. Because of the close feelings that develop between golfers who play together, the game often transcends into business relationships, and a considerable amount of networking and dealmaking takes place on the course. Thus, com-panies often write off country club memberships since these are used to take clients out for games, or take them on retreats that include a heavy dose of golf. Incentive trips to golf resorts also are commonly given as rewards for sales staff who exceed goals. These trips usually include lots of partying and other activities that serve to strengthen friendship bonds, loyalty to the com-pany, and a commitment to work harder the coming year to earn another chance to have fun with a lot of buddies.

From my first study of golfers around 1970, I learned an important point: golfers may lean toward the dependable side of the scale, but they differ from most of their dependable counterparts in an important way—they spend more freely than most dependables when they travel. As a result, they make won-derful guests for resorts. Most want lots of extras when they travel, enjoying many of the comforts available at a destination. They like to select some of the best hotels (24-hour room service is a must), especially those that they can talk about when they return. After a round of golf and some extended friendship at the 19th hole, they'll likely look for a great restaurant. And they might also try to find some good entertainment spots or interesting bars before retiring rather late in the evening to get ready for another round of golf the next day and more living the high life. It all adds up to good money for the hotels and restaurants that serve this group. Smart hotels do everything they can to capture these high spenders and keep them from leaving the property by having quality restaurants and entertainment on the grounds. What golfers want most, similar to most dependable types, is warm weather, pretty scenery as a backdrop to their daily rounds of golf, and lots of good living that includes great food, drinks, and entertainment. It's such a good market for those in the travel business that a number of companies specialize in golf tours. They set up golf packages that include travel to some of the world's best courses in Europe, Hawaii, and the Caribbean.

Golf offers one primary advantage to specialty tour operators and others trying to make a good living serving their interests: Recognizing that money can be made from this market, the golf resorts designed by top PGA pros expanded dramatically in the last 15 years in the United States and around the world. When baby boomers were in their 20s and 30s, they had active lifestyles and took up tennis with a passion. Investors expected them to move into golf as they aged and became less active. But that hasn't happened at the level anticipated. The number of persons in the United States who play golf at least occasionally has remained relatively constant since about the 1980s, at somewhere under 26 million, with only a slight rise in recent years. With more courses and a constant number of players, each golf resort must now compete fiercely for the same market. Overall, golfers are a great market to serve, but not one with high growth potential. The best-known resorts will continue to do well, such as Pebble Beach and the various venues used by the PGA. However, places with less prestige will have to struggle mightily for visitors. Myrtle Beach, South Carolina has about 130 golf courses, an amazing number. But it also is forced to offer deeply discounted package trips that include air, hotel, and golf privileges. The prices make it difficult for local resorts to make money. The current situation should last well into the year 2020 and offers great opportunities for vacation packagers to put reasonably priced trips together that include a good markup in price by concentrating on second-tier golf destinations rather than the famous links that will always draw a crowd.

Tennis Players

Over the years, I have had to explain to clients developing resorts that golfers and tennis players don't mix very well. An avid tennis player has a very different personality than a good golfer. Some developers had planned single clubhouses to serve both groups. Don't do that, I had to tell them. Each wants separate but equal facilities, including pro shops, restaurants, and dressing rooms. Golfers resent tennis players to some degree and don't even particularly want to be around them. The feeling may not be quite mutual on the other side, but you don't see many people carrying a tennis racket talking with a group of golfers heading out to the first tee.

In general, dedicated tennis players make lousy guests at resorts. Although they typically place on the venturesome side of the scale, some even at the extreme end of the curve, they hold on to their wallets more than most venturesome types. They lead more Spartan, disciplined, and health-oriented lifestyles than golfers. Tennis players may take a bottle of water onto the court, but not beer. Golfers frequently pick up a can of beer at the changeover from the front nine to the back nine. Tennis players have no equivalent of a 19th hole, where friendship bonds can be extended. In fact, it's more difficult for tennis players to establish a large circle of friends, for two reasons: little conversation occurs during a match, and a good handicap system to equalize differences between player levels, as used in golf, doesn't exist for tennis (awarding "bisque" points to less capable players seldom is employed in tournaments). When one player wins consistently, it frustrates both players. The better player wants more competition. The consistent loser feels deflated, frustrated, and a failure.

After the tennis match, a small snack bar may serve up a soft drink and a light snack, but little alcohol gets consumed. Now it's time to shower and maybe explore the town for a while. But big meals at the best dining places and late-night entertainment or bar hopping generally don't follow. These would interfere with the competitive edge needed for the match planned for the next morning or the health-oriented lifestyles of better tennis players. Tennis players also spend less for food and services at resorts where they stay and are away from its premises for more daytime hours than golfers. Tennis is a cheap sport. A pair of tennis shoes, a can of balls, a polo shirt and shorts, and a premium racket and you are ready to play. And all of this costs less than a good driver from Callaway or TaylorMade. And use of the courts usually costs nothing at most resorts. The reasonableness of the sport compared to others fits with tennis players frugal approach to life and may explain why they spend less on the good life when they travel. I play both sports, but I like tennis better. It always pains me a bit when I must advise resort developers not to put much hope in attracting a very lucrative tennis crowd. That means that tennis players won't get separate but equal facilities at many places that I would also like to visit. But separate they generally must be—pro shops/clubhouses, the teaching staff, and the memberships and privileges (at private country clubs). An even bigger problem is that tennis is a declining sport. During baby boomers' younger years, it seemed like their ranks might swell to equal the number of golfers. But that never happened. Age has taken its toll. Estimates suggest that only about a fifth as many people play tennis once in a while as compared with those who golf.

Another point for consideration: When tennis facilities are planned for a resort, they must be concentrated in one place, not single courts scattered throughout the grounds. Developers sometimes assume that it would be nice to have tennis courts placed in several locations, close to guestrooms, particularly on low-rise properties that cover considerable acreage. But a couple wanting to play may go to one court and find that it's occupied, go to another and it is also. They may not know that courts on the other side of the complex are open. Placing these together makes it easier to find an open court or be the first one up for the next court that frees up.

Skiers

Skiers also place more on the venturesome side of the scale, and a fair amount of overlap exists with tennis players. But it's somewhat of a one-way street. Many tennis players ski, but not as many skiers play tennis, primarily because tennis players tend to be a bit more active year round than skiers. Skiing obviously includes two groups—downhill skiers and cross-country skiers. Resorts cater most to downhill skiers because they spend more wherever they go. Like golf, it costs a lot to participate. Good skis, special boots, and lots of warm clothing are just the start. Travel to a well-known resort usually means an air ticket, lift fees, and hotel rooms priced high in season, making the trips relatively expensive. Downhill skiers also spend on other items while at the resort. Good restaurants do well with this crowd, with pubs and bars remaining open until late into the night as guests swap stories about their successful runs of the day. Ski villages usually include upscale gift shops. Hot items include clothing featuring the logos and names of the ski resorts. In contrast, cross-country skiers spend less wherever they travel. They don't need expensive equipment or clothes, often take lunch along for a day trip, and tend to use less expensive hotels and restaurants.

Cross-country skiers tend to be more venturesome and independent minded, and less sociable than downhill skiers. They may go out alone during the daytime and enjoy a sense of solitude and escape from civilization as they traverse the lonely hillsides. At night, they will socialize with a smaller group of friends. In contrast, downhill skiers are much more sociable. Groups of friends may go together on trips, and much of the banter back and forth seems similar to what happens between golfing buddies. Downhill skiing promotes strong friendships because it doesn't require an opponent to participate. And families can all go to the same place and enjoy the experience. Varying levels of difficulty on ski runs accommodate the needs of different skill levels in the family (or among friends), enhancing the opportunity to make the entire experience a way for children and parents to feel closer together. The demographics and psychographics of downhill skiers all fall on the positive side—higher incomes and venturesome personalities.

Travel packagers do well with the downhill group. The combination of air, hotel, and lift tickets result in above-average package prices and commission levels. Since more than one person (often a family) typically goes on these trips, the total trip prices can equal some cruises and escorted tours. Many downhillers belong to ski clubs, so it is possible to put high-commission packages together to serve them. With most clients, you can also count on them returning year after year to book more ski trips. But there's also a sour note to consider: The sport is declining. As baby boomers aged, they gave up tennis and picked up skiing. As they continue to age, they now are dropping out of skiing. Some differences exist in the number of skiers reported by two different associations, but they agree on this important point—participation has declined over the past decade or so. The Sporting Goods Manufacturing Association reports that there were 17.7 million downhill skiers and 8.3 million cross-country skiers in the U.S. in 1987, considered a benchmark year. By the turn of the century, those numbers had dropped to 14.7 million and 4.6 million, respectively, during a time that the population continued to grow. The National Ski and Snowboard Retailers Association provides data suggesting that the downhill skier population dropped from 11.4 million in 1990 to 7.4 million by the year 2000. The underlying reason is that the median age of a skier during that period rose from 26 to 30.1 years. Younger persons are not taking up the sport as often as their parents. Rather, they have gravitated to more extreme sports, such as snowboarding. Growth in extreme sports has exploded but, with an average age for participants of just under 16 years, it's tough for any packager to make money on this group. All in all, adult sports participation is on a declining curve.

CRUISERS

More than any segment of the travel industry, cruising has changed its audience over the years. At one time, it appealed almost exclusively to dependable types. The primary form of cruising was trips across the Atlantic on ships featuring an ambience or lifestyle that seems out of character with today's interests. Those who chose it were primarily wealthy dependables, a very narrow audience. Now cruising captures more venturers than dependables, but its true success rests on the fact that it has broad appeal across the board. Its positioning is perfect—something to be studied and copied by land-based destinations with which it competes. Figure 4.2 presents a summary of the psychographics of those that have cruised and are planning to cruise within the next three years. The data show a familiar straight-line relationship. The more venturesome the individual, the more likely that he or she has cruised or is planning a future cruise. Among cruisers, venturers also go cruising more often and spend more on each cruise than dependable types. It's a growth market, powered by strong interest from venturer types.

To understand how a segment could change so dramatically, a little history is useful. At one time, cruising was carriage (i.e., the most common form of travel across the Atlantic, from the U.S. to Europe and Europe to the U.S. and other places around the world). By today's standards, it might not be called cruising, but that was the only way to get across a big expanse of water for most people. Four-engine piston planes introduced by the still very young airlines after World War II (the Douglas DC 4 and DC 6) provided a faster and cheaper alternative to the slow, boring trips by sea. Airlines soon captured a

Figure 4.2   Cruise Patterns (by Psychographic Types)

	Venturers	Near-Venturers	Near-Dependables	Dependables
Average number of cruises taken (total population)	1.0	0.8	0.6	0.4
Average number of cruises taken (of those who have cruised)	3.4	2.8	2.6	2.6
Percent planning cruise in 3 years	5.3%	4.7%	4.3%	3.7%
Amount spent per person on recent cruise	$2048	$1745	$1635	$1666

Source: NFO/PLOG Research, American Traveler Survey.

lion's share of the market on these routes. In the 1950s, the numbers of air travelers swelled greatly. Some small operators who conducted group tours of the U.K. and central Europe realized that they could build a bigger business. They took naïve travelers to the capitols of Europe and used Advance Booking Charters. The ABCs, as they were called, took advantage of a government loophole in aviation laws that allowed these small carriers to provide cheap seats to affinity groups (members of a club or organization) at a low price. The tour companies they founded, for the most part, still exist today. Air travel quickly became the most common way to go across "the pond." Although a few members of the upper classes who had dependable personalities would fly one direction and cruise back, the industry was nearly comatose. Its image was totally wrong. It was a slow and comfortable way to travel that offered good dining and a chance to meet people of your social standing, but it was a boring image to most Americans. They didn't like its formality (tuxedos for dinner) or lack of things to do (shuffleboard and reading on the deck in the daytime).

As an industry, cruising nearly died. But, in 1966, Ted Arison and Knut Kloster had an idea. They bought an old ship at a bargain basement price, redid the interior, and named it the *Sunward*. They literally invented modern cruising with their decision to concentrate on a new market—seven-day cruises to the Caribbean from Miami. Named the Norwegian Caribbean Line (NCL), it didn't matter that the ship guzzled fuel because it didn't have to go very far. And with the warm, predictable weather of the region, it could sail year 'round. This was cruising, not transportation, because it offered more interesting destinations and more activities onboard. Royal Caribbean began a similar operation in 1970, but the bigger revolution occurred when Ted Arison separated from Kloster to start Carnival Cruise Lines. He offered shorter (three- and four-day) cruises in the Caribbean and, with a party atmosphere on board, he named his fleet "fun ships." More than any operator, he lowered the age and income profiles of cruisers by attracting swinging singles. Carnival has changed its focus somewhat over time, but has now grown into the largest cruise line in the world, acquiring multiple other lines in the process. But the primary market for these cruises, even though the demographics had moved down considerably in both age and income, continued to be those with dependable leanings. Both lines offered limited itineraries and a narrow range of activities on board, except to join the party crowd until the early morning hours. Not very appealing to venturers who want variety in their daily lives.

But Kloster and Arison had kicked off a revolution. Other smart people saw that a new market had developed almost overnight and decided to get into the cruise business. Not wanting to compete directly with the guys who started it all, they provided new options. New destinations beyond the Caribbean (the Mediterranean also had warm weather most of the year) and longer itineraries (ten- to fourteen-day cruises became popular) soon followed. And, they began to build ships tailored to their needs, rather than just convert old clunkers. Cruise lines ordered bigger and bigger ships, along with small ships, ones with little draft to get into small harbors around the world, and special-purpose ships. Today's cruisers can choose from ships that carry more than 2500 passengers and offer enough activities to occupy your days and nights throughout a cruise to those designed for less than 100. Cruise activities vary from great entertainment (Broadway musicals, jazz, and big bands, pop singers) to Las Vegas–style casinos, erudite lectures, and wine tasting. Magnificent spas and exercise rooms help get rid of the gluttonous image present at one time, along with onboard rock climbing and golf instruction. Adventure travelers can snorkel from small ships in hidden coves or explore forgotten parts of the world on specially built vessels that can cut through ice flows in arctic waters. At one time, ships primarily served as places to sleep, with activities occurring at ports of call. Today, large ships serve as destinations. These offer so many optional activities that cruisers feel less need to spend an extended time in port. Itineraries now include places not imagined a decade ago—Latin America, Asia, the Pacific, Alaska, the Aegean and Baltic seas, and other parts of the world. With this much diversity, venturers discovered cruising. They tried it, liked it, and came back for more. It offers the convenience of unpacking your bags only once, a good hotel room, top-quality meals, and a chance to visit historic parts of the world not easily reached by air, rail, or motor coach. It's a winning combination. Two simple but interrelated innovations in cruising helped attract greater numbers of near-venturers, the perfect market for most companies: Seabourn Cruise Line established a new-category, ultraluxury to serve the highest end of the market; and another startup cruise line, Silversea Cruises, under the leadership of John Bland in 1994, initiated flexible dining and all-inclusive pricing. Prior to this time, guests were assigned tables for the length of the cruise and ate with the same dinner guests every evening at the same time for dinner. Bland, the former CEO of Sitmar Cruise Line before it was taken over by Princess Cruises, reasoned that sophisticated people want choices. So, ships built for the new line had sufficient dining capacity for guests to come to meals at anytime of their choice, and to choose their dinner companions or eat alone. Bland's related innovation is all-inclusive pricing—no tipping, no port charges, and no cost for wine and drinks. One price includes all.

For these and other reasons, cruising has a bright future. Only a minority of the population has sailed, but more than half of venturers state that they will cruise in the future, according to the American Traveler Survey. They will lead others to follow what they do. Cruising now offers something for everyone, a positioning that destinations and travel providers can use as a model of what is needed for success.

TOURS AND PACKAGES

Compared to cruise lines, tour operators will have a more difficult time expanding their markets. But the opportunities for packagers to grow seem almost boundless. For most of its history, the extreme regimentation and fixed schedules of tours attracted a dependable type of traveler. At first the market expanded quickly and dramatically because escorted tours provided a way for dependable types to visit foreign lands under the protection of a guide. But, because of their early success, many tour operators have been slow to change their approach to the market, as will be seen shortly. First, a couple of definitions will clarify what will be covered.

Broadly speaking, leisure travel includes four types of travel arrangements:

- *Independent travel:* Air tickets, hotels, rail, and other extras are bought separately. It is the preferred way to travel by the three-fourths of all travelers. But it often loses out in the decision process to tours or packages because of discount prices or special itineraries offered that can't be matched through do-it-yourself planning and booking arrangements. The trade also refers to these as FITs, which actually stands for *foreign independent tour.* The label is a hangover from more than a half a century ago, when *tour* referred to plans to explore another county by train or motor car without a guide.

- *Escorted tour:* Although this kind of travel arrangement has been well known since the 1920s, it reached its greatest popularity after World War II when Americans discovered Europe. It's a good choice for novice travelers. They can see the main capitols and historic sites with a guide, who explains everything, handles language problems, and makes them smart about currency exchange rates. In time, some tour operators discovered that many people want more freedom on these trips, and the subcategory of partially escorted tours appeared. These still include guides, tour buses, a hotel every night, and some amenities (meals and entertainment). But they now offer big blocks of free time for travelers to rest, do more shopping, or explore some places on their own.

- *Inclusive package:* Includes just about everything in the price: air, hotel, many meals, and even some amenities like golf or entertainment. An inclusive package often means settling down at one resort in the Caribbean (like Sandals or Super Clubs) or Hawaii (offered by many tour operators). Some ski packages and golf trips where multiple courses are played in different locations also fit into this category since just about everything is covered in the price.

- *Partial package:* Fewer items are included, perhaps just air, hotel, and a rental car or ground transfers from airport to hotel and back again. More freedom is given for the travel party to move around from one location to another. The distinction between *partial* and *inclusive* can fall in a gray area, but it still holds.

Like cruising, the psychographics of those who use tours and packages has changed over the past couple of decades. In my first travel study, completed in 1967, escorted tour takers had dependable personalities. They liked traveling with a group of people on a tour bus, marching as a unit through a city to see the sites, eating lunches and dinners together, and enjoying the same entertainment at night. Even where group participants would shop was predetermined. It may be too routine for most, but it ensured travelers that they would return home after seeing the best of Europe on an "8 countries in 11 days" whirlwind trip. The standard formula moved clients in and out of hotels and onto buses, zipped them through beautiful countryside on the way to the next stop, and provided a quick feeling of local culture with costumed folk dancers in staged events at restaurants or other venues. It's a novice's way to get exposure to whatever seems foreign. Although fully escorted tours tapped a need at the time, tour operators didn't recognize that they ultimately faced a declining market. Since dependables don't influence the opinions of many other people, growth stalled after a large number of dependables had taken their once-in-a-lifetime trip. Escorted tours became the object of derisive humor to the point that people who have never seen the movie *If It's Tuesday, It Must be Belgium* immediately understand its meaning. For a number of years I counseled various tour operators about the need to expand their products and provide more flextime in their schedules. I tried to get them to understand that their tour programs should offer more excitement and diversity in order to capture a broader slice of the market. For the most part, they were slow in understanding the message. First-generation leaders who started a number of today's larger tour companies generally believed that they saw a need and filled it and their vision would carry them far into the future. But while the rest of the travel industry grew dramatically during the late 1970s, 1980s, and into the 1990s, escorted tour operators fought to grow revenue and profits. They lost a lot of market share. In the 1960s and early 1970s, 30 percent of all airline seats between Europe and America were filled with people on escorted tours. Near the end of the last century, that number dropped to 5 to 10 percent, depending on the airline. What took its place? Packages, both complete and partial.

Since the mid-1990s, tours have started to make a comeback. New owners of some older companies, along with business school–trained sons and daughters of the founders, have assumed leadership and made important changes. But the pace has been gradual. Responding to complaints, and fortified with a little bit of research, tour operators now go to less common destinations, offer specialty tours (art, history, wine tasting, horticulture, adventure travel), and provide more free time for individual sightseeing, shopping, or just taking a breather from a grueling schedule. The number of tour companies expanded exponentially during the late 1980s and into the 1990s. The United States Tour Operators Association, which began in 1972, has about 65 members out of approximately 100 companies that have sufficient assets to qualify for its strict rules of membership, representing 150 brands. However, approximately 2500 tour companies exist in the U.S. alone. Their offerings range from rigorous treks with Sherpa guides through Tibet, Nepal, and the Himalayas (Snow Lion Expeditions) to educational tours promoted by university programs that offer faculty lecturers. The very successful Elder Hostel program fills the gap for seniors on limited budgets. Their reasonably priced educational and instructional tours use pensions and vacated university dormitories for accommodations on summer trips. Tour programs have a relatively new image and a broader psychographic appeal than previously. Venturesome travelers buy tours that go to exotic places where some assistance is required in order to see difficult sites or participate in unusual activities.

Escorted tours started on a new growth path around 1997, after losing market share for a couple of decades to travel packagers. Cruise lines serving Alaska have also gotten into the act. They discovered how to increase revenues by offering land tours to the interior of Alaska as add-ons to cruises. With these changes, the psychographics have been moving in a more favorable direction, as can be seen in Figure 4.3. Note that all psychographic types now enjoy tours, a change from several decades ago. But they prefer different types of tours. However, tour operators missed their chance to protect and grow their market share by sticking to old formulas for too long. They will have a bright future if they continue to modify product offerings to attract more ven-

Figure 4.3   Use of Tours and Packages (by Psychographic Types)

	Venturers	Near-Venturers	Near-Dependables	Dependables
Independent travel	84%	84%	83%	86%
Inclusive package	11	8	10	8
Partial package	6	4	6	6
Escorted tour	7	9	6	7

Source: NFO/PLOG Research, American Traveler Survey.

turesome types. They need to counter the image of a herd mentality among those who share the same group experiences when traveling.

Figure 4.3 also points out that all psychographic groups use packages at about the same level, both partial and inclusive. Since these came into true prominence a couple of decades after escorted tours began their rise, they adapted more quickly to the changing needs of the market by offering a broader array of products. The variety is endless. Inclusive packages to the Caribbean attract more dependables because of the chance to lie on the beach and enjoy a warm sun. In the U.S., Branson, Missouri (country music entertainment) is the top-selling packaged destination, with heavy growth occurring for Myrtle Beach, South Carolina (golf trips), Orlando, Florida (theme parks and golf), and Las Vegas, Nevada (gambling), according to the National Tour Association. A London theater package attracts more venturesome types because of their intellectual curiosity and breadth of interests. Partial packages to Waikiki in Honolulu that include air, hotel, and ground transfer to the hotel and back suit the needs of dependables, while air and a rental car on the outer islands allow venturers to explore on their own. The primary point is that packages can be easily assembled by almost any travel organization to suit the specific needs of different kinds of psychographic types.

Although those who use tours and packages have similar psychographic profiles, demographics show differences. The data can be seen in Figure 4.4. It points out that escorted tours (compared with packaged trips) attract older, retired persons with somewhat lower annual incomes, and they are more likely to be female. But escorted tour travelers spent more on their last trip and in total on travel for the year and had more nights away from home during the past year than package users. This chart also contains two important hidden messages: Retirement does not lead to less spending on leisure travel, even though incomes decline for most households. The travel bug has been held in abeyance for years by the demands of raising a family and time restrictions

Figure 4.4   Characteristics of Package Tour Purchases

	Escorted Tour	Packaged Vacations	Partial Packages	Total U.S. Population
Median income	$41,500	$51,000	$51,400	$43,100
Average age	59	44	45	46
Female	58%	51%	54%	51%
% college grads	36%	28%	38%	33%
Retired	43%	14%	16%	18%
Children at home	14%	38%	36%	40%
Average # leisure trips	2.5	2.3	2.8	2.7
Average # nights away for leisure	21	15	16	14
$ Spent past year on leisure—average	$4454	$3292	$3607	$2460
$ Spent past year on leisure—medium	$2417	$2170	$2423	$1491

Source: NFO/PLOG Research, American Traveler Survey.

related to holding jobs. Now, with few economic demands placed on them (the kids have left home) and free time on their hands (retired), they can follow their desires and enjoy the travel they dreamed about for years. Few differences exist between those who use inclusive or partial packages, except that the percent of college/university grads is higher among those who want more freedom and select partial packages. The second message is the obverse of the first: since psychographic profiles are similar between these groups, age and sex do not particularly contribute to a tendency to become more dependable in character.

ADVENTURE TRAVEL

Adventure travel generates interest among quite a few travel suppliers. They hear stories about rapid growth of the market and, as a result, new companies continue to appear, serving different niches. Data confirm most of these points, except one: profitability eludes most who enter the field. Some facts need to be considered before any company launches new programs targeted at this market. As would be expected, the more venturesome an individual, the more likely that person also pursues adventure-related activities on trips. It fits their personalities and lifestyles. Figure 4.5 presents the percent of each psychographic group that participated in an adventure activity during the past 12 months while on a leisure trip. These data do not cover a broad range of

Figure 4.5   Percent Participation in Adventure
Travel Activities (By Psychographic Type)

	Venturers	Near-Venturers	Centric	Near-Dependables	Dependables
Soft Adventure Travel					
Nature travel/eco tours	19%	17%	13%	12%	6%
Exercise/health club	14	7	6	3	2
Snorkeling	7	5	4	2	1
Sailing	4	2	2	2	1
Total soft adventure	44%	31%	25%	19%	10%
Hard Adventure Travel					
Hiking/backpacking	17	14	13	9	6
Bicycle touring	6	3	3	1	1
Scuba diving	5	3	2	1	2
Rock climbing	2	3	3	1	1
White-water rafting	2	2	1	1	<1
Total hard adventure	32%	25%	22%	13%	10%
TOTAL ALL ACTIVITIES:	76%	56%	47%	32%	20%

Source: NFO/PLOG Research, American Traveler Survey.

pursuits because the ATS survey does not include questions about activities of interest to very small groups of travelers. But the data confirm the finding that the more venturesome the person, the more likely that he or she will pursue adventure activities when traveling.

Adventure travel is defined loosely in the industry. Some tour companies label their city walking tours as adventure travel because the word seems attractive. An academic researcher even called bird watching in city parks as adventure travel because it involved "adventures of the mind." So, some clarification is in order before getting into the topic in greater depth. Adventure travel is leisure travel with several distinguishing characteristics: it requires a level of energy by participants beyond normal travel. It usually takes place outdoors in more natural—not manufactured—settings. And it may involve some element of risk. In addition, *hard adventure travel* can be distinguished from *soft adventure travel*. Hard adventurers do more on their own with less backup support from tour organizers and are generally more physically active on trips, and the element of risk can be higher. Soft adventurers exhibit less of each of these characteristics. Soft adventure travel provides a sense of thrill and excitement to the traveler, but with a lower level of effort, less potential danger, and more comfort provided throughout the trip.

A couple of examples can clarify differences. A hard adventure whitewater rafting trip down the Colorado River might start with an individual or a couple of friends, each carrying his or her own kayak or small rubber raft. The individual will take along all needed supplies, such as freeze-dried food and a sleeping bag for a night's rest under the stars. A soft adventure rafting trip is more likely to be organized by a tour operator, who picks up a group of people at a central location, drives them to the starting point, and offers many support services. The tour organizer provides large rafts to handle 6 to 12 people and a guide, and chooses less dangerous rapids to navigate. Guests don't need to carry much more than a camera and wear a life vest. At dinnertime, the raft may pull into a cove, where an advance party has set up tents for sleeping and has dinner prepared, perhaps even with a little wine and cheese to sample. Bicycle touring has grown in popularity in recent years, and it shows similar differences. A hard adventure tour might include several buddies or couples going through New England in the fall. They'll travel on their own, stop where they wish, and sleep out at night. They may buy most of their groceries along the way for convenience, and every couple of nights will check into a motel or bed and breakfast (B & B) to clean up and get a good night's rest. With soft adventure tours, the organizer maps an itinerary, has preplanned lunches at quaint inns along the way and comfortable hotels at night. A van follows to pick up stragglers and their bikes.

Figure 4.6 presents information on the demographic, psychographic and travel characteristics of these groups as compared to the total U.S. population. Three types of groups are included in this summary. Hard adventure travelers participated only in hard adventure travel during the past 12 months and have no future plans for soft trips. Soft adventure travelers chose only soft adven-

Figure 4.6   Characteristics of Adventure Travelers

	Total	Hard Adventurers	Soft Adventurers	Adventure Seekers
Percentage of adult population	100%	3.6%	18.5%	4.6%
Demographic characteristics				
% Male	49%	60%	55%	61%
% college graduate	33%	47%	32%	37%
Average age	46	43	43	40
Number leisure trips (12 months)	2.7	3.5	3.1	3.4
Percent above leisure spending				
Last trip	N.A.	18%	5%	26%
Past 12 months	N.A.	26%	3%	26%
Psychographic characteristics				
Venturer/near-venturer %	21%	33%	29%	35%

Source: NFO/PLOG Research, American Traveler Survey.

ture excursions during that time and have no plans for hard adventure travel. The third group, *adventure seekers,* were given this label because they enjoyed both hard and soft adventure travel activities during the year. As it turns out, that distinction is important. The chart helps to place each group in perspective. Common characteristics across these groups include that adventure travelers measure higher on the venturesome scale, as would be expected, are younger than average for the adult population, and a majority are male. For travel characteristics, each group takes more leisure trips than average and also spends more on travel, for the last trip and total for the year. But significant differences exist between the groups that determine their importance to travel providers. *Soft adventurers* are the least venturesome, take somewhat fewer trips, and spend the smallest amount of the three groups on leisure travel. College graduation rates mirror national averages, and they have a lower ratio of men. *Hard adventurers* provide a more favorable profile. They have higher venturesome scores, take more trips, spend considerably more on travel than their soft counterparts, and have the highest percent of college grads. *Adventure seekers,* however, capture the prize in this review. They truly love adventure travel—all forms of it, whether soft or hard—as evidenced by the larger number of trips they take and the greater amount they spent on their last trip and in total for the year. And they are the youngest of the groups.

   Given a choice, the data might seem to suggest that hard adventure travelers (including adventure seekers) represent the best market for travel suppliers, tour organizers and travel agencies to target. But most travel suppliers or travel agents should consider the soft adventure market first for several reasons. The group is four times the size of either the hard adventure or adventure seeker populations, and double those two groups combined. Further, since adventure seekers also take soft adventure trips, a company focusing on soft adventure can reach a potential market of nearly a fourth of the population (18.5% + 4.6% = 23.1%). And, the total travel spending data for those pursuing hard adventure travel is somewhat misleading. Often, they put more travel dollars into air fares because they take more trips and go to more distant places, rather than drive, but they purchase fewer products and services after they land in a distant place on hotel accommodations, meals, and other amenities. Finally, because soft adventure types enjoy the good life with just a feeling of adventure on their trips, smart tour organizers can learn how to motivate them to add comfort features to their trips.

The points to remember from this review are that adventure travelers have different psychographic profiles from the general population, and the market divides into three types. Knowledge of these differences is essential for any company or organization that wants to focus on adventure travelers as a market. As the population ages in most countries throughout the world, soft adventure travel will increase in size, while other more strenuous forms of outdoor travel will decline. The impact of these changes can be seen in the interesting story of Ron Barness, founder and president of two successful adventure travel companies. He has used the concepts of venturesomeness for years to target his market, create collateral marketing materials, and develop his product. He first contacted me in late 1992, when he wrote an interesting letter that demonstrates how even a travel product can change its character as it moves from attracting pure venturers to more main stream soft adventure travelers. In the following quote, I have changed only the names of the psychographic types to match my current designation.

Dear Stanley:

I have finished reading your book *Leisure Travel* and I want to commend you! I was engaged from start to finish and had a difficult time putting it down. In fact I have recommended it to a dozen friends who work in the travel and/or advertising industries.

I have witnessed southern Utah go from being a haven for venturers to being discovered by the mass market. . . . In 1983, I founded a niche agency called High Desert Adventures, which sells whitewater rafting vacations in Grand Canyon, Southern Utah and in Idaho. Back then, commercial outfitters on the Colorado River sold fewer than 50 percent of their annual seat allotment and I perceived an opportunity: excellent destination, lack of marketing and infrastructure to get people to the river. I linked up with Western Airlines and we were off and running.

The commercial river industry was still a young industry then. Between 1869—the year when John Wesley Powell made his first historic voyage—and 1969, fewer than 1000 people had ever rafted the Grand Canyon. The whitewater experience through Grand Canyon was venturesome in those days . . . and even up until the mid-1980s. Although things changed fast.

In 1992, High Desert Adventures handled 2500 clients. This gave the company an 8% market share for Colorado River trips and it was the fifth largest purveyor even among the river's 48 outfitters. As you probably know, the Interior Department placed limits on the number of commercial passengers who can raft the Colorado in 1972 and it remains to this day a "flat" destination which cannot grow beyond the ceilings imposed by the Federal Government. . . .

Between 1983 and 1992, I noticed that High Desert Adventures' market was changing. What I am not sure about is WHY it changed. In the beginning years, we only advertised in *Outside* magazine. In 1989 we broadened our frequency and reach. We added many more publications such as *Sierra, Backpacker, Audubon, New York Times, Utne Reader* and *Travel & Leisure.* With the exception of *New York Times* and *Travel & Leisure,* all publications seemed to zero in on our niche.

WHAT changed was our clients' expectations about river rafting. In the past three or four years there were more complaints even though our river outfitters had made sophisticated improvements to their operation. Complaints included sleeping outside, sand, being uncomfortable, and the latrine. Many people complained about not having air conditioning in the vans for the two hour ride back to their cars which is curious since they just spent up to two weeks camping out in 100+ degree heat! . . .

Today, I am launching Snow Lion Expeditions, another niche agency which specializes in the Himalaya, India and Tibet. . . . Your book was also very helpful in conceptualizing our new company. . . . I am not sure whether I believe that all of Nepal is a venturesome destination. I think some parts of Nepal are venturesome, such as the newly opened Mustang and Manaslu regions, but I believe the Khumbu (Everest) and Annapurna regions have begun to move up the curve toward the mass market, which is unfortunate. Hotels are being built in the villages at a very rapid rate.[2]

Ron Barness sold his whitewater rafting company in 1989 to a large mainstream tour company in Utah. Obviously what happened was that word of mouth by venturers influenced others around them to try the same experience. Over time, the sport attracted near venturers and, ultimately, centrics with venturer leanings who wanted more amenities and comforts on their trips. That changed the nature of the experience. Like destinations, tour operators must decide which market(s) they want to target and then ensure that they continue to offer a product that will attract those target segments. Barness's new company, Snow Lion Adventures, achieved great success and he now understands what he must do to maintain its original character and purpose.

A market for adventure travel will always exist, but its growth potential is more limited than many may recognize, particularly as the population ages. And, caution should come into the minds of many when they consider that an entrepreneur entering the market must target a segment of it, not the entire

[2]Letter dated November 8, 1992.

Figure 4.7   Size of Total Niche Markets

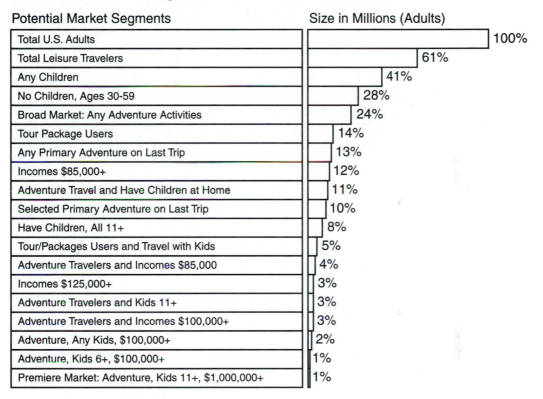

Potential Market Segments	Size in Millions (Adults)
Total U.S. Adults	100%
Total Leisure Travelers	61%
Any Children	41%
No Children, Ages 30-59	28%
Broad Market: Any Adventure Activities	24%
Tour Package Users	14%
Any Primary Adventure on Last Trip	13%
Incomes $85,000+	12%
Adventure Travel and Have Children at Home	11%
Selected Primary Adventure on Last Trip	10%
Have Children, All 11+	8%
Tour/Packages Users and Travel with Kids	5%
Adventure Travelers and Incomes $85,000	4%
Incomes $125,000+	3%
Adventure Travelers and Kids 11+	3%
Adventure Travelers and Incomes $100,000+	3%
Adventure, Any Kids, $100,000+	2%
Adventure, Kids 6+, $100,000+	1%
Premiere Market: Adventure, Kids 11+, $1,000,000+	1%

market. That can make the prospect base extremely slim. Figure 4.7 provides a picture of this difficulty. Note how the percent of the total population declines quickly as various selection criteria are used. For example, targeting adventure travelers who have double the annual household income (a minimum criterion used by a majority of travel suppliers) narrows the available target group to 4 percent of the population. The inclusion of other criteria, such as type of adventure trip offered, reduces that base further—to 1 or 2 percent, or less. Few companies can afford to develop effective marketing programs that target such a narrow base, especially for inadequately funded startup ventures.

CHAPTER FIVE

The Demographics of Travel

Although psychographics explains much about travel patterns, it will never replace demographics as the primary tool to segment and target different groups of travelers. Demographics is embedded in the fabric of business worldwide. Every nation can be described in terms of its percent of young vs. old, educational levels, household income, and related characteristics. All media use these data to define the special characteristics of their audiences, especially age, income, and family composition. Television especially gears its shows—sitcoms and sports programming—to capture young viewers. Most product manufacturers operate on the assumption that if you can capture a young market, this group will remain as customers for decades. And, young people typically spend most of their incomes on impulse buys, making them easier to motivate for purchases. So the interests of people above 40 years generally get ignored when television networks prepare the lineups for each new season's shows. But the tables get turned for leisure travel. Mature individuals travel more and spend more on travel than their younger counterparts. This chapter looks at two market segments where demographics provide very meaningful comparisons: family travel and mature travel.

FAMILY TRAVEL

Periodically I read studies that suggest that the family travel market is a growing and highly profitable segment that deserves special interest and attention from most travel suppliers and travel agencies. And, periodically, I have felt obligated to tell clients that "It ain't necessarily so." A limited number of travel providers can make good money catering to the special needs and interests of families. Others will die on the vine because they don't recognize how the presence of children in a home limits travel choices. But what can't be forgotten is that the market is huge. Adults with children at home comprise the largest group in virtually every nation. Some of the problems associated with the family market will be reviewed before covering the benefits for companies that learn how to target their products and messages properly.

- *Demographics continue to move toward the empty nest era.* During the decade of 2000 to 2010, the number of adults in the child-bearing age will remain relatively stable, not grow. The U.S. Census Bureau indicates that the country currently has approximately 108 million people aged 18 to 44 years, the age at which families are formed and raised, and that number will shrink slightly to 107 million by 2010. There is a small boomlet in the 18 to 34 age category (this group will increase by 8 percent during the decade), which is more than offset by a 14 percent decline in the 35 to 44 group. In contrast, the aging baby boomer generation, as we all know, continues to make its impact on our nation's economy. The empty nester segments (45 to 64 years) will show an increase of 29 percent during this same time period, and retirees (those over 65) will jump by nearly 14 percent. The action is primarily at the upper end of the age chart.

- *Families have less money to spend on travel.* Those with young children generally have not reached the peak of their careers and, as a result, earn less. Thus they have less disposable income to set aside for travel. Figure 5.1 summarizes data on the percent over or under that is spent

Figure 5.1   Family Leisure Travel Patterns

	Total Population	Any Children Under 10 Yrs.	Older Children Only (11+ Yrs.)	No Children at Home
Percentage of total adults	100%	29%	10%	61%
Average number, leisure trips	2.7	2.7	2.6	2.8
Percentage taking int'l trips	9%	7%	5%	10%
Nights away for leisure	14	11	11	17
Average nights per trips	5.3	4.1	4.3	6.2
Percentage above/below for travel spending	N.A.	−14%	−8%	+8%
Number destination Visitors (3 yrs)	6.1	4.6	5.4	6.4
Percentage have taken cruise	21%	16%	15%	24%

Source: NFO/ PLOG Research, American Traveler Survey.

on travel by families with younger or older children vs. those with no children living at home who have just reached the empty nester stage (45 to 64 years) or are likely to be retired (65 +). As can be seen, spending on travel increases as a family ages, and especially when the last child has left home or the wage earner has retired.

- *Families travel less.* Figure 5.1 also indicates that not only do families spend less on travel, they take fewer trips. This point, and the previous one, may seem to make the same statement, but there is a difference. Some households take fewer but grander trips—longer in duration and more expensive. In the data, note that families stayed away fewer nights in total *and on each trip*, took fewer international trips, and visited a smaller number of destinations during the past three years.

- *Money spent on travel must cover four or more people.* Some experts, when they discuss the virtues of the family market, overlook the fact that family travel typically involves two adults and two or more children. Families not only spend less on a trip, but that amount must cover an average of four travelers, not just two adults. Thus, a family spends less per person on meals, hotel rooms, shopping, and other items. This fact explains why so much of family travel is by car. It costs the same to drive four people to a destination as it does to drive one. Not true for air travel, obviously. Families contribute heavily to what is called the "rubber tire crowd" in the industry.

- *Families use travel agents less.* All of the preceding statements point to why families appear less often in travel agents' offices than their representation in the general population: They don't have the money to buy the kinds of services agents offer as much as most people, and they don't travel as often. From a travel agent's perspective, it's more difficult to convert someone to use travel agents than it is to convince current customers to take more trips. Agents face difficulties trying to make money from families.

- *Families primarily travel during the busiest season.* An obvious point, but often overlooked, is the fact that families travel primarily during the summer months. Parents generally will not take children out of school except for very special reasons. Thus, summer travel remains the time for them to get away. It's harder to find accommodations then, most destinations are crowded, and higher in-season prices mean that families must pay more than those who can leave town during off season or shoulder months. Travel providers that focus primarily on families hustle to keep up with demand during the summer, but face down times during the rest of the year.

Figure 2.3 (p. 29) dramatically presented these conclusions. It pointed out that the presence of children can deter travel by an average of nearly 50 percent during school months, with an increase by more than 75 percent above normal in the summer months when school is out. In contrast, child-free homes vary at the maximum by less than 20 percent from one month to the next in the amount they travel, regardless of the season of the year. Children restrict travel more than most people recognize. Older children put a greater damper on travel patterns than the presence of younger children. Stated differently, parents are more reluctant to take teens out of school than their younger children.

- *Planning family travel is a difficult task.* Couples that have only one child, or two that are nearly the same age, have a relatively easy time in planning vacation trips. For the most part, the children will enjoy the same activities. With broad age spans in the household, especially with teenagers and kids under the age of ten, interest patterns vary greatly. It's difficult to find a destination that offers a broad range of activities that will meet the needs of diverse ages. Travel agents and suppliers sometimes get trapped in this morass, spending a considerable amount of time helping parents reach a decision about where to go.

In spite of these problems, the family market also provides some great opportunities. As the largest single segment, tapping into even a portion of it can support of very large business model. And targeting selected niches can lead to strong profits. Travel agencies in affluent neighborhoods, for example, have a good future. These families take more frequent vacations, and they spend a lot. They bring the kids along—to international destinations, dude ranches, adventure trips, and on skiing trips—each of which can use a travel agent's services to facilitate all arrangements. The commissions are sizeable because these families buy top-end products, typically for four people, not the common two travelers. Travel agencies that heavily promote Disneyland and Disney World also can do quite well. Considering the limited financial resources of families, it always amazes me when I look at the cost of trips to theme parks. Steep admission prices, expensive hotels, and pricey restaurants make this a big-ticket item for most couples who decide to give their children a special treat by visiting a theme park. A new trend has emerged that will increase in the future—intergenerational trips. Grandparents now frequently take their grandchildren on trips without the parents. Grandparents relish the opportunity to spend fun time with their grandchildren, and parents appreciate the chance to get away together without having to worry about who is taking care of their kids. The older generation has the equity to afford trips of this type, and they love to travel. They might make the trip to a theme park, or take a cruise where babysitting services are offered, or go to a sunny location where they can lie on the beach while the grandchildren romp around in the sand and water.

MATURE TRAVELERS

The word *seniors* should be dropped from every marketer's vocabulary. It offends some in this category, and it leads to a tendency by younger creative types in advertising agencies "talk down" to this very important group of travelers. Far too many agency folks don't understand the motives and needs of people over the age of 55. More important, many travel suppliers don't realize that today's mature travelers differ greatly from those of the same age who preceded them a generation or more ago. Travel is a more important part of their lives, and they are more active when they travel. For this reason, I have divided the market into two groups: the *new freedoms group* and the *mature explorers*.

New freedoms fall into the age range of 45 to 64 years. Their children have left home and they now have an empty nest. They can participate in many things that interest them without the responsibilities of raising families. That freedom allows them to take the kinds of trips they want without having to think about what the kids would like to do. The freedom to travel when they want, and to where they want, has been a goal for a long time—a new freedom that they haven't been able to enjoy until now. This is the boomer generation passing into its middle years. Its members have retained their yearning for exploration and discovery enjoyed when they were in their late teens and early 20s and toured the world, often with just a few dollars in their pockets. They have built up good equity over time, are at the peak of their earnings careers, and financial obligations have declined after they paid for the kids' college education. They view their situation as a wonderful time in their lives, and travel ranks high on their list of things to do. They are physically active and take more energetic vacations than 45- to 64-year-olds a generation ago.

An even bigger change is apparent in the *mature explorers* group, those aged 65 and above. Although most in this group have retired, I have labeled them as mature explorers because they generally lead less sedentary lifestyles than similar-aged generations that came before. Travel also has a new importance to them. They seek more active vacations. Today you can find them signing up for soft adventure tours and going to more distant lands. They often avoid group travel and choose to go with a spouse or friend. They especially like programs that have some educational content, such as those provided by alumni associations of colleges and universities. Although incomes decline when retirement begins, these folks spend a higher percent of their household income on travel than any other demographic group. In fact, they spend more on travel than any other group reviewed in this section.

Figure 5.2 contains similar data as were presented in Figure 5.1 for families, but this time only for the new freedoms and mature explorers groups. In looking at the data for the *new freedoms group* (comparing them to the average), they

- Take an above average number of trips (2.8 vs. 2.7 average), and more than the family groups (See Figure 5.1).

Figure 5.2   Mature Groups Leisure Travel Patterns

	Total Population	New Freedom Group (45–64 Yrs.)	Mature Explorers (65+ Yrs.)
Percentage of total adults	100%	16%	23%
Average number, leisure trips	2.7	2.8	2.5
Percentage taking int'l trips	9%	10%	10%
Nights away for leisure	14	15	22
Average nights per trip	5.3	5.5	9.1
Percentage above/below for travel spending	xx%	+12%	+24%
Number destination Visitors (3 yrs)	6.1	6.4	8.1
Percentage have taken cruise	21%	24%	33%

Source: NFO/ PLOG Research, American Traveler Survey.

- Are away from home somewhat more than average (15 nights per year vs. 14), and each trip is somewhat longer (5.5 nights vs. 5.3)
- Spend above average on leisure travel (nearly 12% higher)
- Have visited more destinations (6.4 vs. 6.1)
- Have cruised more than average (24% vs. 21%)

Not only does this group have favorable travel habits, but it will experience a tremendous increase in size through the first couple of decades of the 21st century as boomers reach the empty nester stage.

Even more dramatic are the travel patterns of mature explorers, again as seen in Figure 5.2. They

- Average the fewest number of trips (2.5).
- Spend 50 percent more nights away from home than typical travelers (22 nights away vs. 14). They take longer vacations because they have the free time.
- Spend the most on travel (about 24% above average) than any of the groups reviewed so far, even though most of them are retired and now live on reduced household income.
- Have visited the greatest number of destinations in the past three years (8.1 vs. 6.1), and a larger number of the group have taken cruises (33% vs. 21%).

The message is that life doesn't stop at retirement. Rather, a new lifestyle begins for many. Mature explorers should be a prime target group for most travel providers. Travel has replaced many other priorities in their lives and will continue to do so for the foreseeable future. This age category will expand dramatically during the first couple of decades of this century.

CHAPTER SIX

Why Destinations Decline in Popularity and Nobody Ever Does Anything about It

As has been pointed out, leisure destinations, like people, have predictable life cycles, including birth, a growing up and "teenage" phase, maturity, and, unfortunately for too many destinations, a relatively slow, lingering decline into old age. The speed of this process depends on a number of factors, but it almost always follows a straight-line path. Unlike humans in this analogy, however, smart planning can prolong the decline or even erase the potential for an ultimate demise. The reasons for this decline and what to do about it mystify most destination planners, as evidenced by their futile attempts to revive their dying patients. They try a number of remedies, each pulled out of the air with little forethought about the root causes of the problems. This chapter provides a conceptual framework to understand why so many leisure destinations are allowed to go downhill and nobody seems to know how to stop this progression.

The problem is serious. By my estimate, at least 30 percent of the world's best spots are in a state of decline that will spell trouble for everyone at those locales. The overall impact of these problems leads large numbers of potential visitors to decide that they no longer want to visit formerly popular places.

These destinations provide only marginally satisfying trips. I estimate that growth rates for leisure travel have been reduced by about half on a worldwide basis because too many places have lost their allure. Make no mistake, travel is still a growth industry because of the tremendous influx of the baby boomer population moving into their most travel-prone age, the empty nest years. But if these boomers followed their previous lifestyle choices at the same rate in the future, travel in North America would grow at a rate of 5 to 6 percent a year for the next dozen years or so. And international travel could jump to high single digits or low double digits, depending on the country. The cumulative impact of mounting problems, however, reduces travel demand by about half. Justification for these estimates comes from data in the annual tracking study of NFO/Plog Research, the American Traveler Survey. For several years, a scale that tracks the importance that people place on travel in their lives declined and only showed a modest improvement during the mini-recession in the early years of this century. In contrast, products and services that compete for household discretionary dollars have shown strong growth rates. These include purchases of new cars, electronic equipment (including computers), RVs, homes, and home improvement. Leisure travel has lost some of its allure, and too many people involved in the supply and distribution of travel products need only look in a mirror to see who's at fault. And one point cannot be overlooked: the population bulge narrows down as the younger generations of today reach maturity. As these young people move into the empty nester stage in the future, a stage when travel propensity picks up, there will be fewer of them. Reduced interest in travel because of destination decline and fewer people who want to travel spells trouble for the industry by the middle of the second decade of this century! Perhaps today's travel industry leaders don't care much about events that far out in the future. But they should. Deterioration of once scenic or historic places around the globe means that the world is less beautiful for all of us, and our children!

THE PATH OF SELF-DESTRUCTION

Destination growth begins, as was indicated earlier, when venturers return from a new place they have visited and tell their near-venturer friends about the great trip they had. The near-venturers are likely to put that on their list of the next place they want to visit. Near-venturers, in turn, talk about their fabulous trips to their centric friends, a number of whom have venturer leanings. Very rapid growth now occurs because venturesome centrics total slightly over 30 percent of the population. Until now, everything seems rosy at the destination. Each year, tourist arrivals increase as more people learn about the exciting new place to visit. Hotels spring up, quality restaurants follow, roads and airports get upgraded because the tax base has increased, and ground transportation companies and other related services spring up. The newness of all improvements also casts an ambience of freshness and youth. More important, local citizens typically find better-paying jobs in hotels and restaurants than what were available previously in their relatively Third World economy. Everyone seems to like the benefits of tourism. Politicians congratulate themselves on how smart they are to manage growth so well, and they expect each year to produce more tourists and tax dollars than the previous one. They believe there's no end to this gravy train. They feel comfortable and secure in their elected positions since the citizens vote them back into office year after year for the seemingly intelligent way they have brought growth to their communities. But the seeds of destruction and decline have already set in, unnoticed by almost everyone. Specifically,

- As tourism development occurs in a largely unplanned and uncontrolled manner (nobody knows that it should be controlled), a growing amount of excess commercialism and a touristy feel turn away the venturers, who now seek different, more natural places. Near-venturers follow the same path somewhat later. With further uncontrolled growth, centric-venturers also decide that the place has become too touristy, and they look for more interesting locales. As was mentioned, when the appeal of a destination passes the magical midpoint (see Figure 3.1 on p. 51), in terms of the kind of audience it attracts, it now has a smaller and smaller base of tourist prospects from which to draw. The number of tourist arrivals will gradually decline over time.

- Related factors compound the problems. Also reviewed previously, those with dependable tendencies travel less, stay fewer days wherever they go, spend less on a per diem basis, and stay closer to home—preferring the family car to air travel. All of these factors make them poor tourists for most places. A destination that once had everything going in its favor now faces a declining and difficult future. Smaller numbers of tourist arrivals, and an even greater drop in tourism revenue because the new group opens their wallets less often, spell disaster for most places caught in this spin. With the influence curve headed in the wrong direction, attracting the previous and more desirable types of tourists becomes a difficult task.

- Since changes occur gradually, typically over several decades, few notice what is happening. Local tourism bureaus, which get established sometime during the growth cycle, usually feel in the dark. They have been tracking numbers of arrivals and daily expenditures—which had been increasing for some time—without looking at the gradually changing character of the tourists who now arrive.

The continuing decline transforms the character of the destination. It no longer provides the experiences that made it unique and special to its earlier visitors. Too many hotels now dot the landscape, and high-rise properties that come later (as land becomes expensive) block views from most directions. Walking down major streets, visitors can smell the burgers and fries cooking at fast food outlets. They can buy souvenirs and trinkets made in China or elsewhere at numerous shops or drug store chains located on just about every corner. When the kids get bored, they'll drop into a local video arcade or play miniature golf. Their parents might go shopping at the mall, and all will meet later to go to a first-run movie. It sounds quite a bit like home, and that's the problem. It is! In fact, it may even look worse than home because uncontrolled tourism growth often leads to seedy and run-down districts as newer hotels and resort properties steal guests away from the hotels that developed first but now lack the amenities of what is new and fresh. The destination has lost its reasons for existence. Travel writers, who constantly look for unique angles as they spin tales about old places, are reduced to talking about a new restaurant that has become the "in" place or the opening of a luxury spa and resort farther away from town. Three interrelated factors describe what is happening: a decline in the quality of the experience at the destination, a drop in yield per visitor, and continuing reductions in the numbers of tourist arrivals.

Figure 6.1 presents the first of those variables—changes in the *quality of the experience.* It demonstrates what was reviewed earlier. Early in a destination's development, the quality of experience offered to visitors usually improves, rather dramatically during Stage 1 and more gradually during the

Figure 6.1   Quality of the Experience

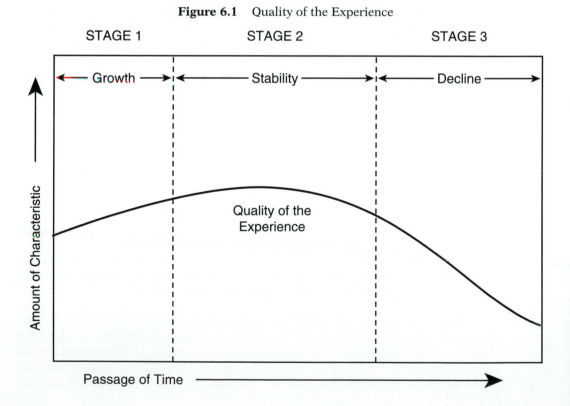

early part of Stage 2. The first group to visit, the venturers, prefers almost everything in a natural state. If they use a hotel, they'll likely select one that has a history reaching back into an interesting period of time, or a converted old castle or public building that now provides rooms and accommodations. Otherwise they'd just as soon go native, sleeping and eating at places used by locals or even staying in someone's home. They'll buy native crafts to take home, especially if these seem primitive or different from what they can obtain elsewhere. Near-venturers who follow in their footsteps, however, want at least some minimal comforts—adequate hotels, food that is safe and tasty, and the availability of some ground transportation to get around and see how the place differs from other spots they have visited. As mentioned, the first hotels typically are low rise, built below the level of the tree line, and don't block the sight line. These offer the best views with panoramic vistas from most rooms. Souvenir shops, fast food outlets, and video arcades haven't arrived yet because the relatively small numbers of visitors won't support the investment. It's a great time to be there! A comfortable room at night, adequate meals at the hotel or elsewhere, and the unspoiled scenery and friendly local people make for a grand visit.

But that high-quality experience typically won't last long. The destination, now attracting more and more visitors, also creates interest among developers. New hotels, shops, and related visitor facilities spring up. These fill in the landscape and spread out to cover hillsides and valleys that previously contributed to the panoramic views and overall feeling of isolation and privacy. As land prices increase, hotels become towers. Guests in some of the upper floors may enjoy the sunrises and sunsets, but people in the streets are likely to miss what they had before the new development took place. Overall, the quality of the experience has begun its long decline. Venturers and near-venturers left long ago, leaving centric-venturers to take their places. A touristy feeling may have started, but it doesn't dominate the destination's more natural qualities—yet. And the large size of the centric market provides a good tourism base to support continued growth for a while. This period, Stage 2, represents a long period of stability, and most local politicians and citizens think that everything is going well, and will continue to do so for the foreseeable future. But even as they feel comfortable in how their community has handled tourism growth, the forces of change begin to work against them. Development continues unabated, with more of the new infrastructure focused on the interests and habits of traditional tourists. Fast food restaurants, souvenir shops, conventional forms of entertainment, and even the opening of discount and closeout stores add to a realization among locals that the place has lost its original character. Although a few may grumble about what has happened, most accept it with a smile because the tourists keep coming and their dollars provide good jobs and help fill the tax coffers. Largely unnoticed, however, is the fact that overdevelopment has changed the character of the place from what was once unique and picturesque to something that has a touristy look resembling so many other places around the world. Most important, the character of tourists who arrive also has changed. Those with more dependable leanings begin to replace even the centric crowd. From almost all perspectives, the place is not what it used to be. A homogenized form of modern civilization has taken over. The presence of bars, comedy clubs, and street hawkers and the continuing growth of some seedy areas around town indicate that good tourism has surrendered completely to bad tourism. The destination now confronts its self-made death spiral (Stage 3). But most people who live and work there don't recognize that. The gradual nature of the changes masks the fact that the quality of the experience has declined to levels that make recovery very difficult, if not impossible.

Figure 6.2 shows the *visitor yield curve* (i.e., per diem expenditures by each tourist). As was mentioned earlier, pure venturers may not damage the character of a place because they like its natural feeling, but they often don't spend the most because there's not that much there to spend it on. Their willingness to experience things much like the natives do, stay at older but inexpensive hotels or go native, and avoid buying trinkets and souvenirs means they dig into their pockets less than most tourists. They're not skinflints. They simply don't require all of the comforts demanded by the groups that follow. However, as their near-venturer friends arrive (who learned about the destina-

Figure 6.2 Visitor Yield

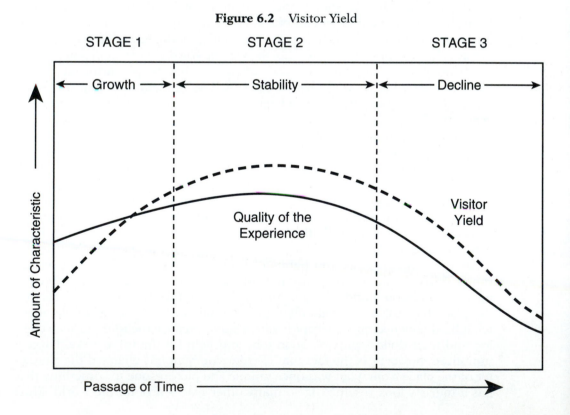

tion in conversations at the office or at cocktail parties), these new folks want some amenities and helpful services to make their trips more comfortable (late Stage 1). Because these near-venturers also are successful, they willingly pay for hotels, restaurants, and other services. They represent the best kind of tourist possible. Their per diem expenditures are the highest among all psychographic types *and* they want the place to retain its unique charm and character. For a considerable period of time during this stage of development, the near-venturers who continue to come and centrics with venturer leanings who now also begin arriving (early Stage 2) produce an ideal mix of visitor types. And the yield curve maintains a relatively high level. Prosperity now seems endless. But the decline starts as overdevelopment and excessive commercialism take hold. Near-venturers begin to leave, and centrics with venturer leanings gradually follow in their footsteps, to be replaced by centric-dependables and, ultimately, pure dependables (Stage III). Now the worst of all possible worlds happens. These new arrivals, as will be remembered, spend less, stay fewer days, travel less often, and prefer traveling to destinations they can reach with the family car. Destinations dependent on a heavy mix of passengers arriving by air face a particularly difficult time. The primary saving grace of dependables is that they will return often to a place they like because they don't want novelty in their lives. But tourism revenues have started to drop, and that path will accelerate in the future.

Figure 6.3 charts the rise and fall in the *number of visitors* over time. During the early discovery period (Stage 1), visitor counts rise rapidly. Word-of-mouth influence from venturers and near-venturers with friends and associates convinces an ever-increasing number of people to find out what is special about this place. Stage 2 represents the relatively long period of stability and economic health that local tourism officials believe will go on forever. But Stage 3 looms on the horizon. Referring again to Figure 3.1 (p. 51), the pool of potential visitors continues to increase as the type of person attracted to the place moves from right to left on the psychographic chart—up to the midpoint on the curve. From then on, the destination's appeal is to smaller and smaller audiences. Since the direction of influence can't be reversed, the problems created by tourism begin to mount, while its benefits wane. Fewer visitors, most of whom spend less money while they are there, and a now spoiled destination create nearly insurmountable difficulties. The number of visitors does not decline in direct relationship to deterioration in the quality of the destination or visitor yield, however. In fact, a place can continue to grow in visitor counts at the time it is already on a downhill path. The lag time between word of mouth about the changes that have taken place as repeat visitors discover that the area no longer appeals to them, and when they tell others, accounts for this discrepancy. But the number of unfavorable reactions to the destination will continue to build over time, and this rising chorus will ultimately overwhelm what previously had been very positive experiences. This image lag time creates a false sense of security for most locals. Like two pebbles thrown into a pond, one after the other, the waves of the first one con-

Figure 6.3   Number of Visitors

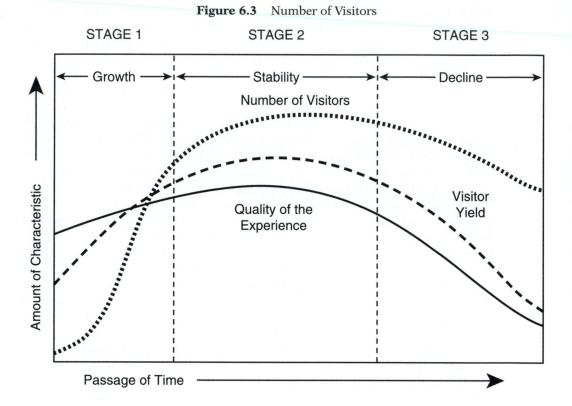

tinue to expand until the second pebble overtakes its predecessor. This critical period of change can take many years or decades, depending on a number of factors, and it helps to explain why the rising problems largely go unrecognized. If the number of visitors keeps growing, how can anyone question that problems exist at the destination?

The closest parallel perhaps is the all too typical history of new restaurants. They often follow a similar path, but in a condensed time period. When a great new eatery opens, word gets out about its greatness, including its fabulous food, attractive décor, and impeccable service. Customers begin to crowd through its doors, and having reservations is a must. It can seem like an overnight success. But, far too often, success leads to inattentiveness to the details that made the restaurant great. After a while, the food may seem less tasty as the original chef moves on to better pastures, and its presentation may be less original or attractive. Service has become slow and inconsistent. And the décor now looks somewhat frayed at the edges and a bit dirty. Old guests have dropped the restaurant from their list of favorite places and now seek out new dining establishments. Few will actually complain to the owner that the food and service no longer measure up to previous levels. They simply "vote with their feet." They don't return. A small number of diners may tell the owner about the decline. But his reaction usually is, "How can that be? Look at how busy I am." The lag time in image development grows out of the fact that negative word of mouth has not yet overtaken the amount of positive word of mouth that had spread among local diners. But reputations catch up. Ultimately, the image waves of the second stone in the water grow larger and overtake the positive impressions from the first stone, and decline sets in. Very few restaurants revive after they have started downhill. A new restaurant with new owners must take the place of the previous establishment. Unlike restaurants, however, destinations can't close their doors and, in a few weeks, open with a new look created by a new owner. Too much infrastructure is in place to make drastic change possible, and multiple special-interest groups come forth with conflicting suggestions about what is needed.

THE DECLINE THAT NEVER SEEMS TO STOP

If those responsible for tourism, both paid tourism professionals and elected officials, recognized the signs of this decline early on, presumably they would take steps to control the situation and reverse the tide. But too late they discover that something has gone wrong—too late for them to have much impact, even if they are wise. As year over year numbers show a pattern of continuous decline in the number of visitors (and visitor yield), a series of very predictable steps follows:

1. Tourism leaders typically first assume that they need more advertising. As a result, the advertising budget gets increased to get out a stronger message in today's cluttered media world. Direct sales campaigns might also get a lift, with a larger sales staff calling on travel agencies, tour operators, and package providers. But travel agents recommend what's hot to their clients or simply fill their requests, so it's tough to get their attention when a destination is in free fall. And tourism wholesalers will gradually change the destinations they promote most heavily as demand decreases, unless they get deep discounts that give them a strong competitive edge in the marketplace. As mentioned, deeply discounted packages usually bring more of the wrong types of tourists.

2. Increased promotion may help some, but not enough to overcome the growing decline, and the next step typically is to change the ad campaign. The tourism bureau directs the ad agency to come up with a new theme and spirit for the place. Make it livelier and promote the new or refurbished hotels, the agency is told. But clever new advertising can't overcome serious deficiencies in the product (i.e., the low-

ered quality of the destination experience). So visitor counts and yields per visitor continue to go in the wrong direction.

3. You probably guessed the next step: Someone suggests that the advertising agency of record has grown stale. They no longer have the sparkle and creative sizzle they once demonstrated, and they need to be replaced. An ad agency review takes place, and the new agency gets a chance to change advertising directions. The long-term public relations (PR) firm may also get the axe, and a new one is selected or the tourism bureau decides they will take the account in-house because they can do a better job for less money. A new ad campaign comes forth after a lot of effort, and the advertising budget gets a temporary increase to support extra promotional effort. The new approach usually gets extensive local press coverage because tourism is important to the economy. But the new advertising campaign seldom produces the desired results. You can't change the destination experience through advertising sizzle alone.

4. Now the local tourism bureau begins to feel the heat. When all seemed on track during the growth period, few civic leaders questioned their actions. But when times change, tourism and convention and visitor bureau (CVB) directors face a familiar chorus of complaints. Those who contribute financial support to the bureau begin to wonder aloud about the bureau and its staff. Has it been making the right decisions (or is it even smart enough to make good choices)? Does its staff seem committed and put in enough hours? Does it spend too much on overhead (especially salaries and perks) rather than on advertising and promotion? The director of the CVB may get replaced, along with a couple of his or her handpicked associates, and a search begins for a new director. That takes time and further deflects thoughts about fixing fundamental flaws of the destination before future tourism growth can be assured. The new director will face the same difficulties and, most likely, without any greater success. And that person may even decide to leave after a short and unsuccessful attempt at rejuvenation. And, during this process, critical time was lost without addressing the important issues related to destination quality, further frustrating and confounding local leaders all the more.

   And who applies the greatest pressure to tourism bureau directors? Most often, it's hoteliers—the owners and managers of local hotels. They pay membership fees to belong to the tourism bureau/CVB. However, their real clout comes from the fact that room taxes, which vary from 11 to over 20 percent of each hotel bill, make up the majority of the tourism budget. For this reason, hoteliers believe that they should wield the most power over the tourism bureau and its course or direction. They want warm bodies in rooms next week or next month, not next year or beyond. Often they won't support a new advertising or promotional campaign that promises to create a new, revitalized image some time next year, even if it can produce the greatest long-term benefits. Destination image change takes time, but few will wait very long. Hoteliers may even force the issue by leading a movement to oust the local CVB director and install one of their own as executive director to ensure that all advertising focuses on their immediate needs. In regional groups, such as state tourism bureaus, provinces, or even entire countries, power may get dispersed more broadly among airline members, tour operators, and large hotel chains, but the pressures felt by tourism directors from their members remain the same. Make something happen now, not later! And tourism bureau members and local politicians won't consider any plan focused on fixing the true problems of the community and its need for revitalization. That's too expensive and takes too long.

5. The strategy of a new tourism director typically concentrates on short-term solutions—get more tourists soon. But that strategy does not address fundamental problems, and the number of new arrivals continues on the path of decline. A feeling of desperation begins to set in. Hotels start discounting room rates, and low-end consolidators put together deeply discounted travel packages that include air fare, three nights' hotel, and perhaps ground transfers, or some golf, or a couple of meals. When discount packages account for 15 to 20 percent of total visitors, that number will undoubtedly rise in the future because few travelers want to pay full price for something they can get at a discount. The destination now faces deep problems, especially as these deep discount packages approach 25 to 30 percent of total visitors.

6. At destinations where tourism contributes a third or more to the local economy, regardless of the size of the destination, the fate of tourism gets talked about by just about everyone. So, as problems mount, a blame game will likely ensue, more public and vicious than anything heard to date. The board of directors of a tourism bureau may publicly blame its new or old executive director, who, in turn, fires back some salvos accusing the directors of meddling and not supporting needed changes. Local politicians point their fingers in all directions to avoid standing in the line of fire. It makes for wonderful headlines in newspapers and lead stories on nightly TV news. Political leaders will begin to feel the heat at some point and face greater difficulty in their reelection campaigns because of voter backlash. Someone has failed to do his or her job, and someone must take the blame. Tourism jobs have gotten more scarce with the downturn, and tax dollars from tourist spending have fallen. This may force elected officials to cut back on needed services or begin talking about a tax

increase. Sometimes politicians push to develop or expand a convention center, assuming they can bring corporate and association meetings to town. But that solution is similar to a couple trying to solve their difficult relationship by deciding to have a baby. Both situations seldom work as planned. A place that doesn't appeal to tourists also has a difficult time attracting meetings. The new convention center, started during the beginning of the downturn, fails to meet projections for revenue growth. Now taxpayers will have to kick in to meet the city's obligations on public bonds that were supposed to keep tourism on a growth path. On the other side of the coin, some local citizens may lead a movement to kick out any politician they feel supported uncontrolled development because they don't like what has happened to the place where they grew up.

Throughout the slow decline, self-interest has dominated decision making of just about every group that lives on tourism. All have a vested interest in keeping things the same, until the downturn becomes painfully self-evident. When times were good, they felt comfortable in owning or working at hotels, souvenir stores, and local restaurants. They could see no need for change. Now with dark clouds hanging overhead, someone must take responsibility for what has happened. But few will look at their own short sightedness.

THE ECONOMIC BASIS FOR PLANNED TOURISM GROWTH

Since the process just described may take decades to occur, tourism planners, elected officials, and property owners typically don't recognize they have a problem until tourism revenues have declined for a number of years in a row. And those who try to determine what has changed are perplexed by a simple fact. Looking again at Figure 6.3, note that *the number of visitors may actually increase on a year to year basis but, during that time, the total amount spent by these visitors gradually declines!* Why? The new group, more dependable in character, doesn't spend as much on a per diem basis as those who preceded them. This fact is evident in Figure 6.4, which summarizes, on a percentage basis, the amount of leisure spending by each psychographic type—for last trip and total spending for the year. These data also come from the American Trav-

Figure 6.4   Percentage above/below Leisure Travel Spending by Psychographic Type

	Venturers	Near-Venturers	Centric	Near-Dependables	Dependables
Last trip	+51%	+24%	Average	<−12%>	<−40%>
Total 12 months	+38%	+28%	Average	<−23%>	<−44%>

Source: NFO/PLOG Research, American Traveler Survey.

eler Survey of NFO/Plog Research. Both spending patterns show a straight-line relationship (i.e., the more venturesome the traveler, the more they spend on travel for both the last trip and in total for the year). So, as a destination loses venturer types, it must increase its growth rate even more rapidly than in the past to make up for differences in spending patterns of the types of travelers it now attracts. Stated differently, *it takes 2.5 dependables to equal the spending of each venturer that a destination loses!* Multiply that number by thousands of never-returning venturer types and the task can seem impossible. A declining destination must replace lost visitors at an ever-increasing rate to make up for the good spenders it has lost—to stay even in revenue totals. Almost universally, those responsible for guiding destinations to bigger and better futures do not recognize this fact. They are doomed to failure and they don't know it! Even if successful, they have added to the miseries of everyone involved. Since there are no additional tax dollars in the public coffers, the infrastructure to support heavier demand won't keep up with the need. As a result, crowded roads, more people on the streets, more discount stores and curio shops that appeal to a lower-end crowd, increased smog, and other undesirable outcomes confront both tourists and local residents.

Other factors compound the problem. During the heady growth years, property values rise rapidly. Old laws of supply and demand mean that each new hotel, retail center, or entertainment complex costs more to build out because land prices have been rising rapidly. And, the most desirable locations already have buildings on them, leading to an urbanlike sprawl of tourism facilities as new resorts must go farther out of town. Hillsides get dotted with new developments, contributing to the loss of the vista views that once enhanced the visitor experience. Once grand resorts situated in spacious park-like settings now face a different future. High-rise tower wings get built and fill in the open space in the push to add more guestrooms and conference and meeting space. Nearby older properties do the same, or even construct totally new hotels on the same grounds. The stately Royal Hawaiian in Honolulu, Hawaii now suffers the indignity of having a Sheraton tower, a multistory parking garage, and a large retail center (fronting on Kalakaua Avenue) crowd its entrance and rob it of its more serene beach. Good locations may become so scarce that some developers plan to tear down the old buildings to put up newer and more grand structures—in a declining market. Throughout the community, older but still serviceable buildings get demolished to make way for larger, taller structures that offer more efficient use of space so that a new project can pencil out. This seems to be a regular occurrence in Las Vegas as newer, glitzier gaming palaces replace older, smaller hotels that the new owners feel don't deliver the maximum return on investment. Las Vegas, however, only partly presents the case because it lacks most of the criteria for what makes a destination great—natural beauty and scenic vistas, a long and interesting history, interesting natives, and unique things to buy. It can get away with these actions because it primarily appeals to the gaming crowd, largely composed of dependable types who like to experience all of the comforts of home wherever they travel. They enjoy being indoors to play the tables and take in great entertainment. And they get all that at very reasonable rates for both food and lodging.

As these changes make a destination less unique and less desirable, an even greater problem surfaces. Each new hotel or resort costs more to put up than others that preceded it because of rising land values. But that message doesn't occur to banks or investors that finance new projects because the destination has a history of success with previous projects. Tourist arrivals and receipts have increased consistently for years. If a slight downturn occurred for a couple of years, not to worry. That's only temporary, and things will soon turn around. But, unfortunately, they probably will not. The newer, taller buildings with their citylike atmosphere have made the place less desirable, turning away the best psychographic types. Fewer visitors who spend less and who are more likely to travel on discount packages mean less money for everyone to share at the destination. Rack rates begin to drop at hotels, more restaurants offer "early bird" meal specials and seniors discounts, and discount outlets crop up to entice these skinflint travelers to spend more freely while they are there. The destination begins to have a bargain mentality about it. On a percentage basis, the deepest discounts usually appear at the newest, most expensive resorts and hotels because the owners have got to put warm bodies in their beds to help meet debt payments. Not having been around for very long, they lack financial reserves from years of profitable operations. Investors let their impatience be known to their hotel managers and may even seek to reflag the hotel with another chain's name, thinking that a different brand can do a better job of marketing. The banks also begin to show their impatience since underperforming loans on their books don't cast a positive image when bank auditors come by. But it's a trend that can't be stopped without concerted, unified action on the part of a lot of people, something that's not likely to happen. As revenues at hotels, resorts, convention centers, and other tourist facilities decline, mortgage payments may be difficult to meet. So what happens next? The obvious. Hotels cut scheduled maintenance, delay upgrade projects, and reduce restaurant hours of operation (24-hour room service often goes out the window). Tourist-oriented businesses follow the same path. And local governments scramble to cut their budgets, or may increase the hotel tax, as falling tourism revenues cause a shortfall in tax receipts. But the gradual deterioration of the product that visitors see and experience continues. It may not be very obvious to those who remain since they don't notice these changes on a daily basis, but visitors who come back over the next year or two react to the subtle differences. They don't like what they see and are less likely to return. The little remaining allure of the resort or destination gets obliterated at an accelerating pace. Since it usually impacts most of the destination, the entire area typically deteriorates and its declining reputation continues to spread. Now, everything works against local planners—unfavorable economics for new development, wrong groups of travelers arriving, too many discounted packages filling the hotels, a bad image, negative word of mouth, and a hostile press. An American investor in a five-star hotel in Acapulco who wanted me to help guide tourism development for the city (but he could not convince local officials of the need for help) expressed it clearly one day in a phone conversation: "I knew I was in trouble when I walked out to our pool area and saw guys with tattoos on their arms and wearing tattered cut off jeans lounging in deck chairs. That's not the kind of crowd I can afford to have in my hotel."

Most people in tourism planning don't recognize the fact that larger and larger numbers of tourists do not automatically translate into increasing revenue and tax dollars for an area. For most mature destinations, an unseen limit exists in the number of tourists that can be successfully accommodated. If surpassed, a downward spiral usually begins that leads to deterioration of just about everything that residents, local politicians, and planners hoped to accomplish. Setting future limits on the desired number of tourist arrivals seldom crosses the minds of local officials, but it should. If not, problems can occur, and sooner rather than later because of the accelerating pace at which events happen today. Mass media can work for the good or the ill of any place, depending on its qualities. Even more fundamental, good word-of-mouth advertising can contribute to rapid growth that is difficult to manage. And, conversely, bad press or bad word of mouth will impact in the opposite direction, usually not as rapidly but with more lasting negative results.

The path of self-destruction outlined here need not happen. Destinations can control their development progress, but only if they wake up to the fact that they should. And, equally important, they must decide how to position the place—typically toward the near-venturer side of the scale, which usually offers more potential for growth because of this group's influence on the broad middle portion of the curve. But, in a number of cases, the positioning should be toward the dependable side. Whatever the choice, healthy destination growth depends on constant attention to planning and control of new development to ensure that the destination retains the qualities that brought people there in the first place. How that can be done most effectively is covered in Section IV of this book.

LEARNING FROM PAST MISTAKES

Several very simple messages grow out of this explanation, which is based on more than 30 years of consulting experience in travel. Those who have responsibility for a destination must think far in the future and address important critical questions. "What makes this place special and unique?" "How can we preserve or protect those qualities?" "What must be done to convince others where we live and work about the benefits of destination preservation?" "How can we get more people to be aware of what is happening when a destination reaches a turning point and could be heading downward, even though everything seems to be going quite well?" Good tourism planners must have sufficient self-confidence to stand up and speak out on these issues long before others recognize the dangers. The forces of resistance they face will likely include local hotel owners and managers, shopkeepers, and restaurateurs, whose perspective typically is to get tourists in their doors next week or next month. They will worry about next year or beyond when that time gets closer. Politicians, who tend to have a next-election perspective, may be the least willing to take risks. But all suffer when a destination goes downhill—those who have invested locally, those who live and work there, and the visitors who come to enjoy the benefits they have heard or read about but now may find it doesn't live up to its reputation. How to protect and enhance a destination is covered in greater detail in Section IV.

CHAPTER SEVEN

Some Overlooked Elements of Good Promotional Strategies

Sun Tzu, the revered Chinese philosopher who lived around 400 B.C., produced the first essays on the art of war. His writings influenced military strategists for centuries. Recently he has gained popularity among corporate marketing executives who seek a strategic advantage over competitors. He believed in understanding your enemy so that you can win with inferior forces through deception, controlled communication, and very focused strategies. He wrote, "The supreme art of war is to subdue the enemy without fighting."[1] During World War II, B. H. Liddel Hart, a scholar of Sun Tzu, was visited by a Chinese Military Attache and pupil of General Chiang Kai-shek. The Attache remarked that Sun Tzu was considered "out of date by most of the younger [Chinese] officers, and thus hardly worth the study in the era of mechanized weapons."[2] In contrast, Mao Tse-Tung was "strongly influenced by Sun Tzu's thought [and] between 1930 and 1934 . . . inflicted repeated defeats on Chiang Kai-shek."[3] Ultimately, Chiang Kai-shek lost the war with Mao and the communists and

---

[1]Griffith, Samuel B. (Translator), Sun Tzu: The Art of War, Oxford University Press, Oxford, 1963, p. vii, quoted in an Introduction by B. H. Liddell Hart.
[2]*Ibid.*, p. vii, words of B. H. Liddell Hart.
[3]*Ibid.*, p. 45, words of translator, Samuel B. Griffith.

was driven to the island of Taiwan. Chiang should have paid attention to the master. Clear strategies and clear messages mattered then, and they matter now.

It may seem trite to repeat that sales and marketing programs require good, well-thought-out battle plans to be effective. However, that message often gets lost in the pressures imposed by today's business climate, in which fewer people must handle ever-increasing responsibilities. Without time to think and plan, simple mistakes get made—and repeated over and over again—by very bright people. Sun Tzu was a philosopher, not a general, but his clear thinking led to his appointment as head of all generals. His successes grew out of careful planning that focused on knowing his armies' strengths and the weaknesses of his enemies. During a very busy career, I have worked with hundreds of companies. Most often I focused on how to make advertising and promotions more effective. I have seen the creative process executed extremely well, but I have also witnessed millions of advertising and promotional dollars wasted on ineffective campaigns. Marketers didn't develop a clear strategy that targeted the needs of their consumers with clear messages about the benefits offered vs. competitors. Even worse, some campaigns harm the organizations doing the advertising. My first recognition of the negative impact of improper advertising campaigns occurred when I worked with Pat Frawley, former owner and CEO of Schick, the company that makes razor blades. His technicians developed the first chromium blades, which cut closer and last longer than the blue blades of market leader Gillette. Frawley designed his own ad campaign, "The end of the blues!" In full-page newspaper ads, a sequential series of drawings pictured a Gillette blue blade gradually turning into a new Schick chromium blade. In tests, however, readers mostly remembered an ad that featured Gillette blue blades. Frawley paid millions of dollars to build up his dominant competitor! I have also witnessed numerous auto ads that compare a manufacturer's new car to a particular BMW model. My follow-up research almost always indicated that these ads strengthened BMW's image, not the competitor's. BMW has received a lot of free advertising since most people assumed BMW produces the best cars if others only present themselves as equals.

Advertising, sales, and marketing require clear thinking in order to be effective in today's media-intensive culture. Too often marketing programs are pasted together without an adequate understanding of what needs to be communicated, how it should be presented, and the intended audience. Over time, I have learned much from the brilliance of a few individuals, and I have developed some concepts of my own as I have counseled with clients. Effective marketing may not be science, but a few principles exist that can help to ensure more consistent success. It's useful to review some concepts that I consider basic before proceeding with a detailed discussion of positioning and branding travel products. These ideas should be kept in mind when developing new advertising and promotional campaigns. Not all will apply to each new ad or marketing campaign, but a consideration of the relevance of these topics can help ensure a greater chance of success. These ideas also complement much of what will be discussed in Chapter 9, on using psychographics as a basis for promoting travel products.

TALK TO YOUR AUDIENCE, NOT DOWN TO THEM

A commonly repeated story about David Ogilvy, the brilliant founder of Ogilvy & Mather Worldwide, illustrates an important point. Frustrated with inadequate messages prepared by his creative department for an advertising campaign directed to housewives, he reportedly shouted at his team, "That woman is no dummy. She's your wife!" Perhaps Ogilvy understood the need for respect of an audience because he began his career in the research department of an ad agency. Anyone who completes a number of studies among consumers will come away with a healthy respect for the common sense of most people, rather than their dumbness. Most consumers make rather rational decisions, not crazy ones. Unless absolute proof exists that the target audience lacks brains, the conceptual work and lines of copy should convey a feeling of talking with a respected friend. To think otherwise could make the ad miss its target. In some work with Molson's Brewery in Canada, using my psychographic system to position their products, the execution of the ad campaign that I reviewed had wandered far off target. I asked to meet with the ad agency personnel assigned to the account to learn why this had happened and to help them understand the goals of the repositioning effort. I quickly learned what had gone wrong. The creative director assigned to Molson's came from a working-class family, but felt he had risen above his more humble beginnings when he obtained a college degree. Asked to create a campaign targeted to blue-collar workers, his own dislike for this group came across in the silly and simplistic way he approached the assignment. Ultimately, the agency had to assign a new person to the account who could empathize with this very important group for Molson's.

The opposite also holds true. Don't talk above your audience with big words or by presenting convoluted concepts. As will be seen, good presentations require clarity and simplicity, regardless of the educational level of the target group.

THE IMPORTANCE OF VALUE FOR MONEY

In all my years of research, and hundreds of studies, I have found just one variable about which almost every consumer gives the same answer. Regardless of age, sex, income, education, or psychographic characteristics, 95 percent of all people state that getting "good value for your money" is *very important* when purchasing a product or service. But the meaning of *value* differs dramatically among different groups. Those at the lower end of the income ladder tend to equate it with lowest price. Thus, they will often buy whatever is cheapest to spend less of their hard-earned wages, regardless of the brand name, quality, or features offered. At the opposite end of the spectrum, high-income individuals may spend a lot more for just about everything they purchase but, surprisingly, they also want to feel they got good value. For them, it means that they bought at a discount or that the product is worth the extra cost because of its extra features or built-in quality. A fine tailored suit fits this example. It may cost multiples of one purchased at a department store, but its wearer believes that the attention to detail, better fit, and higher-grade fabrics warrant the extra price. Most people belong someplace in the middle of this spectrum, trading off price and quality with their own internal formulas. I have a hobby of photography. I own several Pentax 35-mm camera bodies and multiple lenses. They serve my purposes very well, but I didn't pay the extra to go to a Nikon system. When I want to add to my system, I look for sales at camera stores or buy through discount mail order houses to avoid paying full price.

If everyone wants value for their money, how should this fact influence ad campaigns? The answer is relatively straightforward. When low price dominates a campaign, advertising should suggest that a lot of features have been built into the product or service at that low price. In other words, the buyer can enjoy the benefits of much more expensive products or services at a very reasonable cost. At the high end of the pricing curve, buyers need to be convinced that they made smart decisions. They may pay more, but they also get features and quality not available on lower-priced models. I love the instruction booklets and videotapes that come with new luxury cars. These universally begin by congratulating the buyer on having made a smart choice and point out the unique features of the car that the buyer just purchased. But subtlety must dominate the messages. Too much advertising for luxury cars suggests that those who buy brand X are successful individuals who have risen above the level of their peers. Purchase of brand X becomes a demonstration of that fact, the copy implies. This approach talks down to its audience. They recognize that it's a cheap ploy to play on their egos. For those products that are widely distributed in the marketplace (i.e., commodities), high-income households also look for discounts, especially on high-end items. Even if they can afford to pay full price, they feel a bit like fools if they did. Few wish to discover during a conversation at a cocktail party that a friend got the same new Mercedes coupe at a much deeper discount. That knowledge can make a person feel somewhat humiliated. He or she is not as good a good shopper as the friend! For those in the middle of the income spectrum, the best messages often focus on the concept that this product offers the best tradeoff between price, product quality, and features. Home sound equipment does a good job on this score. Most companies that make high-end home audio receivers and speakers for surround-sound systems also offer moderately priced lines. And they rather uniformly suggest that the technology developed for top-end speakers and receivers is incorporated into their more moderately priced units. In other words, the intelligence of the buyer indirectly shows up in having made this kind of a smart decision.

The concept of emphasizing value for the money applies to a wide spectrum of ads. Most often, however, it should get very subtle treatment—simply stressing the quality of the product or service, or that a particular destination is truly out of the ordinary. Some destinations truly are expensive—London, Hong Kong, Paris, New York, Bermuda, and others. In each case, the prospective traveler must believe that the vacation experience will surpass most other trips so that it is truly memorable and worth the price. In contrast, places that offer lots of discount packages, like Myrtle Beach, South Carolina, Branson, Missouri, some inclusive resorts in the Caribbean, and sections of Spain, face a difficult time if they try to stray from a primary message that emphasizes how much is included in one price. Value as a message carries considerable weight, but the type of message must always match the audience.

RELEVANCE FIRST

If we continue to believe the proposition of Sun Tzu that we need to plan our strategies carefully, it certainly applies to clarifying what we hope to accomplish in each new ad campaign. Good advertising offers a benefit to the reader or viewer. Otherwise, why should the person pay attention to the ad? The glut of commercials presented every day in developed countries results in most consumers "tuning out" the clutter, unless something of value is presented clearly and effectively. When I see image advertising, designed only to create a good feeling about a company but lacking a motivational message, I wonder what the company hopes to accomplish. I generally tell my clients not to prepare these kinds of ads. Save the money. Spend it only when you know that what you will say offers a real benefit to your target audience.

Tony Antin, a long-time personal friend, presents seminars and counsels companies and ad agencies about good advertising techniques. I place him in the genius category, though he describes himself as "a totally pragmatic, solely bottom-line devoted advertising expert."[4] He constantly asks the question, "will the advertisement get people to do/think what you want them to?"[5] As Vice President and the first Director of Creative Services Worldwide for *Reader's Digest,* he has demonstrated that specific ground rules exist for creating effective ads. He refrains from calling these rules because most advertising executives believe that the way to be creative is to break rules. But they don't understand the difference between a trite execution of a rule and learning how to show a product attractively and consistently. After a review of over 400 ads

---

[4]E-mail correspondence to the author, October 5, 2002.
[5]Ibid.

that achieved the goal of moving a large amount of product, Antin concluded that effective ads have several elements in common. Their simplicity can hide their importance. His book *Great Print Advertising* belongs on the shelves of every ad agency and marketing director of destinations and travel companies. Many of the concepts he presents apply not only to print ads (magazines and newspapers) but also to broadcast media (TV and radio). He writes, "The primary objective of an advertisement is to communicate its Propositional Benefit quickly, easily, fully, and memorably."[6] He states that a company that doesn't have something worthwhile to say to its markets shouldn't advertise. It should be able to answer the questions as to why it wants to advertise and what it hopes to accomplish through the ads.

In his book, Tony Antin offers far too many insights for inclusion here. But, summarizing some of his material, he presents three essential questions that must be answered in the affirmative for an ad to achieve its desired goal. If it falls short on any one of these, it will likely not measure up. Also, the questions must be addressed in the order presented to maximize chances of success. In other words, don't move on to the second question until you have adequately answered the first. And don't consider the third unless you have fully addressed the second.

1. Is the message *relevant* to the interests of your market?
2. Is it presented *clearly?*
3. Will the advertisement *stand out?*

Relevance

If you target a group that takes leisure trips, you can assume that they like to travel. But you can't also conclude that they have any particular interest in your destination, hotel, resort, or airline. You have to create the propositional benefit that will motivate them to consider a trip to your place or use your airline. What advantages do you offer that make you stand out from the crowd so that your target audience should pay attention to what you have to say? The propositional benefit must offer the strongest message possible to the target group.

Clarity

Even when a benefit has relevance for its intended audience, the message too often gets muddled and confused in the presentation. The ad loses out because the primary proposition wasn't stated clearly. Tony asks, "Do all the elements of the advertisement work to make it easy for people to understand that

---

[6]Tony Antin, *Great Print Advertising,* John Wiley & Sons, New York, 1993, p. 24.

Propositional Benefit quickly, clearly, and fully?" As a beginning, at least show your new ad campaign to friends or associates who don't have intimate knowledge of how you run your business. Do they understand the message easily and clearly? Ask them for their candid appraisals.

Stand-Out Characteristics

Finally, Antin points out that an advertisement stands out when the presentation of its proposition is in some way unique from everyone else's presentation (often of the same proposition). Sometimes a bit of cleverness does it. Humor works well, especially with more upscale and better-educated groups. And, far more often than most people recognize, a simple but exceptionally intelligent presentation will punch through the clutter of all other ads. It can include meaningful art, perfectly appropriate typeface or voice (the ad copy), or blessedly easy-to-follow language.

Tony Antin points out that the sequence of *relevance, clarity,* and *standing out* too often gets reversed. Ad directors and creative people in agencies *start* with the question of how to make their ads stand out from those of competitors, and far too often think "cleverness" is the only solution. Cleverness becomes *the* objective. In so doing, they lose sight of how to present a clear and relevant message because cleverness alone does not lead to success. The chance to convert prospects into buyers is lost. An ad that offers a clearly stated benefit, even if it lacks a certain degree of sparkle, has a better chance for success than one that offers clever humor but either lacks a propositional benefit or has not presented that benefit clearly.

PEOPLE PAY ATTENTION TO WHAT'S IMPORTANT TO THEM

Tony Antin's emphasis on the need for relevance and clarity gets a boost from science, especially the fields of physiology (the study of perception) and cultural anthropology. In the prehistory of human development, certain senses became key for survival as a species. For ancient humans, movement in the underbrush on the African plains automatically captured their attention because it signaled either an approaching lion or tiger, or game that they wanted to hunt. A soft rustling sound in the leaves of a nearby tree created a similar situation. Approach with caution to determine whether it represents opportunity or danger. Other less relevant sights and sounds get ignored to allow total concentration on significant happenings in the environment. The smell of smoke alerts us to a potential fire that could endanger our lives. When confronted directly with a dangerous situation, psychologists talk about the fight or flight response. A sudden rush of adrenaline instantly provides strength beyond the ordinary to meet the demands of the situation, or a capacity to run faster than we ever have. These senses continue today. A tired mother can sleep through rather loud ordinary household noises, but wake up immediately if her baby lets out a slight cry. You can notice the presence of these sensitive scanning mechanisms in your own life very easily. Walk through a crowded, noisy restaurant and you don't hear any of the ambient conversation. But at a table you pass, someone mentions your first name. In the midst of this din, you immediately turn to see if you know them and they might be talking to you or it's just a happenstance.

What does this have to do with advertising and promotion? A lot! Our evolutionary development provides us with mechanisms to scan our physical and social environments to pick out messages that can offer a benefit or might suggest a potential problem. This conclusion offers hope for anyone creating marketing messages, even those with small advertising budgets. In today's cluttered media environment, you stand a chance of getting noticed if you have something relevant to say to your target audience (Tony Antin). An average motorist might pass hundreds of billboards a day and notice only the one announcing new nonstop airline service to a city where he travels regularly. Someone thinking about a vacation might talk or daydream during a television commercial break but suddenly stop everything to pay attention to a special offer from a cruise line. On average, people turn a page in a magazine every three-quarters of a second. But they will pause or read on when something of interest grabs their attention.

This review points to a fundamental conclusion: Getting a good message heard or seen does not necessarily require huge promotional budgets. In spite of oversaturation by all media, the evolutionary basis of our tendency to scan our environment for important indicators of benefit or danger means that good advertising will always have a chance to stand out and get noticed. But the message should be relevant, stated clearly, and presented in an interesting manner, in that order. Plan well and take advantage of inherited evolutionary tendencies to increase the potential success of marketing programs!

THE IMPORTANCE OF PSYCHOLOGICAL AGE

I don't remember where I read it, but I have used this concept for years. And I know that it rings true. A social scientist studied the perceived psychological age of people vs. their true chronological age. We all know that, from the time people enter their 30s, they become increasingly sensitive about their chronological age and show some reluctance to reveal it to others. But our researcher discovered that most adults actually *feel psychologically younger than their chronological age*. In their 30s, that difference can equal five to seven years. By the mid-50s, the difference grows to 15 years. In other words, most of us at some point believe that we act and move like someone much younger than we are. We may even deny to ourselves that the older-looking face we see in the mirror is ours!

A few advertisers have understood this concept for quite some time. Retirement communities generally know how to do it right. Although the minimum age for entrance to one of these communities might be 55 years, with a true average age of over 65, adults pictured in the ads look like prematurely gray 45-year-olds. A montage of photos shows active couples, playing golf, coming off of a tennis court, dancing at night, and entertaining friends—all within the community. Whether or not most people actually do those things at their age does not change the fact that they feel like they can.

The moral of this story? The graphics and story line of ads should create a younger feeling than the chronological age of a target group. Your own self-perception probably matches this conclusion, so think about your needs as you either create ads or review those presented by your agency. Don't go overboard on the concept. You could end up hitting below the psychological age. As long as you have a good balance of common sense, your ads will probably hone in on age self-perceptions of your market targets quite well.

TELL TRAVELERS WHAT TO EXPECT AND THEN HELP THEM EXPERIENCE IT

A number of years ago, I completed several studies for Chris Hemmeter, who built the luxurious twin-towered Hyatt Hotel in Waikiki, Hawaii. The project examined how to get more people to shop and dine at the Hyatt and his adjacent King's Row retail complex. Prior to the first set of focus groups for the study, I wandered around Waikiki to get a first-hand look at the types of people I imagined I would encounter in my groups over the next several evenings. I wondered how they spent their time during the day and how much they seemed to be enjoying their visit. The images remain planted firmly in my mind—families, young swingers, older couples, Midwesterners, and California surfers. Tourists were easy to spot with their Hawaiian shirts, shorts (most would look better without them), and sunburns. Farmers from the Midwest created a special visual picture—deep tans on the lower half of their faces but sunburned foreheads and arms because they left their wide-brim hats and long-sleeved shirts at home. What struck me most was how bored most of the crowd looked. Few smiled, there was little laughing and giggling, and no one seemed in a hurry to get to their next exciting venture. Instead they ambled slowly down the street, sat at restaurants or on the edges of low walls, or wandered aimlessly through klitzy souvenir and gift shops almost expressionless. "These people aren't having a good time," I thought to myself. "How can I develop a plan for Chris Hemmeter to bring more of them into his stores if they don't like Waikiki and what it offers?"

My surprise came during the first focus group that evening. In walked the kinds of tourists I had viewed during the day, Hawaiian shirts, shorts, sunburns, and all. When we got to the topic of how they liked Waikiki and other parts of Honolulu they had seen, the feeling was unanimous across all groups. They absolutely loved it. Bored? No, just relaxed. Wanting to go home early? No, wishing they could stay longer. Disgusted with the shopping? No, looking for more places to spend money to take gifts home to family members. My questions to the group then asked why they loved Waikiki so much. I got back a set of explanations that has influenced my thinking ever since. First timers expected Hawaii to offer good, predictable weather that made vacationers relax as soon as they stepped off of the plane. They assumed that native Hawaiians would treat visitors well, and the food would be good and modestly priced compared with foreign vacations. And they came convinced that local stores would offer items to buy different from what they can get back home so that they could return with unique gifts for family and friends. All in all, they anticipated that they would experience a relaxing, stress-free vacation, and it met all of their expectations. They had a clear image of what Hawaii offered, and Hawaii fulfilled on its promise.

That message works for travel and almost all other products or services, including new cars, beverages, technology, and fashion. It may sound overly simplistic, but it gets ignored most of the time. Advertising should establish a clear set of expectations as to what travelers can enjoy while at a destination, a resort, or on a cruise ship. Especially in promoting a destination, collateral materials should indicate not only the kinds of activities available, but the overall feeling of the place. Will it offer lots of activity choices or a feeling of relaxation, or both? Does it have an ambience of culture and sophistication or a down-home feeling? Whatever the glories of the place, expectations should be set clearly in travelers' minds prior to their trips. And, after arrival, travelers need constant reminders about what they should see and do during their visit in order to enjoy the full glories of the place. Brochures and other promotional materials should obviously give the story, but front-line personnel (hotel clerks, waiters, taxi drivers) need training in how to reinforce the image of the special place where they live and work. The more tourists that participate in the full experience of a destination, the more that will go home happy and satisfied and pass on great word-of-mouth advertising.

DON'T PROMOTE THE OBVIOUS

This statement may seem like it nullifies the previous section (set expectations and make certain that these get fulfilled), but the two ideas complement each other.

At the time I conducted a positioning study for Switzerland, most of their advertising focused on the Swiss Alps. Dramatic photography pictured their beauty in the summer and winter in almost every ad. SwissAir planes flying over them, trains going through them, skiers enjoying the challenges they offer—all setting the tone for what Switzerland offers. It seemed like heresy when I told them to stop promoting the Alps. I stated that they could not mention them for the next century and the public would still know that Switzerland has beautiful Alps. That single-mindedness of image development wastes precious space in ads, whether print or broadcast, that could promote other features of the country not commonly known. Reluctantly, they took the advice. You will still notice Alps in their ads, but mostly as a backdrop to the other activities for travelers when they visit the country.

A similar situation existed for Australia. In a speech I prepared for a tourism conference, I pointed out that their promotional materials usually included kangaroos and koala bears. Again, almost everyone knows Australia claims these as natives, and they don't need to be reminded of this fact. And, after travelers have seen a few of them, what else will they do with their time? A better bet is to point out what travelers don't know about Australia. Various provinces I have worked with in Canada have needed gentle reminders that the great outdoors of Canada photographs beautifully, but these ads only reinforce the obvious—Canada is a beautiful country. That message primarily attracts the rubber tire crowd (i.e., people who drive on vacations and take along their campers and spend less on hotels and meals while they are there—dependable personalities). It appeals less to the valuable venturesome types, who fly more often and also spend more wherever they go.

Most destinations and travel products don't have identities tied in tightly to singular images. When these exist, however, decisions must be made as to whether that image should be downplayed in marketing campaigns or used in new and clever ways to develop a fresh identity that appeals to a broader group of people. In most situations, however, the wiser decision is to stop promoting what most people already know and concentrate on what they don't know that might interest them.

THE TEN TO ONE RULE

During the early years of my first company, Behavior Science Corporation (BASICO), I worked as a consultant and researcher on a number of election campaigns for politicians. These varied from local office seekers to high-profile, well-known gubernatorial candidates. I can't locate the reference, but I remember reading an insightful article in a political science journal about opinion formation. The author examined a number of situations and concluded that it takes about ten times the amount of information to change someone's mind than it originally took to make it up. In other words, if someone has not formed an opinion on a subject, whether for a candidate or a preference for a product, a good promotional strategy stands a strong chance of success. If a choice has already been made against the candidate or the product, changing someone's mind becomes a difficult task. Those engaged in politics have learned this little secret. They now start their campaigns very early in an election year.

The concept applies to travel products as well. I remind clients about the difficulties of changing opinion if negative images abound. In such situations, even the best marketing campaign will require much longer to achieve its goals. In helping to reposition and improve an airline, for example, clients can get a bit impatient waiting for preference for their carrier to improve. They note that they have upgraded meals, retrained the inflight crew to provide more helpful and friendly service, and improved on-time arrivals. Ratings for each of these services improve quickly, but overall preference for their airline doesn't immediately follow the same course. Why? Prior negative images about the carrier remain, and fliers must experience multiple contacts with the airline before they become convinced that the airline truly has improved. For example, when someone has a bad flight on an airline that they normally prefer, they usually continue to like that carrier. They rationalize that any airline can have a bad flight once in a while. Similarly, an excellent flight on a carrier that ranks low on their list typically produces a reaction of, "Well, even the bad airline can do it right once in a while." They don't assume that the low-image carrier now offers improved service, consistently. A sequence of bad flights on the preferred carrier, however, will gradually degrade opinions. Similarly, a number of consistently good flights on the lowly rated carrier will also improve fliers' opinions about the level of service that it now provides. Gradually preference will change. The point is that it takes time to alter opinions, even with effective marketing campaigns. Clients need to remember this. If research shows that strong negative images exist, expect a rather difficult road ahead before achieving the desired results. If the image is either positive or neutral, shame on any marketer who doesn't take advantage of the situation to shape opinion along desired lines as quickly as possible.

THE MAGIC BEHIND GOOD ADVERTISING

Turn on the TV or radio, pick up a magazine or newspaper, or look at billboard signs as you drive and you'll have trouble understanding the message in a lot of the ads you see or hear. The confusing and off-target approach makes it difficult to understand the message. Rather than presenting a relevant message stated clearly, as Tony Antin suggests, these advertisers have wasted dollars on silly, mindless campaigns. All industries suffer from this malaise, including travel. A full-page, full-color magazine ad in *Successful Meetings* magazine shows a golfer leaning on his driver at a tee, looking down a fairway. A very small headline reads, "Have you ever won a game regardless of the score?" Large block letters fill the bottom of the page with the word "TRIUMPH," and a much smaller "Barbados" is superimposed across these letters. I have difficulty figuring out the message. Presumably it suggests that the natural beauty of Barbados will make every visitor a winner, but you have to stretch your imagination to get to that point. Most golf courses show well in photos, so the setting does not particularly entice anyone to Barbados. And what information or feeling does the word "TRIUMPH" convey? I certainly don't know. Or consider another two-page, full-color ad in *Condé Nast Traveler*. It lacks a headline but shows a middle-aged couple reclining in a mud bath. Her eyes are closed and she has a faint smile on her face, but his eyes are open and he looks concerned. The only other graphics on the pages are a picture of a hand-held Clie, Sony's personal digital assistant (PDA), along with two superimposed small PDA screens showing how they planned the trip. The copy suggests that the Clie made the trip possible with its ability to plan for everything. I don't think that ad sold many Clies or enticed others to visit spas.

Ask creative directors at the ad agencies as to why they take this tack and most will explain that, in today's cluttered media world, they must create something startling to capture attention. Otherwise, they continue, the ad will never get noticed. But do these really grab attention? And, if so, does it lead people to read the copy? Not likely in either case! Until recently I countered with the argument that our evolutionary heritage sensitizes us to messages important to our survival or well-being. However, some striking new research adds perspective on how we come to know about the world around us. And it has relevance on how to develop good advertising. Two Harvard University researchers, Susan Carey and Elizabeth Spelke, have cooperated for two decades in studying cognitive development among infants. In addressing the question of how humans acquire knowledge, they have come up with the concept of *the logic of the violation of expectancy*. In an interview reported in the *Harvard University Graduate School of Arts and Sciences Bulletin*, they explain their theories. They point out that during the first year of life

> infants seem to treat any solid, manipulable bodies as things that move about in space and bounce off each other, but at about one year of age, they start viewing objects as members of particular kinds. And this notion of "object kinds" does cognitive work for them, when they have to make basic decisions like, "Is the thing I'm seeing now the same individual as the thing I've seen at some other time?" and "If it belongs to a different kind, it can't be the same individual."[7]

They call their finding the logic of the violation of expectancy. Stated differently, cognitive development depends on learning how to place each new situation encountered into a preexisting category or by developing new categories when needed. But the new categories must have some relationship to preexisting categories. The task in studying infants, then, is to learn about what expectancies they have. Learning about these expectancies helps to explain how adults learn and why they pay attention to certain kinds of new information. As Carey and Spelke explain, these "systems of knowledge . . . are largely innate and are supported by dedicated input analyzers (that) are constant through development; they don't change."[8] The way we learn as infants, then, also determines how we take in information as adults. Carey and Spelke were led to their findings by the discovery that babies give close attention to magic tricks. They go on to say,

---

[7]Interview reported in the *Harvard University Graduate School of Arts and Sciences Bulletin*, fall 2001, p. 5.
[8]Ibid, p. 5.

Babies don't stare very closely at controlled events that are ordinary events. Their attention is grabbed by things that violate their expectancies. . . . You show a baby magic tricks [and] the very robust finding is that, if babies have the knowledge of what principle is being violated, they stare at the magic tricks.[9]

This last quote is the important. In essence, it suggests that advertising that does not present new information will usually fail to get noticed because the information offered is already known. So don't promote the obvious. Make certain you offer a Propositional Benefit, as Antin argues. But, to capture attention, create ads that present information in an interesting way, including using the principle of violating common expectancies. *The intended audience must be able to figure out what principle is being violated.* In other words, as humans, we have innate systems that determine what we pay attention to, a finding similar to the conclusions by cultural anthropologists and perceptual psychologists noted earlier in this chapter about how we selectively process information through our senses. Ads that don't conform to this principle will be ignored. Or they could result in a negative opinion of the company providing the message. Thus, *silliness in advertising most often will not even register as a logical event that is being violated.* It simply represents a random occurrence of little importance and not deserving of sustained attention. The research of Carey and Spelke helps to explain why some attempts at cleverness succeed and others fail. Clever ads capture attention by violating an expected principle. The individual will search for the principle violated and, when understood, will fit it into an existing category of knowledge or create a new category to accommodate the principle. English wit and other clever plays on words are popular and useful in advertising, not only in Britain but also with Americans. These represent more sophisticated, subtle ways of violating our expectancies by twisting a phrase or supplying a double meaning. The conclusions growing out of the work of Carey and Spelke do not suggest that all advertising should regularly follow the path of violating expectations. Rather, the concept still holds that a relevant message stated clearly stands a good chance of getting noticed. If it is also presented in an interesting manner—whether through humor, a stunning visual layout, or clever play on words—chances for success have increased. In contrast, silly and grossly distorted messages that may violate an expected principle but cannot fit into any category of understanding will not be remembered. The information will pass unnoticed because it provides no new information or interesting knowledge to its intended audience. Carey and Spelke describe innate tendencies that continue through life. As marketers, we should not ignore these principles or we run the risk of throwing away precious advertising dollars.

---

[9]Ibid, p. 4.

CHAPTER EIGHT

The Importance of Positioning and Branding

The careful analysis of a successful or an ineffective advertisement reveals underlying principles which have been applied correctly or incorrectly, or possibly ignored, as the case may be. Success and failure are not matters of good or bad luck. Complete analysis of a proposition and careful execution of the plans bring results with as reasonable certainty in an advertisement as cause and effect follow each other in any other controllable human affairs.[1]

This comment may seem to have come from Tony Antin, who argues for good planning in all ads, but Dr. Daniel Starch, Professor at the University of Wisconsin, wrote it in 1914. His perceptive book contains a number of principles that continue to have importance today, including a major section on the need for honesty and avoiding unsupportable claims in ads. Interestingly, he also talked about the growth of advertising and, without using the specific media clutter, the need to stand out from competitors. More so than in Starch's time, we need to think in terms of overall strategies and long-term campaigns, rather than just good execution of single ads. To increase the chances that an ad gets noticed and remembered, it generally must have a

---

[1]Daniel Starch, *Advertising: Its Principles, Practice, and Technique,* Scott, Foresman and Company, Chicago, 1914, p. 16.

theme that ties all advertising and promotional messages together under a single umbrella. Usually that theme should arise from good *positioning strategy* and proper *branding*.

In my years in the business, I have heard much discussion about these twin concepts but few definitions. Some books written on the topic have left me confused about the author's thinking on the subject. Two senior executives of Ogilvy & Mather[2] suggest, "Everyone agrees it's important, but there's a lot of argument about exactly what it is. Advertising theorists are behaving like the judge who said, 'I can't define pornography. But I know it when I see it.' . . . When you position your product, you *place it a certain way in the consumer's mind*."[3] Branding as a term, unfortunately, too often gets used interchangeably with positioning. It's not the same. It has its own meaning and importance. I have developed my own definitions of each concept because of their importance in working with clients to develop new, more successful strategies to increase travel and tourism. Specifically,

> **Positioning** is defining the important attributes that characterize a product or service to distinguish it from competitors in a meaningful way to consumers (the propositional benefits).

Stated simply, what qualities should your target market remember most about the benefits you offer? Any company that puts out a series of ads that fail to reinforce a constant theme has reduced its chances that its target audience will remember the message. Developing a word picture of the essence of these characteristics is essential so that all who work on positioning the product will understand the ultimate goals of their efforts. In various ways, advertising copy and graphics must work together to explain, clarify, and reinforce the positioning concept.

Branding works as the second and complementary part of the equation. Without good branding, a strong positioning strategy can get lost in the execution of a campaign. Specifically,

> **Branding** applies a label or short phrase to the positioning concept that conveys the essence of the positioning platform, quickly and easily, making the benefits easy to understand and memorable.

A good branding statement helps establish an identity for a product or service to help consumers call to mind its essential qualities and its position in the marketplace. Repetition of the phrase in each ad and collateral materials reinforces the brand image and builds strong brand equity. Without good branding, even the best positioning strategies can fail.

---

[2]Kenneth Roman and Jane Maas, *How to Advertise,* St. Martin's Press, 1976, p. 10.
[3]Ibid., p. 1.

INDUSTRY EXAMPLES OF SUCCESS AND FAILURE IN POSITIONING AND BRANDING STRATEGIES

Examples of success and failure in branding strategies from other industries can help to clarify the importance of developing a good strategy and sticking with it over time. Car manufacturers demonstrate both the right and wrong ways to accomplish the task. Among auto companies, BMW has established the best positioning and branding strategies, without exception. When I completed my first project with the company in the 1970s, they held a tiny share of market and an even smaller "share of mind," to use an advertising phrase. Most people thought its initials stood for British Motor Works, not Bayerische Motoren Werke. At the time, Mercedes had staked out the claim of having the best engineered cars. That seemed to leave little room for another high-end product from Germany to distinguish itself in the luxury market. But its ad agency discovered an important difference: BMW's designers and engineers truly believed that they designed and built cars superior to Mercedes on an important dimension. BMWs offered greater responsiveness to a driver's actions. Mercedes had a smoother ride, but BMWs had a tighter feel from the car, providing a greater sense of the road beneath. This created the sense that the driver controlled the car more than was true of any other brand. Only sports car aficionados knew and appreciated these qualities at the time of BMW's introduction to the U.S. The new positioning strategy emphasized the car's performance and handling and how it interacts with drivers to provide a better sense of control and feedback about driving conditions. The next question is how to communicate this positioning strategy to the car-buying public. The branding execution did it all in one simple but great phrase, *BMW . . . the ultimate driving machine.* That statement says it all simply, clearly, and memorably. If you want to enjoy driving at its ultimate, you must buy a BMW. When you brand your product well, you should keep that strategy in place until you absolutely know that it no longer communicates effectively in the marketplace. BMW has stayed the course with its emphasis on performance and handling for over three decades. That mantra now also dominates all aspects of the company. Its engineers constantly seek out ways to keep the company ahead of competition. Car buff magazines continue to comment that the BMW gives a greater sense of the driver in control than any other brand. Its success can be measured by the fact that BMWs now outsells Mercedes in the U.S. More to the point, no other company has achieved BMW's success in moving people up its car line. Someone who buys its smallest car, the 3 series, has a strong interest in moving up to its 5 series when they can afford the jump and ultimately to its 7 or 8 series lines. Whichever model they own, they believe that they own the finest in its class. BMW can keep customers in its fold for decades. No other car company can make that claim to the same degree.

In contrast, Ford has neither positioned itself nor achieved the same level of branding success. It faces the problem of what the industry calls the "missing car line." Someone who buys a Ford does not aspire to own a Mercury as a next purchase. Mercurys appeal to a different group of buyers—older, very conservative in their buying habits, and with household incomes not greatly above average. Thus, Lincoln stands alone atop the Ford hierarchy—a luxury car that lacks good feed-in from car lines below it. Ford truly offers great products today—better than most people recognize. However, it has not created a strong positioning strategy and related brand identity to set it apart from most of the competition. Chrysler provides an even more severe example of what can happen when companies don't develop good positioning strategies and establish strong brand identities. Chrysler dropped its Plymouth line because of declining sales. The company did not offer clear reasons for consumers to choose a Plymouth rather than one of its Dodge or Chrysler nameplates. General Motors announced the demise of Oldsmobile in 1999 for similar reasons. Previously the product was known for strong performance (Olds 88 Rocket series). In its late history, however, the Oldsmobile product development and the marketing teams didn't support that positioning adequately. Ultimately the brand attracted an older, more conservative group of buyers, and it had to fight the image that the car belonged to your father's generation.

Hertz has long dominated the short-term market for rental cars. It has a larger fleet, more corporate accounts, and more locations. Since rental car companies tend to offer similar rates, most competitors have difficulty separating themselves from each other. Generally, people like to go with a winner. The biggest company probably is best, consumers assume, because it has earned its top position. In the 1980s, Avis faced that problem as it struggled to stand out against Hertz. And Avis discovered another difficulty it had to address: service levels provided by its employees did not measure up to those of Hertz, as judged by its own surveys. It needed to develop a reason for more travelers to select Avis. It decided that its primary positioning strategy would be to emphasize customer service, especially because it didn't want to start a price war and establish itself as a low-end brand. It developed a marvelous campaign with the branding slogan, "We try harder because we're number two." That phrase addresses two audiences. For consumers, it suggests that you'll get better service from Avis because it tries harder. And Americans like to support underdogs. They can understand why a second-place company would try to give better service to get ahead. The campaign did its job. Rentals increased. Its second audience was its own employees. It reminded them that they must improve their level of service to customers to live up to the branding theme that Avis tries harder. Avis even planned for the counterattack from its primary competitor. When Hertz ran a series of ads showing its superior fleet size and the larger number of services offered, Avis countered with a clever print campaign depicting battleships lined up against each other with the message, "Avis has been attacked by a larger fleet." It played the role of the underdog to its advantage and kept the slogan for years. Many more examples of positioning and branding strategies could be given, but these will be saved for chapters that focus on travel.

USING THE USP

Decades ago, when he worked with the Ted Bates advertising agency, Rosser Reeves came up with the concept of the Unique Selling Proposition (USP). It starts with the assumption that most products in a category are very similar, leaving little reason for a consumer to choose one brand over another. Advertising strategy must identify a unique quality about a product that makes it stand out from its competition. That quality offers an advantage that becomes a reason for consumers to choose a client's product rather than a competitor's. Consider aspirin. Basically, all aspirin is the same, regardless of whether it is Bayer brand or a much lower-cost generic brand with a drug store's name on the bottle. If consumers always watched their pocketbooks, they'd buy the lowest cost aspirin. But generic brands don't sell as well as name brands. Why? Unique Selling Propositions developed by clever marketing create strong reasons for purchase of name-brand products. Bayer promotes its safety, based on the long years it has dominated the market. A competitor claims that its aspirin absorbs more quickly to relieve headaches sooner. Another is buffered and easier on the stomach. And so on. Major pharmaceutical companies work hard to establish strong brand equity through good, consistent positioning of their aspirin products. Without such strategies, aspirin would be purchased truly as a low-cost commodity.

Destinations face a different battleground. Because destinations generally vary on a number of characteristics, multiple advantages can be promoted, rather than a single point. But even here exceptions exist. Much of the Caribbean seems similar to travelers, creating a need to establish a singular reason as to why one spot should be chosen over another. Golf resorts have sprouted in so many places that these also often require developing a USP in order to provide a clear reason why a golfing traveler should select one spot over another. In a similar vein, airlines, hotels, and rental car companies typically must develop a USP strategy. But the primary message of this chapter remains the same: An effective positioning strategy and powerful branding statement must be developed in order to ensure success for any destination.

CHAPTER NINE

Using Psychographics for Effective Marketing

If you understand the personality of your target customers, you can create advertising that meets their needs and interests, target them effectively by selecting the media they prefer, and create marketing programs that produce desired results more often. Psychographics provides a vehicle to accomplish those goals. Demographics does not give many clues about individuals needs and interests, as was seen in the section in Chapter 3 that contrasted psychographic and demographic approaches ("Does the concept of venturesomeness really work?", p. 61). Venturers and dependables approach life quite different-ly and, as a result, respond to different kinds of messages and generally use different media. This chapter presents a more complete picture of the person-alities of the different psychographic types. For the most part, polar opposites will be compared to aid in understanding. This chapter covers three areas of concern: (1) a comprehensive description of the personality characteristics of each personality type, (2) effective marketing approaches for each group, and (3) media choices of venturers and dependables.

PERSONALITY CHARACTERISTICS OF VENTURERS AND DEPENDABLES

Venturers

As individuals, venturers have a strong achievement drive. That need, however, requires further definition. It does not necessarily imply a passion to gain wealth, status, or power. True achievement-oriented persons simply want to do well at whatever they touch. Even in selecting a personal hobby, they rise above average levels of skill, knowledge, and comprehension. They want to be better than others around them and feel a sense of accomplishment when they do. Those who seek wealth, status, or a position in politics generally possess a drive for power, not achievement. With their varied interest patterns, however, venturers often find it difficult to select a single focus in their careers or their non-vocational interests. They can seem like dilettantes to those who don't know them well. Their drive to achieve means that they typically dedicate themselves to their jobs, put in excessive amounts of overtime and willingly take on difficult assignments. But they also expect progress in their assignments. If they feel they have reached a dead end in their companies, they will look for greener pastures. Job hopping, as a result, appears often in their resumes. But each new position seems to rise above the previous assignment. And they often become entrepreneurs because of past unpleasant experiences working under people less capable and less dedicated to their careers than they are. As a result, most venturers have incomes and job responsibilities well above average, again not because of a need for power or status but as a reflection of their belief that they can do just about everything better than others they know.

Self-confidence permeates the venturer's personality. Venturers believe they can accomplish just about anything they undertake, and they usually do. Risk taking is a normal part of their lives. Tomorrow will be better than today, and the day after offers even more promise. For this reason, others look on venturers as influence leaders. Their willingness to take moderate levels of risk also applies to purchasing new, relatively untested products. This is the early adopter personality. Others want to learn from their experiences and emulate what they have done to a considerable degree. To use a term of David Riesman, venturers have *inner-directed* personalities.[1] They like to chart their own course in life and do things their way. Personal goal setting is important to them, and they work hard to achieve those goals. They attempt to clarify how they differ from others, and strive to make certain that they do not follow common paths in life. They believe that success is self-determined and not based on chance.

Because of these characteristics, venturers may seem somewhat aloof or distant. On the surface, they often give the appearance of being gregarious and outgoing, but underneath they probably would often rather be left alone to their own thoughts. As a result, people can sometimes seem like objects to them. They categorize others in positive, neutral, or negative terms related to how much each acquaintance can help them reach their personal goals. They network with business associates regularly to broaden their base of contacts, and ignore others not seen as important in their lives. Their high degree of self-confidence arises from low levels of personal anxiety and a willingness to take risks. These risks lead to greater chances of success and rewards for their

---

[1]David Riesman, Nathan Glazer, and Reuel Denney, *The Lonely Crowd: A Study of the Changing American Character*, Yale University Press, 1950.

efforts. They also are more likely to challenge authority figures and conventional rules and wisdom. They believe that guidelines developed by others often don't make much sense or shouldn't apply to them. They will tell you that they know a better way to do most things. This belief can come close to arrogance at times. They set personal goals more than most people and evaluate these on a regular basis, trying to accomplish the impossible. Their tendency to change directions in life fits well with their desire to avoid routine, boring tasks.

Dependables

Dependables, in contrast, more often seek personal comfort and an easygoing, low-risk approach to life. Often they won't expend the emotional or physical energy required to reach out and achieve greatness. Rather, they measure high on social needs, to be with others—friends and relatives. They seek their support and warmth. Their social skills may lack some finesse, but friendships run deep and can extend for decades. Their tendency to prefer a predictable and relatively unvarying day-to-day life serves them well in their jobs. They often remain with the same company throughout their careers, rising steadily to senior supervisory positions because of their steadfastness and trustworthiness, which they demonstrate over the years. A higher proportion end up in blue-collar ranks instead of executive positions because of their reluctance to accept the risks and difficulties that go along with more senior management positions. However, they can demonstrate great skills on shop floors or at home in such areas as cabinetry and fine furniture making, sewing, and knitting. Because they seek emotional support from people they know, dependables typically have a friendly personality, although they are sometimes a bit reserved around strangers. They don't reach out to others easily but, when approached, they respond with helpfulness and professionalism.

To a considerable degree, these are *other-directed* personalities, again to use David Riesman's term. They look to people around them for guidance and direction in their lives. Conforming to the group seems natural. They don't try to network as often because of some shyness growing out of their insecure personalities and a feeling that to do so is somewhat false and self-centered. They prefer having fewer but deep friendships, rather than a large list of shallow contacts. In many respects, dependables are the flywheels of society. They keep things on track, not allowing it to be pulled off course by those who constantly offer new and untried ideas or suggest that they have better solutions for political and social problems. Dependables don't usually challenge authority. Rather, they accept traditional values and norms. They prefer the most popular consumer brands because these represent safe choices. These brands must be good choices, they reason, because so many people use them. When new products or technologies hit the marketplace, dependables adopt them late in the cycle, and sometimes never. They don't want to take the risk of being among the first to try something that may not live up to its promise. They may also feel that they have no need for the presumed advantages it might offer. Who needs computers, they might ask aloud? They have gotten along quite well without these in their lives until now, and they fail to see how they could benefit at present.

Resistance to change and a reluctance to accept new technologies leads to a belief that much of what happens in dependables lives is the result of chance, not actions they have taken. A promotion or getting a new job offer, making a new friendship, finding the right music teacher for a child—all of these events happen because of unpredictable events. As a result, dependables tend to set few personal goals, believing that accidental events in their lives determine their ultimate level of success or failure. Overall, they have likeable, pleasing personalities. They simply don't have a lot of exciting things happening on a daily basis. More than almost anything, they desire stability in their lives.

ADVERTISING TO PSYCHOGRAPHIC TYPES

With personalities as divergent as those just discussed, it follows that advertising messages to each group should vary in both content and style. Again, the two extreme psychographic types will be reviewed to clarify differences and because, in most situations, good positioning requires that the ads be made a bit more venturesome or dependable in character than the actual audience targeted.

Advertising to Venturers

In general, venturer-focused ads should include fewer people. Since they feel more psychologically isolated as individuals, they don't identify with crowds. They view themselves as leaders, not followers, who make smart, independent choices in their lives. Large numbers of people in an ad suggest that the product advertised has achieved broad acceptance, the opposite of what they want. A sense of exclusivity and uniqueness appeals to them to a great degree. Those pictured in the ad should appear somewhat younger than the target audience, again because of their self-perception. They believe they are physically and intellectually more active than most people. Using models in the late thirties or younger will fit in many situations. It's best when the ad conveys a sense of energy and motion, all part of the emphasis on a younger feeling. Although venturers seek exclusivity in products they purchase and desire to attain higher levels of status and position in life, avoid blatant appeals to their egos. Ads that suggest they have achieved a certain status or position in life and now can enjoy the fruits of their accomplishments if they purchased a certain product seem amateurish and beneath their dignity. Ego stroking must remain more subtle and indirect. Advertising copy can talk about the superior qualities of a product, but not that the person who made the choice has above average intelligence. They already know that. Most often, they simply want the benefits of products explained adequately to help them to feel like they make good choices.

Good venturer ads often concentrate on one person as the center of attention. Such an ad appeals to their drive for achievement and their need to be recognized for their accomplishments by others. Thus, an "aprés ski" setting might include several skiers who focus on a single individual. Standing by a fireplace mantle, that person may be recounting how he or she won a local downhill race or successfully navigated a difficult slope for the first time that day. In general, avoid the use of celebrities, whether stars or sports heroes. Venturers don't identify with these groups and don't look to them for guidance. Rather, they view themselves as equal or superior to most others they encounter, even those who have achieved fame and fortune. Advertising that carries subtle forms of humor has a greater chance of capturing their attention. They believe that someone who comes up with a clever ad understands their needs and desires. Ads must rise to their level of intelligence, not hit below it.

An Example of Venturer-Focused Advertising   Following a speech I gave at a tourism conference in Waikiki in 1970, Boise Cascade, the developers of the new Waikoloa resort on the big island of Hawaii, asked for help. Sales of lots, homes, and condos had not reached forecasts. They asked me to work with their ad agency, Beyl, Boyd & Turner, Inc., to help them refocus the campaign. Their efforts had produced rather standard copy. Collateral materials emphasized the beauty of Waikoloa's beach location (most of Hawaii is beautiful) and its newness (several other resorts were new then). The message also encouraged prospects to buy now while they can still choose an ideal lot for their home (a standard sales pitch for new homes). I reviewed their materials, described my psychographic concepts, explained that they would need to target the venturer group, and discussed how this group needed indirect subtle appeals that suggested they would experience something unique at Waikoloa. After learning more about the development, I suggested that the area had a history that could become the basis for a good positioning strategy. The ad agency, directed by Bill Boyd, understood my concepts quickly. They created some of the best advertising copy targeting venturers that I have seen. References to their championship golf courses, sunny beaches, and other expected attractions were relegated to a secondary position behind an emphasis on the mystique of Waikoloa and its history. The new ads contained more copy than I would usually recommend for two reasons: A description that changes perceptions may require more space. And venturers read more, as has been mentioned. The copy carried the following message:

> **Presenting Waikoloa: Once reserved as a place for Hawaiian nobility.**
>
> Waikoloa: Crown land once reserved as a place of resort for Hawaiian nobility. Now after years of careful preparation it is emerging as a place of resort for you.
>
> Ancient chieftains chose Waikoloa to escape from the duties of their court and to refresh themselves in body and spirit. When you visit here you will discover why they selected Waikoloa Beach as a royal sanctuary.
>
> Already attention to each detail of the overall design is evident. Majestic lagoons that once provided fish for those ancient nobles have been restored and again schools of fingerlings can be seen skimming across the sunlit surfaces.

> Magnificent botanical gardens are being planted around the lagoons. . . . Waikoloa's second golf course is being shaped from the awesome lava flows which jut into the Pacific. No other golf course in the world surrounds ancient burial caves, petroglyph fields, and the King's Trail once used by early Hawaiians. . . .
>
> . . . Ride the rugged rangeland of the legendary paniolos [Hawaiian cowboys] who attended King Kamehameha's vast herds of cattle. Walk the golden beach where only footprints of royalty were once allowed.
>
> Here on the sunny Kohala Coast of the Island of Hawaii, the hand of man moves slowly. In a changed world, the spirit and integrity of Waikoloa remains. For this is a sanctuary where Hawaiian nobility found a place of resort . . .
>
> But why wait? A royal welcome awaits you even today.

Stunning pictures accompanied the four-color ads, all designed to emphasize again that Waikoloa differs from other resorts. It offers much to do, but in a setting of peace, tranquility, and protection of an ancient heritage. A separate booklet that provided even more information on the history of Waikoloa was given to all prospects. Sales at the development quickly picked up after the launch of the new campaign, and the resort has maintained its special status even today.

Advertising to Dependables

Targeting the other side of the spectrum, the dependables, generally requires a different feel to the ads. Although most of the emphasis in this book has concentrated on the venturers, dependable types dominate certain kinds of destinations (such as Branson, Missouri and Las Vegas, Nevada) and some travel products (escorted tours and some cruises and packages). Thus, this group cannot be forgotten in a review of advertising and promotion. Dependable-oriented advertising will include more people, usually with no clearly identified leader or superior individual—unless that person is a well-known celebrity. For the most part, the people pictured are friends or coequal workers. If someone appears to have taken a leadership role in the ad, then dependables might assume that his or her aggressive style does not fit in well with the friendship situations they seek. Dependables want to enjoy the company of people with whom they feel close, not take orders from someone considered a peer. Persons pictured in the group may be chronologically older than in venturer ads, often in their early to late 40s. Individual accomplishment and achievement do not belong as often in these ads since equals don't try to stand out from each other. The people pictured also might have a little more girth around the middle, a sign that they enjoy the good things of life, especially in the company of others.

Well-known personalities and sports heroes, used as spokespersons to endorse products, can add a high degree of credibility. To dependables, a person's celebrity status indicates that he or she has earned a position of public trust deserving of attention when that person speaks. And direct, unsubtle appeals can be effective. Dependables particularly accept suggestions that they should treat themselves to special things in life because others often don't recognize their level of self-sacrifice in helping others at work and at home. Dedication to their jobs, steady performance, and willingness to live with seemingly unvarying daily routines make them valued workers. Because of their trustworthiness, many get promoted to supervisory positions. Thus, ads that show work settings, particularly of blue-collar jobs, often are appropriate for this group.

An Example of Dependable-Focused Advertising   *Reader's Digest* convinced the original group of airline sponsors from the first travel study my company conducted (1967) to back a two-year, bimonthly insert campaign in the *Digest* that targeted dependables. Although it was the first campaign based on the venturesome concept, it still places at the top in motivating dependables to change their well-ingrained habits and try something new. The campaign focused on getting nonflier dependables into the air through eight-page informational inserts. It seems like a difficult task, but Tony Antin (Vice President, Creative at the *Digest* and mentioned several times in this text) followed his time-tested concepts and moved an entire market. He reasoned that getting them into the air would require several steps. Each ad insert would take one of those steps. The first insert booklet asked the question, "Should you travel more?" The goal was to get nonfliers to consider traveling more, and then work on getting them into the air. Inside it asked a series of questions that most people would want to answer in the affirmative, and used professionals and experts to point out the importance of achieving each goal. The opening section began with, "Want to be healthier, wealthier, and wiser?". Quotes from physicians described the benefits of getting out of daily routines to experience something new and novel. A human resources executive indicated that people who travel more also advance more rapidly in their jobs. And the point was emphasized that someone who continues to experience and learn new things throughout adulthood will be wiser and better informed. The next question in this initial insert, "How's your marriage doing?", followed the same format. Statements from top marriage counselors buttressed the argument that couples who get away together regularly have better marriages. The use of experts to mold opinion fits the psychology of dependable types.

The second insert booklet provided an interesting twist in the form of the question, "Should the airlines write you off as hopeless?". That turnabout of expectations by Antin for this ad truly meets the criteria established by Carey and Spelke to capture attention. The copy approached the problem directly. It described the happy, self-confident characteristics of people who fly vs. the rather depressed, anxiety-ridden personalities of those who don't fly. Assuming that most people would rather be happy and approach life with a great deal of confidence, it encourages readers to take a simple test to determine where they fit on the scale and what they can do to better their lives. How? By following "5 Easy Ways to Start Flying." These include talking with friends about flying, planning trips with someone you know, getting excited about a place to go, taking "the hand of an expert" (a travel agent), and making a commitment.

The third insert answered questions people commonly ask about flying. The fourth answered what to expect when you go to an airport, board the airplane, and take off on your trip. Other inserts described how to use a travel agent effectively, how to choose a destination, and other very down-home topics.

According to *Reader's Digest* follow-up studies, the effort resulted in the second best read insert campaign ever, and average readership was double that of a typical ad. One out of four readers (24%) read the inserts. The *Digest* won several awards for the campaign, and various church groups and Boy Scouts/Girl Scout troops requested reprints of the pamphlets for distribution to their members.

Moving Products across the Psychographic Spectrum

Travel providers that offer multiple products usually can achieve greater success by positioning their products to distinct psychographic groups. Escorted tours provide a good example. The industry grew up largely by serving dependables, but it now covers the psychographic spectrum. Venturers select adventure tours, some historic tours, and group programs that require sophisticated guides in order to get the maximum benefit from the trips. Dependables continue to love old-fashioned guided tours to major world cities that visit well-known historic sites.

A product can also be moved across the psychographic spectrum and stopped at a predetermined point by following the advertising and marketing guidelines described previously. Molson's Brewery of Canada has used these concepts to position its beers. They position products across the entire psychographic spectrum because all types of people drink beer. Contrary to what some might assume, beer is not a unitary product. It has a different set of images with each psychographic audience. When a new product is introduced, Molson generally targets it at a venturer audience. Dependables, in contrast, generally want assurance that they are drinking a brew that has been around long enough to prove its worth. In following the concepts presented previously, fewer people appear in Molson venturer-targeted ads. A single person is the center of attention in the ad, and most of the people are younger in appearance. Both men and women are likely to be included. And the ad often has a feeling of energy, with subtle humor in the headline or copy.

As the product works its way beyond pure venturers, it has a more mature feel. Individuals pictured become somewhat older, a bit broader across the middle, and more rugged looking. The ad contains additional people, often just men, and a greater egalitarian feel exists within the group. Friendship pervades the setting, a hallmark of most beer ads. When the proper point on the psychographic chart has been reached, the positioning strategy remains constant to prevent further movement. By following this approach, it is possible for Molson and other companies serving a broad spectrum of the public to introduce and target specific groups to maximize the size of the potential audience covered.

MEDIA SELECTION

Although the most successful media attract the broadest audiences possible, venturers and dependables have distinctive media interests. Knowledge of these differences helps to target each group more effectively. Dependables form the core television viewing audience. They spend more time before the "boob tube" than any other group. They especially like sitcoms. The light-hearted fare of these programs with their not very subtle and often slapstick humor suits their tastes. Dependables identify closely with key elements of these shows. Most programs show ordinary people engaged in everyday kinds of relationships clumsily trying to solve personal problems. And, characters portrayed in sitcoms generally represent friends or relatives, most of whom are seen as coequals in the story line. With their heavier television viewing habits, dependable personalities dominate TV ratings systems. What they like, to a large extent, determines what's available for others to watch. When dependables read, they favor magazines that feature celebrities, such as *People* and entertainment weeklies, along with home fix-up and crafts magazines and supermarket tabloids.

Venturers, in contrast, use print media to a greater degree. They make up the primary audiences for daily newspapers and a broad range of magazines. These include news and business publications, upscale travel magazines, gourmet food and home design periodicals, and technology monthlies. They also buy more books of all types, from fiction to nonfiction, self-help guides, and topics that reflect their special interests. Although they watch less TV, their viewing habits also reflect their personalities. They like prime time news, dramas with an involved psychological plot, informational shows (History Channel, Discovery Channel, etc.), and TV "magazines" (*60 Minutes, 20/20,* Dateline).

Although sports on TV cut across psychographic segments considerably, tendencies appear. Venturers have a special love for football and basketball. Football, to them, possesses the intricacies of a chess match, with two coaches matching wits on a brutal battlefield. Opposing teams use deception, aggression, and defense while capitalizing on their own strengths and seeking to take advantage of opponents' weaknesses. Venturers love the beauty and grace of basketball. Although the game doesn't feature the intellectual challenge of football, the one-on-one match-ups between players in basketball and the fast pace of the game add excitement and drama. Dependables also love these two sports, but for different reasons. In football, they seldom think about the coaching. Instead they love the manliness of the game—the hard hitting that occurs with every scrimmage and the excitement of breakout plays, such as a big run or a touchdown from a long bomb pass. Dependables' love of basketball comes from a focus on the personalities of the players, especially the attitudes conveyed by some of the stars. Baseball would seem to be made for venturers, with its heavy psychological basis in the duel between pitcher and batter and the drama that occurs with a bases-loaded home run. But venturers often find the game to be a bit unvarying and lacking in significant coaching strategy. Instead, the grand old American pastime attracts a greater share of dependables. They like its very distinct American roots, its association with traditional hot dogs and beer, and the storied pasts of many teams. A clearer distinction is evident in golf and tennis on TV. Golf tends to attract dependables in larger numbers; tennis captures more venturers.

Radio reaches a more diverse market and, as a result, is more difficult to define. Drive time news grabs venturers, as do classical and jazz music stations. Most talk show formats capture greater numbers of dependables, as do heavy metal and hip-hop. Classic rock and newer country music tend to cut across both audiences.

HOW TO TARGET PSYCHOGRAPHIC GROUPS IN A NONPSYCHOGRAPHIC MEDIA WORLD

Since all forms of media use demographics to define their audiences, not psychographics, somewhat indirect approaches must be employed in order to match media choices with psychographic-focused marketing campaigns. Although the approach may be indirect, it is possible to combine two demographic categories to approximate the results desired. The results may lack the definitiveness provided by the original set of questions, but it's a reasonable compromise.

Household income forms the first cut. Although income does not predict the types of trips people will take or what they do after they arrive at a destination (see Chapter 3), income at least provides the means to make travel possible. Higher-income households can afford air trips, cruises, and tours of Europe. And luxury travel providers, by necessity, must always target the upper end of the income spectrum. All media have these data available to show to prospective advertisers. The second demographic variable is less obvious. For a long time, educational level has seemed relatively unimportant to researchers and media specialists. Most travel companies don't even measure it. However, they overlook a key element. Education correlates more strongly with venturesomeness than any other demographic characteristic, based on multiple studies I have conducted. Apparently, the more years of schooling that someone achieves, the more that they are exposed to new ideas. This sets the stage for their continued interest in exploring the world around them by traveling to new and unique places.

To summarize, selecting media with audiences that measure high on both income and education (including advanced degree work) produces a greater proportion of venturesome types. In contrast, selecting media with lower demographics for household income and educational attainment (high school degree or less) tilts the scales toward the dependable side of the psychographic curve.

CHAPTER TEN

Repositioning Destinations for Maximum Growth

Adolph Zukor, the founder of Paramount Pictures, lived to be 103. Before he died in 1976, he commented, "If I'd known I was going to live so long, I'd have taken better care of myself." Destinations should follow that advice. Although few places ever disappear completely from the travel scene, they barely hang on. They survive as old, tired spots desperately in need of something more than a face-lift. They have lost their prime markets, their luster, and their allure. Attempts at a revival fall far short because no one can agree on what needs to be done. Planners too often don't consider the long-term future by trying to protect and enhance the special characteristics of the places they represent. By the time they wake up to the problems, it may be too late. After years of declining tax revenues, local governments can't provide the financial help to make needed changes. Their minimal efforts at revitalization have little impact. As punster Dave Falk said, "There is nothing worse than trying to put a *now* look on a *then* face." Planning for the long term seldom occurs because pressures exist to fill hotel beds next month, not next year or the year after. When a slow, steady decline begins, it can be difficult to reverse. The majority of destinations do not age gracefully, unfortunately.

In spite of these problems, most destinations still have much to offer the traveling public and, with appropriate positioning strategies, can ensure successful futures for many years. But attempts at change fail too often because tourism officials don't know how to develop an effective positioning strategy, or they approve an advertising campaign that sends out the wrong message. The most desired psychographic types will either ignore the message or quickly decide that it's not for them.

This chapter reviews how to position destinations for maximum growth by developing effective positioning strategies. A declining destination spreads pain throughout a community. Airlines, hotels, shops, restaurants, entertainment centers, and those employed by these establishments all feel the pinch. A destination that wants a bright future must always convey the right message about what makes it special or it will get lost in a crowded, competitive marketplace. The psychographic concept of venturesomeness forms the backbone of the material to be reviewed in this chapter. The goal is to help destinations know more about what they need to do to turn themselves around by examining case examples from places around the world. Branding also plays a part, as do the ideas presented in Chapter 7, which covered some overlooked elements of good marketing and sales techniques.

Destinations vary greatly in the ease with which a new positioning strategy can be implemented. In the best of all possible situations, a destination has a positive image and only needs a good campaign that will make it stand out among its competitors. Second best is when little is known about a place, good or bad. The situation resembles a *tabula rasa,* a blank tablet on which a new positioning strategy can be written without having to change images from the past. But when negative perceptions abound, the 10-to-1 rule applies (see Chapter 7). Old negative perceptions must be greatly reduced or eliminated before positive messages will have a full impact. Some spots in the world attract the wrong crowds—dependable types when venturers would provide more revenue, or ruffian motorcycle groups to quaint, isolated villages. Often a smooth transition must be planned in many of these situations so that what remains of the desired crowd doesn't stop coming before sufficient numbers of new visitors arrive. These and other problem situations are reviewed in the material that follows. Real case examples illustrate the principles involved. This chapter covers repositioning and branding strategies only, not what should be done to improve the quality of the experience at a place. That topic appears in Chapter 14.

WHAT MAKES A DESTINATION GREAT?

When I work with a destination, I start with one underlying assumption: Every place has something to offer that tourists would like. I must discover those special qualities and help to emphasize these in new marketing campaigns. Some places have so many positive attributes that tourism planners can comfortably select from multiple approaches for a new positioning effort. They may even be able to address the question as to whether they would ultimately like to put limits on the number of tourist arrivals. Others with more limited attributes must make careful choices—target the right segments and give them appropriate messages or the effort may fail. Over the years, I have developed a checklist of the primary types of advantages that characterize a destination. This information helps me determine the size or difficulty of the task I face in developing a proper positioning strategy. A dozen criteria fit on my list—four in Level 1 (most important) and eight in Level 2 (less important). The more qualities possessed by a destination, the easier the task of repositioning.

Level 1: Call these the magic four. A place that possesses all of these qualities has a lot going for it. In relative order of importance, these include the following:

- *Dramatic scenery:* The visual aspects of any journey dominate memories. When given a list of twenty-one reasons for choosing a destination for the last leisure trip, the top choice is always "It's a beautiful, scenic place" (selected by 50 percent in the American Traveler Survey). Tall mountains and green valley floors sloping down to a lake or an ocean beach place at the top of the list, but quaint villages and towns also contribute to excitement and pleasant memories.

- *Perception of lots to do:* The more activities available at a place, the greater the chance it can serve the interests of multiple groups of people, entice visitors to stay longer, and keep them coming back. Variety can include urban attractions (nightlife, museums and art galleries, historic sites, great shopping) and/or outdoor activities (hiking, water sports, golf, tennis, horseback riding).

- *Uniqueness:* The more that a destination differs from others, the more that it seems like an interesting vacation spot to travelers. Unique settings make memories more indelible and provide a reason to choose one place over another for the next trip.

- *Predictable weather:* Predictable weather serves as an important backdrop for most trips. Warm weather, clear skies, and the absence of rain and clouds help to ensure a dream vacation. Visitors can enjoy the outdoors and get to various venues of interest, such as museums, theaters, and restaurants. Similarly, ski resorts that have more predictable snow packs in the winter also do better. They get earlier reservations, can charge higher rates, and are more likely to operate at full capacity during the high season. Utah ski resorts do better than those in California because Utah has more predictable snow cover.

Level 2: Although these eight characteristics don't measure at the same level of importance as Level 1, the greater the number of Level 2 characteristics possessed by a destination, the better its chances for success. Again, these will be presented in their approximate order of importance.

- *Unspoiled environment:* This point has been emphasized repeatedly in discussing the psychographic model. Venturers most seek this characteristic, but others also prefer places that seem natural and not corrupted by commercial development. Highly developed places, like major cities, especially those with historic sites, need to avoid excessive, tacky commercialism.

- *Cleanliness:* Travelers like cleanliness and hate dirt. The top three items that can spoil a vacation, as measured year after year in the American Traveler Survey of NFO/Plog Research, are a dirty hotel room, dirt or filth in the area around the hotel, and an unclean or dirty local village.

- *Friendly people:* Hawaii places high on the scale of providing a memorable vacation for a number of reasons, but its Aloha spirit contributes a lot. People experience a warm greeting when they arrive and depart from the airport, and feel they have been treated well throughout their stay. Friendly citizens enhance any vacation.

- *Favorable price/value relationship:* If a destination possesses many of the aforementioned characteristics and also seems reasonably priced, it can more easily attract an audience. Not many places can make this claim, but it can help. But even high-priced places can do well if they provide a strong feeling of value for the money—a dimension that is distinct from low price (see Chapter 7).

- *Crime free:* Travelers want to feel safe. Places known to have high crime rates face problems in attracting visitors. Mayor Rudolph Giuliani increased tourism to New York City significantly when he cracked down on vagrants and worked hard to reduce crime.

- *The natives speak the visitors' language:* Besides offering so much to do and the fact that it is part of America's heritage, England remains very popular with Americans because English is spoken. Japanese visitors most often select U.S. places where they know that someone can communicate with them in their tongue, such as Honolulu and some major cities in California that have large Japanese populations.

- *Quality hotels:* A hotel seldom determines why someone will choose a place to visit, unless it is a luxury resort. But a hotel room becomes the place of retreat for travelers worn out from the day's activities or too much shopping. A well-appointed room, an attractive lobby, and manicured grounds all get noticed by guests. Good destinations offer choices among quality hotels.

- *Good food:* Restaurants also add significantly to the vacation experience. Fine dining ranks as one of the most frequently enjoyed activities, especially in places that seem very different from home. This characteristic is the least important of those listed, however.

SETTING THE STAGE FOR TOURISM DEVELOPMENT

Neil Armstrong, the first human to set foot on the moon (July 20, 1969), had lunch with the famous portrait photographer Yousuf Karsh and his wife. Armstrong questioned the couple about the various countries they had visited. "But Mr. Armstrong," Mrs. Karsh responded, "you've walked on the moon. We want to hear about your travels." Armstrong replied, "But that's the only place I've been."[1]

Pity the poor astronaut. He saw the moon before he saw the world. Given a choice, most people would probably choose differently. Travel offers excitement, personal enrichment, and the opportunity to recharge our psychic batteries. Its multiple benefits lead many to make travel the dominant focus of their lives. Robert Louis Stevenson expressed that feeling in his statement, "For my part, I travel not to go anywhere, but to go. I travel for travel's sake. The great affair is to move."[2] As travel becomes more accessible to the middle class, larger numbers of people worldwide lock the doors of their homes to visit one exotic place after another for months on end. Others take to motor homes, either not caring where they will end up or following only loosely planned itineraries. Cruising has attracted that kind of a crowd also. I can remember a lunch with the director of hotel operations for Crystal Cruise Lines on the ship *Harmony* when it docked at San Pedro (Los Angeles). The director pointed to a woman in her mid-80s who cruised with the line for 10 to 11 months a year, regardless of the ship's itinerary. It offered her a comfortable lifestyle, like an elegant retirement home but one that offers new and interesting experiences every day. Most people, however, choose destinations carefully. They want to see specific historic or interesting sites they have heard about, enjoy a unique festival or art gallery, or lie on a beautiful beach to recover from the stresses and strains of everyday life. Then they can return home with indelible memories.

Since travelers can make choices numbering into the tens of thousands about where to go and what to do while there, the need exists for destinations to clarify what they offer. Without compelling reasons to choose one spot over another, unique and interesting places limp along, suffering from slow tourism growth and disappointing tourism spending. A strong positioning strategy, along with a good branding statement, can alleviate many of those problems. However, tourism planners don't know how to accomplish this task, let alone that they might even need to consider such an effort. Working with destinations to increase tourism has been the most exciting and challenging part of my career. Each situation is unique. Yet similarities exist. And, if local leaders truly get behind a new positioning strategy, they can achieve surpris-

---

[1]Reported in *The Little, Brown Book of Anecdotes*, edited by Clifton Fadiman, Little, Brown and Company, Boston, 1985, p. 21.
[2]Robert Louis Stevenson, *Travels with a Donkey*., 1878, Quoted in *John Bartlett Familiar Quotations*, p. 667, Little Brown and Company, Boston, 1980.

ing results. When that happens, everyone feels excited and rejuvenated. But multiple pitfalls also exist, which are described in this section.

The following materials cover the development of new positioning strategies for U.S. and international destinations, using case examples to point out how to solve common and not so common problems. Some special situations are also reviewed briefly. Chapter 11 presents a review of considerations in positioning travel providers. Because selecting where to take a trip is the most important part of travelers' decisions, destination-positioning strategies receive more attention in this book than how to turn around the products of travel suppliers. However, the rules that apply in successful tourism development are similar to what should be followed by travel suppliers. The format for presentation in this section on destinations includes an overview of the situation, a summary of the problem, a review of the approach used, and a summary of the outcome.

Planning and executing a strategy for tourism growth doesn't come easily. In all of the situations where I have worked, probably fewer than half achieved maximum results because of a variety of problems. The ten to one rule (Chapter 7) points out the difficulty for those places that start with a negative image. But the greater problem lies with the conflicting forces operating in most communities.

In my work with a variety of industries and hundreds of clients, I have developed a great empathy for a special group of people. Tourism directors stand in the line of fire of just about everyone in a community. Whether they direct a local convention and visitors bureau (CVB) or a state or international tourism bureau, the conflicting pressures remain the same. If tourism growth declines for any reason, these directors get blamed first. And they will be replaced if things don't change—soon. The number of ideas about what's wrong and how to fix it seem to equal the number of members of the CVB or tourism bureau. One faction believes that the ad campaign has grown stale. Another concludes that they need to look for a new ad agency. Some suggest reallocating the CVB's budget by cutting back on overhead to put more dollars into promotion. And, far too often, a growing consensus will come to the conclusion that the director and staff are incompetent or have become too comfortable in their jobs. They simply fill their days pushing paper around. Surprisingly, even the local press frequently takes pot shots at the tourism board and its staff, especially after the launch of a new image campaign and slogan. I watched a local TV show in disbelief when a roving reporter asked people on the street, "What do you think of the new silly tourism campaign created by our convention and visitors bureau?" A tourism director described his problems succinctly: "I'm battered, hung out to dry, I can't play golf any more, and I work seven days a week." Yet few ever retreat from the field. Like most in the travel field, they find their work interesting and challenging. If fired, they typically look for another place to land where, they hope, it will be a less stressful and less politicized environment than in their previous assignment. That may not happen, but hope springs eternal.

Obviously, some tourism directors don't perform up to expectations. But more often the problem rests at the feet of the board of directors of the tourism organization and local politicians who seek scapegoats when tourism revenues decline. In seeking easy answers, fundamental long-term problems often get ignored. The quality of the experience at the place may have declined over the years and it is less competitive in the marketplace. Or perhaps the positioning strategy completely misses the target. Few consider the need to reposition a destination to achieve long-term growth. Rather, they tend to emphasize short-term promotions to fill hotel beds over the next three to six months. Repositioning may take a year or two to achieve desired results, far longer than most will wait. And if a local convention center has booked fewer meetings than last year, then a tourism budget may get diverted to support a new campaign to bring in meetings and conventions business. Each new special marketing campaign adds to the problem because the separate campaigns carry conflicting messages and a needed solution has been delayed to a more distant point in the future. Although I will give some examples where striking results occurred within six months, two messages should be kept in mind. First, an image makeover usually requires many months before the most positive results are prominent. And, second, don't blame the tourism staff before reviewing all other contributing factors.

REPOSITIONING DESTINATIONS: CASE EXAMPLES

The destination examples described in this section feature international and U.S. locations, but the primary target group is U.S. travelers. However, the same concepts apply elsewhere in the world, as shown in Chapter 3. Various academicians have successfully tested the concept of venturesomeness in Europe, the Pacific Rim, and Asia.

SWITZERLAND: Just Passing Through

Background

The invitation to conduct a positioning study for Switzerland came in 1992 from Armin Baltensweiler, the brilliant Chairman of SwissAir who developed the carrier into international prominence during his tenure. It later went into bankruptcy when it failed to follow the growth principles he established (now it is simply called *Swiss*). I was a member of the North American Advisory Board for the airline and had given a presentation to the Board about Swiss-Air's potential markets. Baltensweiler had a special concern—declining tourism from the United States, especially since other European countries had enjoyed healthy increases in recent years. Recognizing that it would require a cooperative effort, he pulled the Swiss National Tourist Office and Swiss Federal Railways into a three-way partnership with SwissAir to fund the project and jointly implement the results. During my entire research career, I never had the luxury of a situation in which the stars seemed to line up so favorably. The major players that would implement the conclusions had agreed to a cooperative effort, the project had adequate funding, and it was set to begin quickly.

The Swiss are model clients. Whatever I requested, got done—and on time. They prepared well for each meeting, and their attention to detail made my job easier. They quickly understood the logic of the novel approach I presented to them in our early discussions. They also demonstrated a self-deprecating humor that added to the fun on the job, making jokes about how they think others see them (stiff, reserved, formal, rigidly on time, etc.). However, their cautious and orderly approach to life, which contributes to their successful business ventures, also makes them reluctant to change their thinking. They need to be thoroughly convinced about new ideas before agreeing to a new course of action.

The Problem

At the time of the repositioning effort, Europe had experienced four years of strong growth in traveler numbers from the U.S. However, Switzerland's tourism industry had not participated in that increase. Its numbers remained flat. Prior research pointed out that the country attracted an audience four years older than average for European visitors with household incomes 21 percent higher than those who visited other parts of Europe but not Switzerland. To get on a growth curve, it needed to broaden its market by lowering its visitor age and income profiles. In other studies I had conducted, the country received high marks for the cleanliness of its hotels, city streets, and country highways. And its citizens are viewed as polite and helpful, but reserved. These are nice traits for any destination to possess, but not very exciting.

It faced a much bigger problem, however. Visitor stays averaged one to two days. Because of its central location in Europe, encircled by four popular countries (France, Germany, Italy, and Austria), it was a drive-through area on the way to someplace else. I called it the "Ohio of Europe." The most visited place in the U. S. is Ohio, not Florida or California. With Ohio's central Midwest location, many auto travelers (85% of the leisure market) go through it on their way to their final destination. But few choose Ohio for a vacation. Similarly, only a small percent of travelers planned to stay very long in Switzerland. They were passing through to a place they thought offered more to do. Obviously, a successful positioning strategy would have to place Switzerland higher on the priority list of destination choices.

As usually happens when things go wrong, many people involved in tourism had their own ideas about what needed to be done to turn things around, including hoteliers, tour operators, and tourism officials. The Swiss love their nation, and they could not understand why more people didn't choose it over other destinations in Europe. As they point out, it has unequaled scenery with its magnificent Alps and stunning green valleys. And, since it has not faced war for more than seven centuries, it has a greater concentration of undamaged historic sites and churches than any country in Europe. Tourism officials, in thinking about a new advertising campaign, were primarily considering two themes: "Switzerland is Europe in a nutshell," and "Switzerland . . . Europe in miniature." I quickly rejected these ideas, pointing out that each statement suggests that Switzerland is second best. Both slogans imply that another country has the original version or more of whatever advantage Switzerland would like to promote. Few people around the world want to visit something that can only claim second-class status. Switzerland must find a way to shout that it is "the real thing," "the genuine article," "the real McCoy." It cannot achieve success as a second-place finisher. I pointed out my belief that we must develop a series of *superlative statements, based on fact, that apply to Switzerland.* A new positioning strategy must provide Switzerland with its own unique claim to greatness in order to ensure tourism growth.

An additional hindrance to a good positioning strategy also required attention. Tourism bureaus receive support from multiple sources, including travel providers (hoteliers, tour operators, site venues) and government agencies that collect tourism-related hotel taxes and other taxes from venues. The various groups usually cooperate in some joint advertising campaigns. But co-op ads too often identify all sponsors of the ads, with short, separate messages for each. This approach clutters and weakens the promotional message. Directors of tourism for each of the 19 cantons (provinces) wanted to ensure that their own canton was identified in all ads, along with a brief statement, to increase tourism to their areas. I had to argue strongly that my task was to attract more people to come to Switzerland and get them to stay longer. If that change took place, everyone would benefit. In a small country, tourists who stay longer will travel to more places and, ultimately, all cantons will benefit. With a tiny share of the tourism market and a miniscule promotion budget, by international standards, I pointed out that marketing resources must concentrate on getting out the primary message that will motivate travelers to visit Switzerland. Concentrate resources to get out simple, compelling messages—repeated over and over again—to maximize chances for success.

One final point, a topic I covered earlier (Section III, Chapter 7, "Don't Promote the Obvious"): Almost all promotional materials for Switzerland at the time featured the Alps. Pictures in ads and collateral materials showed their magnificence and majesty: SwissAir planes flying over the Alps, Swiss Federal Railways trains running through Alpine passes, tour company brochures with quaint villages situated in the Alps, and so on. I stated that the space used to picture Alpine settings left little room to indicate what else Switzerland offers tourists. If the country stopped promoting its Alps for a century, travelers would still know that Switzerland has magnificent Alps.

Tourism officials had it right on one point, however. Switzerland is a wonderful country to visit, far beyond what most travelers recognize. On previous vacations, I had gone through the country like many others and stayed for a day or two. I enjoyed it immensely—some of my most striking color slides come from those trips. But I had gone to the well-known villages and major cities. Following my usual practice on projects, I arranged for Swiss officials to design a custom trip for me. I wanted to see those places that the people who know the country best especially love, but that typically don't get featured in promotional materials. I saw great art galleries and specialty museums that I didn't know existed, and executive retreat centers that created a feeling of repose, unlike most in North America, which use standard hotels with look-alike conference rooms. The varied architectural styles of the different regions give a feeling of being transported into new destinations, often in the same day. Switzerland also has unique wine regions that reflect its French, German, and Italian cultural heritage. The country had much to offer that tourists throughout the world needed to know about.

Situation Summary   Tourism revenues declining for several years; visitors older and wealthier than average narrowing its market appeal; many positives about the country not known by most Americans; location on psychographic scale unknown, positioning strategy ill defined and mostly focused on what travelers already know (the Alps).

Approach to the Problem

Almost always, positioning an international destination allows more limited choices for an approach than positioning a destination for the domestic market. The place must have characteristics that appeal to venturesome types of travelers. Venturers like to travel by air; dependables prefer autos. Venturers spend more on trips and take more trips than dependables. Did Switzerland carry an image that would attract these more exciting kinds of travelers? If it did, it must end up with a visitor profile that is younger and with lower household income. In that situation, it would be on a growth curve, not in a decline. A strategy must evolve to create a new sense of excitement about what the country offers to travelers and with a venturesome spirit to motivate the proper psychographic groups to consider Switzerland for upcoming trips. And, that strategy must be based on fact, not hype. Promotional campaigns built on false promises will always fail. Good marketing research would determine the special qualities of Switzerland that could attract more visitors. That knowledge, in turn, would help develop a new, effective positioning platform.

Venturesome types of travelers like variety—lots of things to do at the places they visit. After my tour of the tiny country and discussions with more than 60 officials involved in tourism, I knew that venturers and near-venturers would like many things about the country that they didn't know existed. I put together a list of 48 activities and things to do for inclusion in the questionnaire, drawn from all that I had seen and experienced during my travels with my client hosts. In the questionnaire, respondents checked off which of these

48 activities they especially like to do on an ideal vacation and which ones they believe they could pursue in Switzerland. The list included such diverse items as interesting architecture, ancient castles and forts, Roman ruins, world-quality museums, quaint villages, beautiful countryside, interesting local food, outdoor cafes, clean environment, wine tasting/winery tours, outdoor markets and bazaars, and outdoor sports. Do people believe that Switzerland possesses most of the qualities and activities that they state they would like included in an ideal vacation? If not, then a marketing gap exists because the country does not get credit for its variety and cultural diversity. To disguise the focus on Switzerland in the research and to provide competitive information, three other European countries were also reviewed. These included England/the British Isles (always the highest-rated European destination), France, and Italy. The questionnaire was long and inclusive to cover multiple issues.

The research plan called for a survey among 3500 air travelers:

- Two-thirds had taken at least two leisure trips by air in the past year, including one or more within two years to Europe, the Far East, or the South Pacific.

- One-third of the sample met the above criteria and had also taken two trips to Europe in the past two years.

These very restrictive criteria ensured that only experienced leisure travelers participated in the project. A return rate of 42 percent, a high return for a questionnaire mailed to a broad sample of respondents, provided 1410 questionnaires (1356 useable for analysis).

The results proved insightful and provided the basis for a new positioning strategy. In looking at the data, the ratio of men and women travelers and the percent married (73%) were similar regardless of which of the four countries were visited. However, Swiss tourists' average age and household income were higher than those who traveled to Europe but had not visited Switzerland, confirming earlier conclusions of tourism officials.

The more important findings, however, related to images of Switzerland among tourists. As was mentioned, all 48 activities listed on the questionnaire are available in Switzerland, but not necessarily in some of the comparison destinations. England, for example, is not known for good wine-tasting tours, nor does it offer skiing. Visitors to Italy don't usually give it high marks for having a clean and pure environment. But *travelers believed that fewer of these activities were available in Switzerland than in any of the three comparison countries.* Figure 10.1 presents the answers to 18 of the items in the list. As is evident in the chart, Switzerland was seen at the time as a country of considerable beauty with quaint villages, beautiful mountains and lakes, snow-capped Alps, and as having a clean environment (neatly kept city streets and homes). But it offered little else, in their eyes. Although it has the highest concentration of *fully preserved ancient castles and forts, along with old churches,* only a minority knows about this. And less than one out of ten (9%) had

Figure 10.1   Activities Desired at Ideal Destination and Perceived
to be Available in Switzerland (Percent Choosing Each Item)

	Ideal Destination	Switzerland
Beautiful countryside	91%	85%
Ancient castles & forts	86	33
Outdoor cafes	82	38
Interesting museums	80	29
Quaint villages	79	67
Beautiful mountains & lakes	78	76
Interesting architecture	74	37
Train rides through beautiful countryside	68	60
Outdoor markets & bazaars	66	33
Clean, pure environment	66	63
Old churches	65	26
Roman ruins	64	9
Beautiful parks & gardens	63	40
Important art galleries	62	17
Snow-capped mountains	56	58
Wineries/wine tasting	51	11
Skiing	28	34
Golf resorts	20	5

knowledge of the fact that the Roman empire extended its influence well into the borders of this tiny nation and that remnants of its occupation still exist. Also, few suggest that Switzerland has good wineries, quality museums, or important art galleries. And, in spite of having four dominant architectural styles reflected in its various regions, only 37 percent believe this to be a fact. Probably most think that a Swiss chalet is its only unique architectural form. In the report for the project, I wrote, "Switzerland's image presents a cultural void in the minds of international travelers. Each of the other countries reviewed (England/British Isles, France, and Italy) measures much higher on possessing ancient buildings, forts and castles, old churches, museums, and art galleries." On an open-end question, a miniscule 1 percent stated that the Alps was the most memorable part of their vacation trip. In other words, the Alps may define Switzerland's beauty, but other countries also posses these (Austria, France, and Italy). And, of the nearly 1400 respondents, only 86 selected Switzerland as their favorite destination. Although those who had visited Switzerland selected more activities as descriptive of the country than those who had not visited it, differences in the items selected were not great, and the rank order of what was chosen was identical across the two groups. In other words, both groups held similar impressions of the nation. That finding confirms the conclusion that its visitors did not travel through many cantons nor explore its museums, art galleries, historic sites, and old churches because they didn't know that these attractions existed. Images not only influence whether someone will select a destination for the next trip, but also what they do when they get there. As pointed out earlier, travelers who believe that a place offers little variety or choice of activities typically will participate in fewer activities while there because preconceived ideas limit their choices. Conversely, those who have rich expectations for a destination tend to explore it to a greater degree and participate in a larger number of activities. Images of Switzerland were so narrowly focused that they created the impression Switzerland was a beautiful country that had pretty valleys and mountains, and little else.

The national character of a country can also contribute to enjoyment of a vacation. Those places that have interesting, unique, and/or friendly citizens help to make a trip more memorable and create favorable word-of-mouth advertising. Part of the project, as a result, required assessing views about the Swiss people. If it came out favorably, it could become part the positioning strategy. A list of personality descriptors was presented to respondents, and they were asked to select those that they believed describe the Swiss personality (they were also asked to describe the English, French and Italians). Figure 10.2 summarizes results on 20 of the items from the total of 39 viewed by respondents. The table distinguishes between international travelers who have visited the country and those who have not. As before, those who have never been to Switzerland select fewer descriptive items than its visitors, but the

Figure 10.2   Image/Personality of the Swiss Character (Percent Selecting Each Item)

	Total	Have Visited Switzerland	Have Not Visited Switzerland
Clean/neat	87%	92%	76%
Efficient	73	79	61
Well groomed	70	75	58
Honest	64	69	51
Courteous	62	67	51
Trustworthy	60	63	52
Reliable/dependable	60	64	49
Helpful	58	63	49
Friendly	52	54	47
Reserved	40	43	34
Cheerful/happy	31	31	33
Relaxed/casual	19	18	22
Flexible/adaptable	17	17	18
Sense of humor	16	16	17
Outgoing	16	15	19
Lively	13	14	12
Arrogant/rude	9	11	6
Excitable	7	6	8
Flam boyant	3	3	3
Discourteous	2	2	2

rank order of what is selected tends to be very similar. In other words, *a trip to Switzerland reinforces preconceived images.* And what did they think of the Swiss as people? Figure 10.2 indicates that travelers view them as clean and neat, efficient, reliable, dependable, courteous, friendly, and trustworthy. But only a minority thinks of them as cheerful and happy, relaxed, casual, flexible, adaptable, and outgoing. Though few consider them arrogant, rude, or discourteous, they seldom describe them as lively or excitable, flamboyant, or having a sense of humor. All in all, these descriptors present a picture of a nice group of people, but not very exiting or interesting. In contrast, the English (reserved, proper, and with a dry humor), French (lively and arrogant but with a *joie de vivre*), and Italians (romantic, approachable, and unconcerned about tomorrow) all had distinct and interesting personality profiles. The Swiss personality could become a backdrop to a new positioning proposition, but not a central part of it.

Research and discussions with tourism officials pointed to the final positioning strategy, based on the following conclusions:

1. No true negative factors exist about Switzerland that must be addressed before a positive image could be presented. This fact allowed more freedom in determining final directions.

2. The most important recommendation was that the image of the breadth and depth of what Switzerland offers to its guest must be expanded. The tightly focused and narrow view of the country limited what visitors expected to see and do as they passed through the country and, as a result, what they actually experienced while there. This self-reinforcing and self-limiting cycle of image formation reduced the potential for increasing the number of visitors and the length of time they planned to spend in the country. The new positioning platform must break out the image boundaries to create a new more inclusive identity.

3. The destination has much to offer that U.S. visitors to Europe traditionally seek during their trips that they do not associate with Switzerland. This includes well-preserved historic sites (old castles and forts, medieval churches, interesting public art galleries, museums, and more). These advantages need emphasis in developing a new positioning strategy.

4. Switzerland's highest-rated item is its scenic beauty, placing it above all competing destinations. This characteristic should continue to be emphasized in promotional strategies, but the Alps should become a backdrop to scenic views of magnificent valleys and quaint villages, rather than the primary focus of the photography.

5. Since Switzerland is considered to be very expensive, two simultaneous strategies must be considered: first, lower the perceptions of what it costs to visit the country through promotion of lower-cost

vacation packages. This helps create an image of affordability. Second, emphasize that the unique characteristics of Switzerland make trips seem more worthwhile because of the enduring images these create among visitors. This approach can provide a stronger sense of value for the money, regardless of the cost of hotels and food. Both strategies will help to lower the age and income profiles of visitors.

The final report pointed out that Switzerland needed a "unique focus . . . different from any other country in Europe, in order to make it memorable" and to attract more visitors. I commented again on why the second-best phrases would hinder, not help, their efforts at repositioning ("Europe in a nutshell," and "Europe in miniature") because these statements relegate Switzerland to second-class citizenship. In the clutter of advertising that exists, particularly in the U.S., superlatives are required. This does not suggest developing unrealistic claims, since these will ultimately damage credibility. Rather, it means determining in what ways Switzerland can make leadership statements. The goal is to produce advertising and marketing messages that will be more **hard hitting,** in order to be heard and be effective. And there must be a consistency in the message, along with a **commitment** to a long-term program in order to accomplish a permanent change in perceptions about Switzerland.

The basis for a new positioning strategy now rested on the fact that Switzerland offers visitors much more than they probably expect. Its variety of leisure time activities far exceeds what is available in countries many times its size. Friendly, but reserved, the Swiss greet tourists with a quiet warmth and a spirit of helpfulness and hospitality. As a nation, it has led the world in protecting its environment, providing cleanliness and neatness in all cantons. Its undeniable and almost unequaled scenic beauty helps to ensure a memorable experience for all visitors. Further, it has much of what tourists traditionally seek when they visit Europe but do not know exists in this small nation—historic sites and old churches, interesting architecture, good wines, interesting food, art galleries and museums, and much more.

In brief, advertising and promotional strategies must emphasize the full diversity of the country, in addition to its natural beauty. Since an advertising agency had not been selected for the worldwide campaign at the time, I offered several suggestions for the promotional (branding) theme for consideration so that the new agency would not face a situation without any structure or guidelines. The suggestions included the following:

- The magnificence of Switzerland
- Switzerland—in all its diversity
- Switzerland—an enchanting place
- The eight wonders of Switzerland

These suggestions were considered a start, but not the final branding statement. Of these, I considered the "eight wonders" theme the most viable because it could accomplish several tasks simultaneously. It suggests that Switzerland offers superlative sites and activities for its visitors, the destination has great variety, and the theme provides multiple opportunities for promotion. Most people in developed countries know the meaning of the "Seven Wonders of the World." The eight wonders plays off of this statement and challenges travelers and travel agents to name the wonders of Switzerland. My suggestions for the list of eight included the following:

1. *Scenic beauty*—Switzerland measures higher on this characteristic than any other destination, a true superlative that it can claim as its own and the highest-rated item for what makes a trip memorable, in the eyes of travelers.

2. *Small, picturesque villages*—Although these interest travelers considerably, the research pointed out that most persons did not know that Switzerland had so many that varied dramatically in architectural style because of its mixed ethnic heritage. These create an ambience of their own and a reason to get around to more cantons.

3. *Swiss cultural heritage*—This is probably the most unknown characteristic of the country, that it has the highest concentration of preserved historic buildings and sites in Europe, including Roman ruins. These all rank high on activities desired by international visitors. Top-rated museums, art galleries, and a variety of architectural styles also fall into this category.

4. *Clean environment*—As environmental issues become more important worldwide, Switzerland can claim a leadership position. The cleanliness of the country and its efforts to develop a green environment send visitors home talking ecstatically about how the nation differs from most places they have visited. Zurich residents, for example, can swim in the river that runs through the city and eat the fish that they catch. This is not true for rivers in most big cities.

5. *Good transportation*—Switzerland can claim a superlative on this characteristic. Universally, people know that its trains run on time. But few are aware that its transportation network provides access to cities, the countryside, lakes, and resorts and mountain villages. Most of the nation can be enjoyed without the need for a car. The emphasis must focus on accessibility of most regions through public transportation, rather than on the known quality of on-time trains.

6. *Swiss food and wine*—Switzerland receives little credit for its interesting, tasteful, and varied food, or its excellent local wines from three dominant ethnic regions (Swiss-German, French, and Italian). Switzerland has much more to offer than chocolates and watches.

Emphasizing other qualities can broaden its image and create a warmer, more interesting feeling about the country.

7. *Adventure sports*—Switzerland offers more opportunities to participate in soft and hard adventure sports than most countries. Although only small numbers of people seek these activities when traveling, promotion of their availability can help create a view that the destination provides excitement to venturesome travelers. The concept is similar to Nissan, which puts more weight in advertising behind its Z car than actual sales would justify. The company wanted the sporty, performance Z image to create a sense of excitement about its entire line-up, much of which included conservative sedans.

8. *The Swiss people*—The fact that the nation has multiple, diverse nationality groups provides an opportunity to promote the varying qualities of the Swiss people. Contrary to expectations, visitors should expect to see different Swiss character types, not the bland unitary personality they imagine of the Swiss-Germans. The Italian and French heritage groups in Switzerland definitely are more lively.

My primary goal was to get all parties involved to forget about the traditional ways they promoted the country in the past and to consider a fresh positioning strategy. The new concept would point to the amazing number of experiences an informed traveler could enjoy. My presentations in Zurich and New York City convinced tourism representatives of the need for a new positioning strategy based on the broad diversity that the country offers to its guests. Now, the question remained as to how well the suggestions would be implemented.

The Outcome

During my final presentation to Swiss tourism officials in New York City, I knew that implementing the project could be problematic. Why? A U.S. ad agency, formed by a Swiss national, had been selected to handle the worldwide account. But neither the head of that agency nor any of his staff were in attendance at the beginning of my presentation. More than halfway though, the president of agency and his account executive walked in. The president offered no apologies or explanations for his absence, but he exuded an air of supreme confidence. When I finished, I asked him if he could stay a while and I would fill him in on what he had missed. "No need to, " he responded. "I understand everything perfectly and I know exactly what to do." "Uh-oh," I thought. He made up his mind before he got here, and all of my hard work would have little impact. At that point, I decided to maintain contact with Swiss tourism officials in the hope of having some influence on the final directions of the campaign. But it's usually difficult to change the course of an ad agency that doesn't want interference from outsiders, including the client.

The outcome demonstrates the good and the bad that can come from positioning efforts. On the positive side, the Alps got dropped as a featured emphasis (the agency complied gladly because it allowed them more freedom to follow other alternatives), and it decided to select six themes (rather than eight) to emphasize in its campaign. Great! That's a start. But it put together a multipage slick paper insert campaign to appear in major consumer-oriented travel magazines, such as *Travel & Leisure*. Although the American Express travel card supported half of the cost of this campaign, it still had a huge price tag for a destination with a limited budget. Worse yet, insert booklets included in travel magazines featured more than a dozen small pictures on every page, with lots of white space in between. Beautiful photography went largely unrecognized because of tiny photos. And, the campaign consumed most of the ad budget up front, providing few remaining dollars for a continuing effort to woo people to Switzerland. I also had suggested a concentrated effort to educate travel agencies about the wonders of Switzerland. Not much money left over for that either, unfortunately. And, little thought was put into what I consider a critical element of any good campaign—the branding slogan or theme. Lacking any good suggestions on that score, the home office of Switzerland Tourism in Zurich decided to develop a common theme to use in all countries. Apparently it translates well into German and French, but not into English. The final slogan? "Look no further, Switzerland." That doesn't say much about what Switzerland offers to potential travelers or why they should visit. Nor does it provide a platform to develop a broad array of advertising messages to different audiences—escorted tour groups, travel agents, incentive travel, and the corporate meetings market—a necessary condition for any good positioning strategy.

In spite of these problems, offering a broader view of Switzerland and deemphasizing its commonly known qualities produced results. This fact demonstrates that not all conditions have to be perfect in order to achieve gains. The program launch began in early 1993 with the American Express cosponsored ads. The tag line has changed over time, but the campaign continues to emphasize the variety of vacation experiences available in Switzerland. Joseph E. Buhler, the North American Director of Switzerland Tourism, continued to emphasize the key points of the findings of the study and, on his initiative, developed a program focusing on travel agents. Annual tourism growth began slowly at first, but increased to high single digits (average of 8 percent) after a couple of years. And the characteristics of the tourists it attracted also changed in the desired direction. In early 1998, Buhler had me give presentations on the new Switzerland to tour organizers in Palm Springs, California and travel agents in Atlanta, Georgia. I was able to report on the progress in repositioning the country in several ways. Based on results from the large annual tracking survey of Plog Research, Inc. (the American Traveler Survey/ATS), Switzerland had broadened its market considerably during a two-year span. Average age of a traveler had dropped by seven years, household income declined by 9 percent, and the number of leisure trips taken annually by its visitors also declined. In other words, Switzerland now was capturing younger, less wealthy, and less sophisticated groups of travelers who no longer considered the country too expensive for them to visit.

Further progress is evident in other data. ATS also measures satisfaction levels with trips and the potential for growth of each destination. Out of nearly 80 international destinations, Switzerland measured in at 18th position at the time that ATS began in 1995 (still a strong number by any standard). By 1996, it moved to 15th place, and 13th in both 1996 and 1997. It achieved 12th position by 2000 and has remained near that level since. Household income continues to be somewhat below average for European visitors. On another important dimension of ATS, the growth potential index (a measure of how many travelers plan future trips to a destination), it moved from 40th position in 1995 to 37th in 1996 and to 20th in 1998. Consistent with the idea that travelers will see and experience what you tell them to see and do, its tourists now measure higher on having an interest in enriching their perspective in life, especially through visits to historic sites, old buildings, and churches. At the time of the positioning project, the highest measured item for the country was the opportunity to experience its natural beauty (the Alps and picturesque valleys and villages). The escorted tour market has grown in concert with the increase in independent travelers and continues to account for about 15 percent of visitors. And tour takers also have younger and lower income demographics than previously. Undoubtedly even greater growth could have been enjoyed if the ad campaign started in the right direction, but changing the emphasis for Switzerland at least produced satisfying results.

GRANDE LISBOA AND THE ESTORIL COAST: Not for My Group!

Background

Few people in the travel world recognize that a strong interrelationship exists between leisure travel and the corporate meetings/incentive travel market. An abundance of quality hotels and top-of-the-line conference facilities alone do not make a destination competitive for meetings and incentive trips. With few exceptions, *destinations that attract large numbers of leisure travelers also book more corporate meetings and incentive group travel.* Conference organizers learned long ago that they can expect more attendees if they choose places that business travelers would also like to visit on a vacation. Attendees don't want all work and no play. They also hope to enjoy themselves when they have free time away from meetings. At places they like, they may stay an extra day or two, especially if they bring along a spouse. Orlando, Las Vegas, Honolulu, some Caribbean destinations, London, and Paris book conferences more easily than competitive cities that suffer from plain Jane images. The need to offer a cafeteria of choices for activities and sightseeing simply makes a better draw.

Only mandatory sales and training meetings can fill a Chicago airport hotel. Book it downtown and you might get a few more to come. But choose Monterey, California, and you'll probably turn away late registrants. And incentive travel truly belongs in the leisure category. Salespeople and other employees work harder to win contests if they know they can play golf in Maui or enjoy a trip to Paris, rather than a jaunt to a crowded big city.

John Pelletier, founder and CEO of Equation Communications, called in 1992 and asked me to join his team on a project for Grande Lisboa, the tourism bureau that handles the region of Lisbon and the warm, sunny Estoril coast in Portugal. His ad agency, based in Pleasantville, New York, had made a name with its innovative direct marketing campaigns for tourism clients. We had worked together for several clients in the past. Pelletier possesses an incomparable creative mind and a rare willingness to be guided by the findings and conclusions of research. Unlike some ad people who fear that research will point them in directions they may find difficult to handle, John believes that insights into traveler motivations and perceptions help him design more focused campaigns. The Grande Lisboa area faced stagnant growth, and its tourism bureau wanted to increase its incentive travel and corporate meetings market to fill hotel rooms and restaurants.

The Problem

Portugal came late to the table to enjoy the post–World War II European tourism feast. It had faced internal problems for decades, starting with a military coup in 1926 that overthrew an unstable republic. Dictator Antonio Salazar ran the county until 1974, when a bloodless revolution established a constitutional, socialist government that presented a new constitution in 1976. But political instability continued. Between 1974 and 1987, Portugal endured 16 changes of government and a series of severe recessions. It became the poorest nation in Western Europe. Economic progress finally began in the late 1980s and continued through the 1990s. But tourism, which had dropped during the difficult times, didn't improve with the economy. The country continued to suffer year by year declines into the early 1990s. Travelers avoided it, perhaps from a belief that years of oppression and decline left nothing worthwhile to see or buy. Or, possibly, they feared they would confront dirt and poverty wherever they went, the two conditions that can easily spoil a trip, as was pointed out earlier. Whatever the reason, the country needed tourism. And the best place to begin was its major city, Lisbon, and the nearby lovely Estoril coast.

Even a casual visitor could recognize that Portugal has much to offer. It has a warm, sunny climate, beautiful scenery, and sites and monuments commemorating times when Portugal was a world power. Because it lagged on the tourism growth curve, it also had relatively inexpensive hotels, modestly priced restaurants, and friendly ingratiating people who still welcomed visitors. And, since it had been bypassed for several decades during the tourism boom, tourists had not changed the character of its cities and villages. These qualities rank high on what near-venturers seek when they travel. So why weren't they coming? Research had to find out.

Situation Summary   An Old World country bypassed by the tourism boom that desperately needs tourist dollars to help the economy. Because of past political and economic instability, it has retained a charm that high-tourism nations no longer offer. It can offer much to travelers but seldom is considered for upcoming trips. This image also reduces the demand for incentive travel and corporate meetings.

Approach to the Problem

One way to jump-start tourism is to attract more corporate business. Incentive groups and corporate meetings can fill entire hotels more quickly than waiting for leisure travelers to change their minds about where they want to go next. At the time of the project, the lead time for planning an incentive trip or corporate meeting had dropped to 4–8 months from 9–12 months or longer a few years earlier. In contrast, it can easily take 12–18 months to increase leisure travel significantly, if image problems exist. And, corporate meetings and incentive travel usually provide more perdiem revenue than leisure travelers. Incentive trips, for example, include multiple add-ons, such as golf, entertainment, sightseeing trips, catered meals, and even some activities for spouses. Meeting rooms are also used to ensure that the Internal Revenue Service counts everything as a business expense, not unreported personal income. Corporate meetings may not provide quite the same amount of revenue per person as incentive travel, but there are many more of them. And, marketing programs targeting meetings and incentive trips can operate on smaller budgets than those that go after leisure travelers. However, the axiom still holds: A destination will have difficulty attracting incentive travel or corporate meetings unless it has a strong, positive leisure image. The research would have to discover the views held by meeting planners about Portugal, especially Lisbon and the Estoril coast, and what assurances they required before they would consider the destination for their companies.

Detailed questionnaires were sent to 1600 corporate travel executives, half of whom had responsibility for incentive trips and the remainder for corporate meetings. The anticipated response rate of about 40 percent would produce somewhat more than 700 questionnaires, more than enough for all planned analyses. However, over 800 useable questionnaires came back, providing even more stability to the data results. The survey instrument covered a range of topics, from images of Portugal and awareness of Lisbon and Grande Lisboa, to necessary requirements before considering Portugal and who makes decisions within their companies about where to book upcoming meetings. As with Switzerland, the Portugal questionnaire presented a long list of activities, historic sites and buildings, and cultural events, all of which are available in and around Lisbon and the Estoril Coast. Respondents were asked to indicate which activities are part of an ideal corporate trip, which they associate with Lisbon and the Estoril Coast, and which they associate with three competitive European destinations. Because the project focused on handling groups of people, participants also stated which destinations they believed had luxury and first-class hotels, along with the high level of service and amenities that they require for their corporate programs. The results proved to be a wake-up call to tourism officials. They believed that they only needed to promote tourism to a greater degree. Until they saw the results, they did not recognize that they also must create a distinct image and overcome a view of Portugal as a very backward country if they hoped to achieve their goals. The report of the research pointed out the following:

- Very little specific knowledge existed about Portugal, including Lisbon and the Estoril Coast. Most did not even know the location of the Estoril Coast area.

- As a result of this lack of knowledge, Portugal was not in consideration for upcoming incentive trips or company meetings. Most meeting planners only choose destinations about which they have adequate knowledge so that they feel comfortable about the level of service and amenities their company employees will receive. Meeting planners feel at risk when they select a hotel or venue. If something goes wrong, the blame rests on their shoulders, even though they don't control the hotel staff. Attendees and senior executives feel that the meeting planners should have known about potential problems in advance and not selected the place. That's their job. It's what they get paid for.

- Most important, a strong majority of planners believed that Portugal lacked quality hotels. They did not select it as a destination because they believed its guest facilities did not measure up to the standards they require. Without a guarantee of inviting rooms, good meetings facilities, and well-prepared meals, Portugal did not appear on their radar screens.

- A Latin bias also was evident. Planners assumed that Portuguese hotel staff were indifferent, inefficient, poorly motivated, and inadequately trained, all of which could ruin a program regardless of how well it had been planned. In comparing competitive destinations measured in the questionnaire, Spain also carried some of this negative baggage, but not to the same degree.

- The Grande Lisboa area also had few amenities necessary to run a successful incentive or conference program, according to the planners. They did not believe it had many golf courses, tennis courts, great restaurants, museums, unique entertainment, or interesting sites to visit. In truth, Portugal has a rich cultural heritage that includes interesting and quaint villages, old churches and historic sites, museums and galleries, and countless golf courses and other outdoor recreation facilities. The planners simply lacked knowledge of these advantages.

- A major reason for their lack of knowledge about the destination was the fact that Portugal had not enjoyed the fruits of the tourism boom. Having been bypassed for decades by tourists because of internal problems, most Americans assumed it was a cultural backwater. Meeting planners, in turn, concluded that the entire country was so primitive that it would be difficult to find anything that would interest attendees at their meetings. Portugal's failure to promote itself since World War II, in contrast to its European neighbors, further convinced planners that it lacked most of what they required in a destination.

- On the positive side, planners viewed the country as less touristy and more native and natural than most other countries in Europe. And, its people enjoyed a reputation of having a relaxed and joyful spirit that would make visitors feel welcome and accepted.

- Portugal also enjoyed a reputation as being less expensive than most international destinations, providing good value for the money for any incentive or meeting event. Planners, while trying to provide top-quality venues, also look to stretch their budgets since they continually face the problem of rising travel and hotel costs.

- Finally, and also on the positive side, as the closest point in Europe to the U.S., Portugal could be reached within an acceptable flying time. Distance also contributes to decisions about where to go for the next event.

Several interrelated problems had to be addressed concurrently in a marketing campaign. The program would have to convince planners that Portugal offered everything that they required for their meetings to ensure a great event. That meant convincing them that Lisbon and the Estoril Coast had four- and five-star hotels, fabulous restaurants, and challenging, beautiful golf courses. And, the message would also have to convey a theme that Portugal can deliver impeccable service. In truth, the Grande Lisboa area contains many fabulous hotels with international reputations, along with restaurants that can compete with high-end establishments in France and Switzerland. And, its sites and outdoor recreation offerings, including championship golf courses, measure up to the best anywhere. But how can old images be changed quickly to ensure a successful campaign within a relatively short period of time? It would require a targeted marketing effort that conveys a strong and believable message. Fortunately, most images about Portugal were based on minimal knowledge of the country, rather than direct experience. People knew about its past instability. They did not know about its charm and beauty. Although the repositioning effort did not start with a complete blank slate (*tabula rasa*), at least a new marketing program would not have to overcome decades-old negative images based on direct knowledge with the country.

The positioning strategy created by John Pelletier of Equation Communications picked up on the elements listed previously with the recommendation that the overall theme would stress *old world charm with new world convenience*.[3] Several salient points from the research defined the message to be conveyed to planners (underlined words from Pelletier's message). Specifically,

- Since Portugal is not well known, prospects must be provided with a considerable amount of information about what Portugal has to offer.
- The primary theme is that Portugal is a <u>unique</u> and <u>interesting</u> country with <u>friendly</u>, <u>relaxed</u> people who are <u>cheerful</u> and <u>happy</u>, and also <u>helpful</u> and <u>courteous</u>.
- Lisbon must stress its <u>top-quality hotels, world-class meeting facilities</u>, excellent <u>infrastructure</u>, and an efficient and <u>well-trained support staff</u>.
- The vacuum of information about Lisbon (and Portugal) should be filled in with details about sports, sightseeing, events, and places of historic and cultural significance.
- The perception that Portugal offers good value for money and that it is less expensive than most European cities should be emphasized.

In short, the conclusion was to present "Portugal as capable of <u>consistently delivering a quality product and consistently living up to the promises</u>" it gives to clients and prospects. The marketing messages should be directed to senior marketing, sales, and general management who are sophisticated and knowledgeable and who are the real decision makers for incentive travel programs. The first phase of the program focused on incentive travel because of the high revenue potential of this market and the ability to produce results more quickly. The meetings market would play a secondary role and come later.

Living up to his reputation for producing results, Pelletier executed the strategy beautifully. The theme line adopted for the campaign, and printed boldly on every ad and brochure, read, "Portugal . . . so much you never expected." In these few words, it invited incentive organizers (and meeting planners) to reexamine their views about the destination. All collateral materials featured four-color, *National Geographic*–quality photos highlighting the variety of venues and activities available in and around Lisbon and the Estoril Coast—scenes never expected by most incentive travel organizers. Collateral materials pictured the old and the new. The old included ancient castles and churches, small villages with fishermen attending their boats, and street scenes with pastel-colored buildings and people in native costumes. The new showed five-star hotels, state-of-the-art conference centers, resorts in beauti-

---

[3]All points listed for Equation Communications come from Equation's December 1993 year-end report containing a summary of the country's marketing needs and recommendations and how to address these needs.

ful settings, high-end restaurants, elegant golf courses, beautiful symphonic halls with full orchestras, and more. Collateral materials consistently emphasized the branding theme—*So much you never expected!* The campaign's essence was to show that Portugal had the facilities and trained, motivated staff that would ensure a successful corporate meeting, conference, or incentive group trip.

The accompanying ad copy also brought the point home cleverly, interestingly, and clearly. Lead-in lines pointed to Portugal's multiple advantages with different taglines such as

- Somehow, just being in Portugal makes the castles more magnificent . . . the wine more exhilarating . . . and the incentive program more successful.

- Lisbon and the Estoril Coast . . . old world charm with an attraction for every travel taste.

- Some people have the idea it's behind the times. Then again, they may have a point . . . Grande Lisboa . . . a perfect blend of the old and the new.

- Come in. An extraordinary incentive travel experience is waiting.

- Incentive travel's most misunderstood destination . . . has modern hotels, swift transportation, incredible wining & dining, fantastic shopping, fashionable resorts, heady night life, & professional expertise.

- The one thing you shouldn't have to do at your incentive travel destination is . . . travel.

- We'd like to set your meeting or incentive program back a few hundred years (when) Kings used to party like this.

Often a theme line presented a single advantage on each of several fold-out pages. An especially clever teaser appeared on the address side of a mailed brochure and said, "Dated material inside—(15th Century)."

I repeated a number of the theme lines used in the campaign to emphasize how following the conclusions growing out of research leads to creative solutions, not slavish conformity to narrow guidelines as so many advertising people seem to fear. Classical musicians consider Bach to be one of the most creative musical geniuses of all time. Yet he chose the most restrictive idiom available for much of his work—the fugue and contrapuntal forms. Understanding what needs to be accomplished leads to a clearer definition of the objectives of any marketing campaign. Then creativity can take over.

The campaign targeted incentive and meeting planners through ads in core market publications and a direct marketing campaign with a call center to handle inquiries to be passed on to appropriate Portuguese travel suppliers. The ads appeared in publications like *Successful Meetings, Corporate Meetings & Incentives,* and *Sales & Marketing Management.* A list of 20,000 corporate meetings planners, provided by these publications, were targeted for a direct mail campaign that included colorful, odd-sized fold-out brochures that used the themes mentioned previously. The fulfillment center established by Equation for the project received all mail and telephone inquiries, mailed out information packages, and verified all leads with follow-up telephone calls.

The Outcome

The budget for this promotion was infinitesimal by all standards. It began with only $600,000 for the first year and was reduced for subsequent years, hardly an amount that anyone could expect to get noticed in a cluttered media environment. Most destinations spend millions yearly to stand out in the crowd. Yet the May 1996 Program Evaluation pointed out that

> the original program objective was to generate a response of 1,200–1,500 sales leads per year. In 1993–94 the promotion program generated a tremendous total of 3,871 responses which yielded 2,800 sales leads (after duplicates and/or illegal reply cards were deleted). In Phase 2, 1994–95, the smaller program budget produced comparable results: a total of 2,867 responses which yielded over 2,203 sales leads. Over 5,000 prospect-buyers identified themselves as being interested in Grande Lisboa and wanted more information. This is an incredibly positive response.

Total bookings are usually difficult to track in situations like these. Qualified leads typically get turned over to travel suppliers and they seldom report back their results. Hotel occupancy rates could tell the story, but no central reporting system exists in Portugal. Only idle conversation can bring out case examples. Equation was able to confirm over 12 million dollars in bookings during a two-year period, probably a fourth or less of what actually came through. But even at the minimal amount, it represents a very strong return on the investment from a small promotional campaign.

Creating a strong incentive and meetings program represents a quick and efficient way to jump-start travel to a destination. But it has less long-term impact than efforts to reach the broad leisure travel market. People who plan a vacation to a destination of their choice generally return home more impressed with what they saw and experienced than those who traveled as part of a program selected by their companies. But any program that sends visitors home with a positive message helps in the long run, including bringing them to destinations that exceed their expectations while on business or incentive trips.

Object Lesson Learned   Vague images with some negative overtones (Old World, behind the times, not much to do there) can be made positive relatively quickly by filling in with information that addresses primary concerns. Small marketing budgets can have a significant impact when the money is used to target niche groups through direct marketing campaigns and selected media (travel trade magazines). Research can help to make the creative portion of ad campaigns more on target, more creative, and more effective.

HONG KONG: The British Have Left! What Do We Do Now?

Background

My staff said I would stub my toe on this assignment. Regardless of how many destination-repositioning projects I had worked on before, nothing could turn around Hong Kong tourism, they believed. Now that the British had left, the city had lost its charm, its uniqueness, even its reason for existence. The urgent call for help came from the Director, the Americas of the Hong Kong Tourist Association (now called the Hong Kong Tourism Board), located in Los Angeles, California. He visited my offices in September 1997 and provided a good description of the problem faced by this incomparable international city. Tourism had grown every year since 1989, but declined by double-digit amounts from nearly every country after China resumed sovereignty of Hong Kong several months earlier on July 1, 1997. The situation was considered desperate and called for immediate action. Part of the problem obviously derives from the fact that every big event, such as the Olympics or centennial celebrations, results in steep declines in tourism after the conclusion of all ceremonies. These venues steal from future visitor streams by focusing promotional efforts on attracting visitors for the big event. But in the current situation, the decline in visitors measured much higher than would normally be expected.

Hong Kong held a unique position among world-class cities with its fascinating mixture of East and West. Tom Brokaw, the NBC news broadcaster, aptly called it a beginner's guide to Asia. It has the flavor of the East but the conveniences and familiarity of the West. Its citizens speak English (and Mandarin), it follows a Western form of civil service administration (the British system), it is a shopping and dining mecca (the Chinese always excelled as merchants and restaurateurs), and it had panache at the time not matched by any other city in the world. Formal British mannerisms and structure overlay the city in interesting ways. Streets and buildings had names or carried symbols that recognized both cultures. Festivals varied from celebrations of the Chinese New Year to recognition of the Queen's birthday. Large, bright neon signs, cluttered together in commercial districts, vied for attention in both English and Chinese. Along with London, I always considered it to be one of my two favorite international cities. It had a unique feeling not found elsewhere. I was constantly amazed at the flexibility and adaptability of Hong Kong residents. Its population density didn't seem to faze them. They accepted that as a matter of course. In spite of seemingly limited ways in which to make a living, the entrepreneurial spirit of its citizens produced countless numbers of multimillionaires and even billionaires.

But July 1, 1997 changed everything. On that date, after more than a century and a half of colonial rule, Britain turned over the Hong Kong territories to China. During a 24-hour period, what is now called a city-state changed its identity. The event had been anticipated since December 19, 1984, when Britain signed an agreement to hand over (the common term for the event)

Hong Kong to China in less than 13 years. Uncertainty and anxiety ran high. During the several-year period of time leading up to the event, the Chinese government had not announced its plans for Hong Kong. Would it allow its citizens to remain free, democratic, and entrepreneurial, and elect their own government and follow their own rules? Or would it impose a communist form of government on Hong Kong? What about property rights? Would Beijing take away private ownership of all land and improvements or allow private investors to keep their hotel empires and business conglomerates they had developed over the years? And with its known tendency to use force when confronted with a problem, did China plan to occupy the territories with its army and security forces? Thousands of wealthier Hong Kong residents didn't want to take a chance. They sold their buildings and moved their business operations to other countries. Vancouver, Canada, which already had a large Chinese population, experienced a huge influx of immigrants from Hong Kong for several years prior to the handover, dramatically pushing up real estate prices throughout the city. The worst scenarios envisioned China's People's Liberation Army (PLA) storming into the city to take control of all operations and converting the government to the socialist form enforced by Beijing throughout the rest of China.

The Problem

None of the dire predictions happened. The PLA sent in a small garrison and stationed them out of sight, not even allowing troops to leave their barracks to mingle with Hong Kong residents. Beijing didn't want adverse publicity through unfortunate incidents or awkward photo situations. In the months prior to the handover, China gradually made its intentions known. Hong Kong would operate as a Special Administrative Region (SAR), allowing it to operate with a high degree of autonomy. Landowners would retain their holdings, and a high degree of freedom would continue for its citizens. Its chief executive was now selected by an election committee of 400 local pro-China leaders and appointed by the Central People's Government. And the press would remain uncontrolled. Although many complaints have surfaced since about a puppet mayor who accedes too often to the wishes of the central government, Hong Kong has continued to function largely in an independent manner, free from day-to-day influence by the mainland. And it is guaranteed a high degree of autonomy for 50 years by the basic law of the Hong Kong SAR.

But Hong Kong has changed. Most outsiders did not know in what way that might have occurred, but they assumed it would never again be as interesting without a British presence. The unique mix of East and West made it a travel writer's delight. Endless reams had been written about its exotic and sometimes unfathomable social customs and ways of doing business. But many travelers saw little reason to visit if it had lost its previous allure. It now seemed a shadow of its former self. It had a reputation for expensive but high-quality hotels, and shopping no longer was cheap, so it had little to fall back on to generate new tourism. Although the Chinese government took a light-handed approach in assuming authority over Hong Kong, it was clear that they were in control.

The situation was desperate at the time I received the invitation. Hotels faced revenue problems if the trend continued very long. Shop owners reported huge declines in numbers of tourists and the amount they spent while there. Hong Kong's economy was heavily dependent on tourism. The bump in the number of visitors that occurred in the first half of 1997 covered over other developing difficulties that pointed to a future slowdown in growth. For example, The American Traveler Survey of Plog Research pointed out that during the three-year period covering 1995, 1996, and 1997, Hong Kong had declined from 16th to 48th position as a favorite international destination for leisure travelers. Other reports from the Hong Kong Tourism Association indicated that a similar scenario was developing among visitors from other countries.

Hong Kong had also contributed to its own problems. Promotions by hoteliers and others encouraged people to visit before the British left to see the Hong Kong that no longer would be. Someone who liked the old Hong Kong knew that this was the last chance to see a part of history that would soon pass. That helped create a feeling that the new Hong Kong would not be as good or as unique as the old. The worldwide press picked up on the topic too, suggesting that the new city-state would be more drab and boring than what it replaced. And, knowing that they had a good chance to increase occupancy prior to the handover, the hotels also bumped up room rates dramatically. That left visitors with the feeling that they had been gouged and they came home with the impression that the city was even more expensive than before. Thus, tourism dropped by double digits after July 1, 1997 from just about every country. Adding to the problems, the Japanese press discovered later in the year that tourists from Japan paid more for hotels in their tour programs than package users from Australia. In an interview with the head of the Hong Kong hotel association on the topic, he made the grand faux pas of stating that the policy was part of a good business practice of yield management, similar to the approach used by airlines. As he indicated, airlines charge business fliers higher rates for the convenience of booking at the last minute for flights that depart at the busiest times. If you could get more from one group than another group, he reasoned, then you should take advantage of the situation. His comments added to the dropoff in tourist arrivals from Japan.

Clearly a fresh start was needed. Hong Kong had to get a new identity. But what could it be? How can a destination remake itself completely, dropping the most important features of what it once represented to present a new face to the traveling public? What if the new identity didn't work? If so, how long would it be until the right formula could be found to bring back tourism? A sense of urgency permeated everyone concerned with tourism. In spite of the enormity of the task, I remained confident that the right repositioning formula could be found. Every destination that I had ever worked with had qualities that would interest tourists, if these were presented properly through good marketing programs. I soon discovered something else that would help too. More so than most American clients, the staff and members of the Hong Kong Tourism Association listened carefully to all suggestions I gave and understood that effective repositioning doesn't happen quickly. Perhaps it's the patience of the Chinese compared to the do-it-now philosophy of many Americans, or the fact that they truly recognized change would take time. I felt confident we could all work together and achieve a lot.

Situation Summary   After several years of strong tourism growth, boosted by the July 1, 1997 handover from Britain, Hong Kong experienced a dramatic double-digit drop in visitors from its most important arrival countries. All problems were compounded by previous feelings of many travelers that hoteliers and others gouged them in the months prior to the handover. A change in its previous identity as a unique combination of East and West, old and new, created a sudden need to establish a new identity and new reasons for travelers to see Hong Kong as soon as possible.

Approach to the Problem

During my first trip to Hong Kong on the project in October 1997, I had two goals in mind: first, meet the tourism staff and learn more from them about the situation and their needs. I found an impressive group of people, uniformly well trained and dedicated. They work longer hours than any other tourism bureau I had previously encountered. Lily Shum, who was General Manager of Marketing Communications for the HKTA and has since moved over to direct North American tourism, has more energy and puts in more hours on the job than anyone I have ever met. I also believed that this group would follow through on recommendations growing out of the project. I also wanted them to become comfortable with me, which was accomplished through formal presentations on my plans and personal conversations. For the second point, I needed to learn more about the city and what it offered, beyond my casual acquaintance with it as a previous visitor. I was given an in-depth tour that covered two days and nights. I would use this information to develop the questionnaire for the project. And I was provided with copies of other studies conducted within the previous two years to gain more understanding of the images of Hong Kong in its key markets.

Hong Kong wanted one positioning strategy that would work on a worldwide basis. Particularly in a makeover situation like this, a new identity must be built on a single platform, not with confusing multiple messages. Thus, the project had to determine the universal qualities of the city-state, post handover, which would appeal to everyone. The attempt at a makeover received considerable attention in the press. The *South China Morning Post*, the primary English language paper in Hong Kong, ran regular stories on the challenges faced by the HKTA and dubbed me "Dr. Destination" for my efforts in turning around other destinations.

The project focused on the four most important countries where tourism had dropped significantly—Japan, Taiwan, Germany, and the U.S. A total of 450 telephone interviews were completed, 100 in each country except for Japan, where the sample was increased to 150 because of special concerns about the destination and that it contributed about 20 percent of the tourists. Initial screening provided a structured sample for each country. All respondents had sufficient income to travel internationally, with quota samples for age groups. Half had visited Hong Kong within the past two years, and the remainder had traveled to Asia in the past two years or planned to visit the area within the next two. I developed a common questionnaire for use in all four countries, which was translated into the four separate languages. Its topics focused on travel habits and plans, and important inhibitors to future Hong Kong visits. Similar to other positioning projects, the questionnaire compared Hong Kong to three competitive destinations. And, as usual, all destination descriptors in the questionnaire applied to Hong Kong, but not necessarily to the other destinations. In developing the questionnaire, my main concern was to represent the full diversity of Hong Kong. Although it has a reputation for world-class hotels, fabulous restaurants, exciting nightlife, and high-end shopping, it has so much more to offer. Unknown to most, visitors can enjoy a feeling of peace and serenity at Aberdeen Bay, a Buddhist temple, or in the quiet and isolated forests of the New Territories. And it provides easy access to China, and day trips to Macao and other nearby places of interest. Creating a new identity rested on the ability to design a questionnaire that would cover all possibilities. And, the final positioning strategy would have to focus on more venturesome types. They have the greatest interest in learning about a place that had seemingly changed its soul overnight.

The project was fielded in early December 1997 and, because of the urgency of the situation, a report was issued later that month. Although it covered a number of topics, the essential data are contained in Figure 10.3. It summarizes the top 12 descriptors about Hong Kong (from a longer list) by residents of the four countries targeted in this study. Several conclusions can be derived from these results. Specifically,

- The most positive views about post-handover Hong Kong come from German residents. Americans also see it in a relatively favorable light. Asian countries rate it lower, with Japan generally at the bottom and Taiwan somewhat above it.
- The British may have left, but Hong Kong retains key elements of its former image. It provides good shopping (stores have the world's best brand names, and has good bargains), quality restaurants (only Japan rates it relatively low), and is a unique combination of East and West, old and new. And it also provides good entertainment. The strength of these qualities indicates that these need not receive heavy emphasis in future promotional programs. Visitors from around the world know

Figure 10.3   Descriptions of Hong Kong by Residence in Each Country (Percent Choosing)

	From Japan	From Taiwan	From U.S.A.	From Germany
Can buy the world's best brand names	52%	78%	78%	88%
Is the events capital of Asia	73	74	50	77
Is the hub of Asia	61	81	70	65
Offers contrasts of East/West, old/new	51	79	64	70
Is dynamic, vibrant, & exciting	53	51	63	77
Has good entertainment	65	46	44	75
Has good bargains	62	64	50	56
Lots of good restaurants	31	56	71	81
Lots of things to do there	30	62	72	68
Has interesting people	25	16	72	80
A place I'd like to visit	35	15	56	59
Modern and up to date	7	28	61	72

that Hong Kong hasn't lost these characteristics. Other qualities need to be emphasized in order to create a new image.

- Some of the strongest geographic differences occur on the dimension of "a place I'd like to visit." Interest remains relatively strong in both the U.S. and Germany, but weak in Taiwan and Japan. The latter two countries would require greater marketing efforts to increase tourism. But the finding provides hope that attempts to increase tourism will not face big obstacles.

- The most distinctive feature in the data is that Hong Kong is seen as a "dynamic, vibrant, and exciting" city by half or more of the sample in all countries included in the survey. Following the pattern indicated, the ratings are stronger in Germany and the U.S., and lower in Taiwan and Japan. Not shown in this table, no other destination comes close to Hong Kong on this characteristic. Singapore and China, the two competitive destinations queried about in all four countries do not, nor does any destination that was specifically measured only in a single country. Thus, Thailand does not have the same qualities (measured in Germany), or Italy (measured in Japan because of the recent growth of tourism to Italy), or England (measured in the U.S.). Other than the fact that Hong Kong continues to have an image as a unique contrast of East and West, old and new, *the feeling of energy and dynamic excitement it still creates in the minds of international travelers clearly sets Hong Kong apart from all competitors measured.* Other places may offer good shopping, quality restaurants or even excel at entertainment, but Hong Kong stands alone for its feeling of 24-hour excitement.

- Related to the previous point, and except for Japanese residents, a strong majority believes that there are "lots of things to do there."

Thus, the city can fill a vacation with many activities. Visitors will not feel bored while there nor return home with an impression that they had to look for activities to fill their time.

If Hong Kong stands above all competitors examined on this dimension, then two questions come to mind. First, do a sufficient number of tourists want to take high-energy trips so that a viable positioning strategy can be built around this concept? And second, can Hong Kong make a superlative claim that it places above any other city or destination? New York City and Las Vegas convey a strong sense of energy and excitement. And Paris, London, Rome, and Tokyo, to name a few, also could be nominated for this kind of recognition. Subsequent focus group research, however, indicated that even New York cannot match Hong Kong in its ambience of energy and vitality. More than any other spot in the world, Hong Kong feels alive 24 hours a day. New York City tends to shut down after show time, travelers believe, and Las Vegas sleeps in the daytime but wakes up after dark. And, yes, the first question was also answered in the affirmative—quite a few travelers like to take high-impact vacations. Obviously, the more venturesome the individual, the more that they like activity and excitement on their trips. The American Traveler Survey of NFO/Plog Research consistently shows that Hong Kong primarily attracts those with venturer leanings. As mentioned earlier, its exotic qualities and the fact that it can only be reached by air appeal to people who want more activity packed into their vacations than sitting in a deck chair on a beach.

With the need to create a totally new identity for the city, Hong Kong placed its advertising account under review. It sent copies to the project report to five large, well-known agencies with worldwide capabilities. Each prepared a potential repositioning strategy, based on findings of the research. I was invited back to Hong Kong to help in a two day review of the agencies. BBDO/Asia WorldWide won the account with their suggestion for a campaign built around the theme of *Hong Kong . . . World City for Life!* Most of the review team agreed that BBDO's suggestion was close but not quite right. But it represented the best start. Ultimately, the final theme line read, "We are Hong Kong . . . City of Life!" The phrase "We are . . ." was added to give a sense of pride and identity to Hong Kong residents, who now faced an unknown future with their new communist leaders. "City of life" more appropriately conveys the energy and constant motion that the city projects to its visitors than "City for life!" Within a couple of years, the decision was made to drop "We are . . ." from the theme line. By then, Hong Kong residents felt comfortable with their new position in the world. They had not lost their identity. The final theme, *Hong Kong: City of Life*, conveys the key message of the city's unstoppable energy and excitement clearly and quickly.

Print and TV ads created for the new campaign were tested through focus group research and refined in a series of stages to ensure that the message got through that the new Hong Kong was different and, in many ways, more exciting than the old version. The new slogan, "City of Life," performed beautifully. International travelers reacted favorably. They felt that it fits Hong Kong and created a new sense of enthusiasm about the city and a desire to take a trip. The ads pictured a variety of Hong Kong settings but always conveyed a sense of its energy and nonstop activity. These included its bustling harbor (with traditional Chinese junks), the city at night (lots of neon lights and people in the streets), dining, sports activities, and shopping (with a huge array of goods). Descriptive words in the ad copy also emphasized the same theme: *energy, sparkle, bustle, exhilaration, fast lane, motion, rush, speed, 24 hours, action, moving,* and *party,* to name a few. Other modifications were made to the ads, but it was clear that the agency had listened to the research and operated within its guidelines. The next step would be to see if it works.

The Outcome

The new campaign was announced on March 24, 1998 in a special ceremony at the very large Hong Kong Convention and Exhibition Centre. Accompanying materials stated that "The campaign focuses strongly on Hong Kong's . . . extraordinary diversity and energy (of) its people and their way of life. . . . The research findings showed clearly that Hong Kong's marketing advantage lay in its image—and reality—as one of the world's most exciting cities." Because of the need to ensure success of the new positioning strategy, particularly in the U.S., Lily Shum was assigned to Los Angeles to direct all North American tourism efforts. Her creative 'round the clock efforts resulted in great gains in the consumer markets, incentive travel programs, and among travel agents. Follow-up research I conducted for HKTA demonstrated that the strategic repositioning campaign had achieved its goals. A June 1998 quantitative study among U.S. international travelers included four specific types of travelers in the sampling plan. These were persons who had visited Hong Kong both *before and after* the Handover, only *before* the Handover, only *after* the Handover, and *never visited.* The report presenting the results stated that

> all groups of respondents believe that changes have happened to Hong Kong, but the patterns are quite different. Those who have *never visited,* surprisingly, believe that the changes are minimal, i.e., they feel that Hong Kong is largely the same as before. . . . The *post-Handover group* of visitors demonstrates a unique pattern. By wide margins, sometimes in the 20 to 30 percent point range, they think that *Hong Kong is a better place* to visit today (post Handover) than it was prior to that time. *Pre-Handover visitors,* however, demonstrate the opposite pattern. They think that their trip was taken at the best time possible and they assume that Hong Kong is not as good a city at present as it was when they were there. Further, the percentage differences are very large, often 20 points or more—always favoring the pre-Handover time.

Elsewhere in the report, it pointed out that those who had visited both pre- and post-Handover had the most positive views. These findings again demonstrate a conclusion presented earlier: Establish expectations for a destination and chances improve dramatically that visitors will return home more satisfied. In this case, the new view of the excitement, energy, and dynamic qualities of today's Hong Kong successfully replaced images of sophistication and panache cast by British rule for a century and a half. That message attracted visitors who want energy packed vacations. Hong Kong met their expectations, and they returned with favorable impressions, becoming goodwill ambassadors. And, on the opposite side of the coin, the advertising messages that previously had attracted the pre-handover visitor group and had not visited since the handover left them convinced that Hong Kong would never be as interesting after the big event. The earlier marketing campaign had undoubtedly reduced future demand!

A June 1999 ad tracking study for Hong Kong produced positive conclusions. Overall, over a third (36%) in the U.S. had seen advertising for Hong Kong. Unaided recall (not prompting respondents to aid their recall) indicated that the primary message presented was that "Hong Kong is an exciting and fun place to visit." Further, when themes from the new campaign were presented to these air travelers, the strongest recall was for "Hong Kong is one of the most dynamic and exciting cities in the world" and that it is also "The most energetic city in the world."

The true measure of the success of a repositioning effort, however, must pass a different test. Assuming that the campaign was handled well, which it was, did it produce higher visitor counts? The answer is yes. By mid-1998, tourism from the important countries for Hong Kong began to pick up, followed by double-digit increases in 1999. In the U.S. during 2000, leisure traveler counts jumped by nearly 20 percent and incentive travel increased by a whopping 46 percent. This growth occurred in spite of the fact that Hong Kong during this period received considerable unfavorable worldwide publicity. More than once its health department issued orders to kill all chickens destined for restaurants because of an outbreak of the "chicken flu" disease. Growth from Western countries continued during the Asian economic crises that occurred at this time, and even during the soft travel year of 2001 until the 9-11 attack on the World Trade Center and the Pentagon. The theme and the campaign have been modified slightly from time to time as Hong Kong seeks new markets, but the vision remains the same. The government also promotes it as "Asia's world city" to position it as the hub for conducting business in China and the rest of the Asia-Pacific region. Shanghai and Singapore both would like to make this claim because of their rise to prominence in the latter half of the 1990s, but research shows that only Hong Kong can continue to claim that mantle.

Other data point to the success of the effort. The American Traveler Survey of NFO/Plog Research includes a measure of a destination's competitive position in the marketplace—the *growth potential index* (GPI). It is a measure of the number of travelers who have visited a destination divided by the number who plan to visit it in the future. As indicated in several sections of the book, turnarounds build over time to achieve maximum effectiveness. In this case, Hong Kong improved its ranking in ATS among the more than eighty international destinations reviewed from forty-ninth position in 1999 to thirteenth position by the 2002 survey. Specifically, its numbers are as follows:

Year	Ranking
1999	49
2000	35
2001	16
2002	13

Its upward curve in visitors from the U.S. continued uninterrupted until the terrorist attacks on the World Trade Center and the Pentagon on September 11, 2001. For example, the data for 2000 from the U.S. are as follows:

Total visitor arrivals: +12.5%

Leisure arrivals: +21%

Incentive travel: +37.4%

Corporate meetings: +34.7%

Cruise arrivals: 14.1%

Until the September attacks, 2001 had also shown strong growth over 2000, with the anticipation that growth would continue beyond that time.

Object Lesson Learned   In select situations, a destination can dramatically alter its identity. It requires a clear understanding of the new qualities it should offer that fit travelers' needs, along with a well-conceived and -executed marketing campaign. In this situation, Hong Kong had mostly positive images. If tourists held negative views, however, the situation would have been much more difficult. Hong Kong's new positioning strategy assured travelers that it is still a great place to visit—somewhat different than before, but with a new sense of identity and purpose.

TAHITI: A Great Place to Visit . . . Someday!

Background

Al Keahi introduced himself after a presentation I gave for *Endless Vacation* magazine in 1991. The time-share publication had conducted a readership study using my psychographic system to categorize their readers and determine if this group also traveled to places other than just their timeshare properties. Because of very favorable findings, *Endless Vacation* had me give a series of presentations to potential advertisers in cities from New York to Los Angeles. Keahi had recently been appointed Executive Director, the Americas, for Tahiti Tourisme. He explained that tourism to the islands had been declining since 1986 and he had been brought in to turn things around. He seemed like the perfect guy for the job. As a native Hawaiian and educated on the islands, he understood the Polynesian culture and what the mainlanders enjoy most about it. Young, energetic, and a former hotelier (with ITT Sheraton), he proposed an interesting approach to a repositioning effort. He liked my psychographic system and wanted to position Tahiti as a destination for venturers (called allocentrics at the time). Tahiti's advertising account was up for review, and he had invited five ad agencies to compete for the job. He ordered six copies of my recently released book that described the concept, one for himself and one each for the five agencies bidding for the account. He directed the agencies to read it before submitting their proposals. The agency that developed the best proposal to position Tahiti on this dimension would win the account. The Phelps Group, a Los Angeles–based integrated marketing communications agency, won the prize.

The Problem

In multiple ways, Tahiti faced a difficult situation. Various studies I had done indicated that travelers thought that it would be a nice place to visit—someday. No compelling reason existed to take that trip now. It seemed like a sleepy place with beautiful beaches, and not much to do. In a review of ads prepared for Tahiti Tourisme, I wrote that

> from a perspective of most travelers, Tahiti does not fit common sense. No rational argument can be given for taking a trip. It's expensive to get there and to vacation while at Tahiti. Many competitive destinations offer much shorter flight times at less cost, while still meeting most of the definitions of providing a quality vacation (such as Hawaii and selected Caribbean islands). Also, Tahiti is relatively unknown and it does not come up for consideration in most people's vacation plans.

On the Destination Positioning Matrix (DPM), its image characteristics placed it as only slightly *unique* but *relaxing*, with no particularly strong appeal to either venturers or dependables. In some ways, it seemed like a crazy idea to position Tahiti for venturers. It offers beautiful scenery (mountains and clear lagoons), along with warm sunny beaches and balmy tropical air. But it lacks a strong cultural history, had limited air service, and was very expensive (over-the-water bungalows go for several hundred dollars a night). And, except for some water sports, it offers few activities for its visitors to pursue. Humorously, a coffee table with a glass top in over-water huts that allows guests to look at the fish below is called "Tahiti television." How could venturers find it interesting? And, at the time, Tahiti didn't seem to be that unique. Adding up all of Tahiti's qualities, it came out second best to the gold standard among tropical destinations—Hawaii. The flight to Tahiti from anywhere in the U.S. required an extra 2.5 hours more than the flight time to Hawaii (most people thought it was four to five hours longer). It also lacked parity on good restaurants and entertainment. In contrast, Hawaii offered lots to do (world-class golf courses, water sports, entertainment, good infrastructure), natural beauty, and a good price value relationship. And the Aloha spirit created a warm and friendly feeling that began as soon as air travelers set foot in Hawaii. Those who knew that the French governed Tahiti assumed that island natives also possessed some of the perceived arrogance of the French. It came out second best on every comparison except natural beauty. But Hawaii had that, too. So why should someone make the effort to go to Tahiti?

Situation Summary A generally positive image but lacking compelling reasons for travelers to consider a trip. Offers few activities for visitors. Not perceived as a destination for venturers. No great negatives to overcome. A place that many people might consider "someday." A need to create clear image and reasons to take a trip.

Approach to the Problem

This situation differed from most assignments. Al Keahi had already decided that Tahiti's positioning strategy would be on the venturesome side of the scale. My job was to provide counsel and ensure that the ad agency understood the concept of venturesomeness and how it could be applied to Tahiti. The Phelps Group did their job—very well. Although it took awhile to come up with the final message, the essential elements included the following:

Positioning Strategy The Phelps Group's review for the campaign stated, "Position Tahiti as unique and stress free compared to other destinations. Highlight the lagoons, over-water bungalows, snorkeling and new cruise options." They developed ad copy describing Tahiti as a place where stressed-out, type A personalities can recover from the constant demands, obligations, and strains that arise every day in work and at home. Visitors can rediscover their inner selves in its relaxed casual environment and come back refreshed and eager to take on the challenges that sometimes seem overwhelming. The absence of radio, TV, newspapers, and other distractions, along with its isolated private beaches, ensures that the relaxation will be complete. The goal was to create a feeling that Paul Gauguin still lives among the natives and that little has changed from the time he completed his famous Polynesian paintings. The campaign would also target honeymooners who seek isolation in a romantic setting. The most important point is that the overall strategy creates a need to visit Tahiti now, not sometime in a future that may never happen. Many people feel stressed out and look forward to the opportunity to recover emotionally and physically where they can experience peace and solitude. Tahiti, more than any other place, provides that opportunity.

Two other issues had to be handled. The first, to convince that travelers that the islands are not that distant. Ads pointed out that it is only another 2.5 hours more than the time it takes to fly to Hawaii. Second, a price value message was needed. In essence, it stated, Yes, Tahiti costs more, but it also offers a vacation of a lifetime. That makes it worth the extra expense. These messages were covered in the copy for the ads, and in various PR releases.

Branding and Advertising Don Lum, Vice President, Tahiti Team Leader headed a group at the agency that understood very clearly what was needed. The branding message created fits the positioning strategy perfectly, "Tahiti . . . Islands beyond the ordinary." This slogan, displayed prominently in all ads, creates the feeling that Tahiti differs from competitive destinations. It provides an island experience beyond the ordinary, therefore worth the extra time and cost. Following Antin's dictum, it presents a benefit quickly, easily, clearly and memorably.

Ads, for the most part, were full page, full color. Also in line with the principles outlined by Tony Antin, a large serif typeface headline graced the top of the page, along with beautiful full color photos of Tahiti. Copy for each ad followed the general theme and ended with the branding statement *Islands beyond the ordinary*. Some examples of the top flight, on-target, interest-creating headlines include the following:

Destination Ads

- "Get there in a night. Remember it forever."
- "Why just vacation when you can live a dream?"
- "Most resorts build spas in their hotels. We build hotels in our spas." (Visual is over-water bungalows in serene Bora Bora lagoon with Mt. Otemanu in the background.)
- "Ordinary" (accompanied by picture of crowded Waikiki beach and high rise hotels)—"Beyond the Ordinary" (second picture of an isolated white sand Tahitian beach).
- "The ultimate adventure is to go back in time" (picture of an isolated island lagoon)
- "It's like heaven with a French accent."
- "The Tahitians had to canoe across an ocean to get here. You just have to call."

Honeymoon Ads

- "Marriages are made in heaven. Honeymoons, in Tahiti."
- "You're not just in love. You're in Tahiti.
- A lifetime of love should start with a week in paradise.
- "After the wedding, only Tahiti can give you a reception like this."

Al Keahi also achieved the extraordinary. In effect, he doubled the size of the advertising budget by securing cooperative dollar contributions from the islands' hotels and tour operators. In spite of pressures from co-op advertisers to micromanage the campaign, he kept the agency focused and on track. He put on special presentations that targeted key travel agents. The June, 1997 issue of *National Geographic* featured Tahiti as its lead article, with a picture of a young Tahitian girl on the cover. And he signed up the *Survivors* series on CBS television with Tahiti as the site for its 2001/2002 programs. He helped start a new airline to serve Tahiti, *Air Tahiti Nui,* and bring in P&O Princess Cruises to operate the new ships (R3 and R4) of bankrupt Renaissance Cruise Lines.

The Outcome

Sometimes a new campaign can have a quick impact, particularly if no strong negative images exist and the right ad agency has been selected. The Phelps Group took over the account on July 2, 1992. The ten-year results show the progress in terms of visitor arrivals from the U.S.:

1992	34,533
1993	42,914
1994	43,179
1995	47,023
1996	49,114
1997	51,376
1998	52,282
1999	71,397
2000	130,000 (est.)
2001	95,000 (Renaissance Cruise Lines in bankruptcy)
2002	100,000+ (est.)

The drop in 2001 resulted from the loss of Renaissance Cruise passengers and the 9-11 attacks, which will jump dramatically as Princess positions the R3 and R4 ships. Correct positioning strategy, based on knowledge gained through an understanding of the psychographic needs of travelers, along with effective ad campaigns can make a difference.

Object Lesson Learned   With a proper positioning strategy and execution, dramatic results can be achieved quickly and relatively continuously for a period of time. Tahiti did not have a negative image in the minds of travelers. Most knew little about it, but their thoughts weighed on the positive side of the scale. Advertising strategy had to provide reasons why this isolated set of islands should be visited soon, not someday! And, because of the long air trip and expense of the vacation, the reasons to visit had to appeal to the motivations of venturesome types of travelers.

DETROIT: Sometimes Progress Takes a Little Longer

Background

Repositioning a destination always involves risk and opportunity. Detroit suffered from such a universally negative image when I was approached to conduct a tourism project in 1996 that I knew that the ten to one rule would apply. The area would require about ten times the effort to turn it around compared with a destination that wanted to increase tourism and had a neutral or somewhat positive image. The city also faced other tasks that made prospects for the future more problematic. Local leaders debated as to whether or not tourism was important for the economy. And some surrounding upscale communities, concerned that they were being bathed in Detroit's poor image, discussed the possibility of disassociating from the Metropolitan Detroit Convention and Visitors Bureau to create their own distinct tourism campaigns. Local leaders also remembered that previous attempts to shore up Detroit's image had produced few results. Believing that previous efforts had wasted taxpayers' money, the local press was also ready to pounce on any attempt to create a new identity for this city that had historically contributed so much to America's economy.

But therein lies the opportunity. If a city and its neighbors can unite in a common effort, the possibilities for success can increase dramatically. Detroit was able to accomplish that goal. It is on the road to improvement, as a city and as a tourism spot. It will take longer than most turnaround efforts, but success is already being noted. The city has achieved a greater feeling of unity and sense of purpose as a result, and its suburban neighbors now feel more comfortable in being considered a part of the greater Detroit area.

The Problem

Few U.S. cities faced problems as severe as Detroit's. Following decades of economic decline, much of its white population fled to surrounding suburbs, leaving a black inner city majority (82%). *BusinessWeek* pointed out that four out of ten residents officially lived below the poverty line and that the city's population had slipped below one million (to about 950,000) during the decade of the 1990s, while other cities grew.[4] About "10,000 abandoned, open and dangerous buildings, and pothole-riddled streets desperately need repair," the *Los Angeles Times* reported as late as December of 2001.[5] Graffiti covered

---

[4]*BusinessWeek*, May 28, 2001, pp. 79–81.
[5]*Los Angeles Times*, December 30, 2001, p. 24.

commercial buildings, and boarded-up houses lined the streets from downtown Detroit to its once grand residential districts. Many areas were unsafe, and cars left on the streets overnight could be stripped of valuable parts. The city led in many crime statistics and more than once had to endure a race riot. The downtown convention hall (Cobo Conference and Exhibition Center) was underutilized, adding to the city's problems. Built in 1961 and expanded in 1988, it offered over 700,000 square feet of space. But associations and corporations too often ignored Detroit as a site for their meetings because of a fear that they would face low attendance numbers if they selected the city. Previous attempts at downtown redevelopment proved largely unsuccessful, such as the Renaissance Center, which included a hotel, a huge amount of office space, meetings rooms, and conference facilities. Most big-name retail stores had left for greener pastures in the suburbs. Upscale restaurants that remained sometimes were at corner locations next to abandoned or destroyed buildings, not a pretty or comforting sight for those who hoped to enjoy a night on the town.

Yet, in my customary review of the city before beginning the research program, I found a surprising amount of positive feeling about Detroit among almost anyone I encountered. Blacks and whites both like the city. They remember its glory days and believe that, in some way, it could return to a better past. Give it a chance, they would echo. They believed that almost everything was improving—economic development, racial harmony, and a new spirit about what Detroit could accomplish. Two-term mayor Dennis Archer had created a new sense of anticipation for the future because of his programs to get people of all races to work together for common goals. And he had secured a considerable amount of funding for new development. Around $4 billion at the time of the project, it later rose to more than $18 billion. New projects included two sports stadiums (for the Tigers baseball team and Lions football team), the corporate headquarters for Compuware, and General Motors' commitment to redevelop the Renaissance Center that it had purchased. Detroit is one of the few U.S. cities to boast four major pro-sports teams (baseball, football, hockey, and basketball). Renovations had already begun for sections along the waterfront that would include a river walk, restaurants, shops, and entertainment.

Detroit also possessed numerous cultural assets, including great science and art museums, a first-rate symphony orchestra, a center commemorating the birth of the Motown musical sound, and a recently opened Charles H. Wright Museum of African American History. And, it could show visitors what the surrounding communities could offer, such as the Henry Ford Museum and Greenfield Village. But the spirit of its people impressed me most. They wanted to bring the city back and would dedicate themselves to accomplish that goal. Their enthusiasm for anything that suggested a new beginning made my commitment even stronger.

Situation Summary   A destination facing decades-old image problems. Has many assets that travelers desire but are unknown to them. Local residents and surrounding communities have great hope for a comeback of the old Detroit. A difficult situation since negative images must be altered before positive attributes can be believed by travelers.

Approach to the Problem

The project had a twofold purpose: specifically to "help develop a clear, positive image of Detroit to increase leisure travel to the area *and* to increase meetings, conference and convention planners' selection of metro-Detroit." As always, it will be difficult to grow the conference and meetings market unless the city could establish a positive image. The Metropolitan Detroit Convention and Visitors Bureau came to the table well prepared. It had done its homework to determine what was needed, secured the funds, and developed community support for the effort. Its cumbersome name reflected the fact that surrounding communities also contributed funds to the MDCVB to help their own growth potential (now called the Metro Detroit Convention and Visitors Bureau). Nearby communities also joined Detroit's efforts at repositioning after they became convinced that, if tourism to Detroit increased, they would also benefit. A very capable MDCVB staff supported all of my efforts. I had a thorough, personally guided metro-Detroit tour, multiple opportunities to meet with Detroit residents and those in nearby communities to explain the consulting process, and visits with city officials to help them understand what was about to happen. My primary contact was the Vice President of Marketing of the CVB, Kim Fitzgerald (now Kim Greenspan). Smart, well organized, good at follow-through, and sensitive to political processes, it was obvious that if anything went wrong, it wouldn't be because she didn't do her job.

Two concurrent surveys were conducted in the October–November 1996 time period. A mail-out of 3500 questionnaires was sent to a random sample of adults aged 25 and above. Over a thousand came back (29 percent return), a good response rate considering the length of the questionnaire. A thousand questionnaires were mailed to meeting planners, with 600 taken from readers of the magazine *Successful Meetings* and the remaining 400 from MDCVB's list developed over the years of companies on their high-priority list. It produced a 20 percent return rate, again a good response since it is possible that some overlap existed between the two lists. The results of both studies mirrored each other. Meeting planners had similar images of Detroit as leisure travelers to the point that I concentrated primarily on the leisure sample in my presentations. I especially wanted elected officials to recognize that they could not count on more meetings and conventions business until the city became more attractive to leisure travelers. That message can never be repeated too often.

In the survey, Detroit was compared with three other cities (Chicago, Cleveland, and Toronto), my usual approach in projects of this type. Without presenting the specifics of these images, a couple of interesting insights came out of these comparisons. On most dimensions, Cleveland looks like a twin of Detroit. It is seen as facing many of the same social and economic problems

Figure 10.4   Activities Desired at Ideal Destination and Perceived to Be Available in Detroit (Percent Choosing Each Item)

	Ideal Destination	Detroit
Quality restaurants	70%	27%
Quality hotels	67	30
Good shopping areas/ malls	63	25
Riverfront attractions/ sightseeing	54	14
Science/ technology museums	47	18
History museums	45	18
Good zoo	45	21
Good local arts & crafts	39	12
Broadway musicals	39	11
Traditional art galleries	37	17
Modern art museums/galleries	24	12
Symphony/opera	22	15

and lacking in cultural resources. Chicago's image includes that it has much to offer visitors—great museums and entertainment, quality hotels and restaurants, and lots to do while there. But respondents also believe that it has a high crime rate, a drug problem, and other social and economic ills. These data confirm that a destination can have some image problems and still attract a large number of visitors if it offers other important advantages. Toronto looks like a dream destination. Travelers consider it to be clean and neat, having a very low crime rate and offering many cultural and entertainment advantages. These data point to the fact that Toronto can increase tourism dramatically if it ever develops a strong positioning platform. As stated before, many places have good image characteristics but have failed to provide strong reasons for travelers to visit—NOW! In today's competitive marketing environment, few destinations can rest on their laurels and expect visitors to find them.

In many respects, the results of the study confirmed what most people expected: Travelers did not recognize that Detroit offers a lot to do, has great restaurants, top-flight entertainment, and unique shopping opportunities. And, more important, they considered it to be unsafe, filled with crime and drug problems. These images provide adequate reason for not selecting the Detroit area for an upcoming vacation trip. Figure 10.4 provides a dozen items, for illustration purposes, of the forty-four characteristics of Detroit (and comparative cities) rated by respondents in the study. They were asked to indicate which activities they would particularly enjoy while on a vacation and which ones they believe Detroit (and the comparative cities) offered. Following the same format as in other destinations reviewed, Detroit possesses each of the qualities. However, as the data indicate, the traveling public did not give Detroit credit for its many positive attributes. Their low image of the city ("Nothing good could come out of there") can be seen in that fact that:

- Only three out of ten travelers, or less, believe that the metro-Detroit area has good hotels (30%) or restaurants (27%).

- Even fewer think that it has good shopping areas and malls (25%) or offers local arts and crafts for sale (12%).

- The city gets little credit for its cultural base, including its world-class symphony and opera (15%), traditional art galleries and museums (17%), or modern art galleries and museums (12%).

- Its world-famous zoo is largely unrecognized (21%), as are the science and technology museums, and history museums in Detroit and surrounding communities (18%).

- Only about one in ten (11%) believe it could produce good Broadway musicals, in spite of the fact that Detroit has several great venues and stages for world-class productions.

- The one lowly rated feature that is not surprising is a lack of recognition for its riverfront attractions and related sightseeing activities (14%). Waterfront areas were part of a more recent development plan and had not received great national attention.

The project also focused on the social environment of the city. This also proved problematic. Six out of ten (61%) stated the city was unsafe and had a crime problem in spite of the fact that crime statistics had dropped consistently for several years in a row. They also believed that it had a huge drug problem (59%) and was grimy and dirty (51%). A third considered it to be an ugly city (33%). Although these data collectively point to the problems faced by Detroit, one hopeful sign came out of the data: More than was true for Chicago, Cleveland, or Toronto, a significant number believed that the city was on the rebound. About a fourth believed that it was "coming back and rebuilding" (24%) and was in the process of "revitalizing and renovating" (26%). And, nearly the same number stated that the city was getting better (22%). *This hopeful sign provided a basis for a positioning platform for the Detroit area.* The need was to convince more people that the city has improved, is continuing to improve, and that much of what leisure travelers want to enjoy and experience on trips is already available in Detroit. It might be a difficult task, considering it was starting from a negative base of opinion, but not an impossible one.

A dual approach was recommended to tourism officials. One part of the effort would focus on a strong public relations campaign to get out the message that Detroit no longer faced the huge economic and social problems of its past. It was changing in numerous positive ways and offered interesting things to do that rivaled other big cities. PR campaigns are especially good in getting out stories, rather than the more limited messages possible through advertising. Renee Monforton, Director of Communications for the CVB, handled the PR task extraordinarily well, getting positive stories placed in various publications and broadcast media. The focus of the advertising campaign, the second part of the two-pronged effort recommended in the project report, should emphasize both daytime and nighttime activities. The feeling of 24-hour activity would help convince venturer personality types that Detroit offered many varied activities for all travelers. This segment will more often take a chance and visit a city that has a long history of difficulties but now is creating a new image out of its storied past.

From the beginning of the project, Kim Fitzgerald planned an ad agency review to ensure development of a hard-hitting campaign that would achieve the needed results. She selected five local and out of town agencies to present their capabilities and describe how they might tackle the problem. These sat in on a presentation I gave summarizing the results of the study prior to submitting their proposals. Irma S. Mann Strategic Marketing, Inc. (ISM) of Boston, Inc., a full-service midsized agency I had worked with in the past, won the review. They possessed the necessary resources and, from previous experience, I knew that they paid close attention to research findings and developed strategies from those findings. Gary Leopold, the President, took a personal interest and directed the account. Throughout the effort, they did a great job. Their creative effort, follow-through, and development of the campaign can't be faulted.

ISM recognized the need to develop a strong branding theme to carry the campaign. Multiple messages about the new Detroit will flow easily from that theme. But the repositioning effort faced a difficult task: It had to please several audiences in order to ensure success. First, the campaign had to convey a positive message to tourists by offering clear reasons to reconsider past images about Detroit and why it should be considered for an upcoming trip. Second, city officials required that Detroit residents must also like the theme. The Mayor's office wanted residents to feel more positive about where they live and work and its prospects for a better future. And finally, since surrounding communities also contributed dollars to support Detroit's CVB, they also should approve of the campaign. These conflicting pressures made the assignment more difficult, but not impossible. I pointed out that other companies had handled similar situations. The "We try harder" advertising campaign of Avis Rental Cars, reviewed earlier, had the dual purpose of attracting customers and reminding employees to focus on customer service. United Airlines decades old "Fly the friendly skies of United" also targeted two audiences. To fliers, the message promised that United would provide friendly, helpful service on their trips. And employees were reminded that they should live up to that promise. Finally, Ford Motor Company's very successful campaign, "Have you driven a Ford lately," targeted two groups of prospective buyers with a different message to each. At the time, Ford faced holdover image problems that it lacked quality, dating from the 1930s when its vehicles were referred to as "tin lizzies." The inside jokes went around that FORD stood for "Fix Or Repair Daily" or "Found On the Road Dead"! With the theme, Ford accomplished a difficult task. It convinced a significant number of prospects who held negative views that they should try a Ford again. Its products might have improved beyond their expectations. And, for those who did not hold long-term negative views, it suggested that they should try a Ford because of the great cars it produces, without creating a feeling that it had any carry-over problems from the past.

ISM commissioned further research to test their creative ideas. Three themes were reviewed in a telephone survey among 275 respondents that included residents of Detroit, those who live in surrounding communities, and states that border Michigan. In the survey, the themes were presented in random order to eliminate bias and included

- Detroit: A City without Limits
- Detroit: A World of Difference
- It's a Great Time in Detroit

Of the three themes tested, one came out the winner among all markets—*It's a great time in Detroit*. It had the highest number of positive votes and the lowest negative totals among all groups. Potential visitors liked it because it fit with the general idea that Detroit had changed and maybe they should consider another visit. Detroit residents felt it conveyed their feelings that the city was improving. And surrounding communities gave a thumbs up based on their belief that they had noticed positive changes in Detroit. The campaign could help their communities since they still get tied into the dominating image that their big city brother casts over them. Research data showed that the theme had the potential to unify the disparate groups in and around Detroit more than had been anticipated when the research began. It suggested to all groups that Detroit offered lots to do (75%), it was a good place to visit (71%), new things were happening (68%), and that there was a new sense of excitement in the city (66%). And, overall, 64 percent of the urban and suburban residents indicated that it gave them a new sense of pride in Detroit. Seldom do theme lines generate so much support and universal agreement on the intended message of the theme.

ISM crafted a promotional campaign with full-page, four-color ads in consumer and meeting planners magazines. The headlines followed the research recommendations:

- "You're just in time to see the new Detroit."
- "There aren't enough hours in the day to see all the difference in Detroit."
- "To create an ideal meeting place, we're moving heaven and earth. Well, okay, mostly earth!"

For surrounding communities, such as Southfield, the theme was expanded to say, "Four times the fun!" representing the four metropolitan districts that make up Detroit. The theme, "It's a great time in Detroit" received prominent display in the ads or was modified to substitute the name of the community for Detroit, thus building on a common theme. Photos of activities, events, and things to do that potential visitors might not have expected for Detroit helped to expand the image that they might have of the area. A musical theme was created for the city, along with a video for distribution to media outlets, including public television. For the launch, Renee Monforton contacted TV stations, newspapers, and community groups for coverage and set up media interviews for me to elaborate on the findings. Three city buses were plastic wrapped in the blue theme color and carried the branding line, "It's a great time in Detroit," on two sides and the back to remind citizens of plans for a better future. The potential for progress had begun.

The Outcome

A couple of months after launching the campaign in the summer of 1998, ISM reported that approval of the theme line had increased, and the new theme song received approval from over three-fourths of residents in Detroit and surrounding communities. Over 10,000 consumer inquiries had already been received as a result of the ad campaign. Further, the new campaign received top honors at the International Association of Convention and Visitors Bureaus (IACVB). The research project also won the award for the best study of the year from the Midwest chapter of the Travel and Tourism Research Association (TTRA). But a fast start from the gate doesn't mean that great success will come quickly. Politicians and residents can express impatience if they don't notice significant increases in tourism, and even local media saw an opportunity to foment controversy by attacking tourism development efforts. The attacks may gain readers and viewers, which helps to sell advertising, but it works at cross purposes in trying to pull a city up by its bootstraps. New campaigns become easy targets for criticism because most people assume that advertising and promotion will produce immediate results. Few recognize that image transformation, especially when starting from a negative base, requires several steps. Awareness of the positive changes must be established first among a prospective audience. Then interest in visiting must be created, followed by increasing the number of inquiries from prospects who are considering a trip until a final commitment to visit occurs. Ultimately, the head of what is now called the Metro Detroit CVB was replaced and a new ad agency was selected. Fortunately, the new Director of the Bureau, Larry Alexander (a hotelier by background), has unified the broad community in multiple ways that some people did not think possible and established the basis for sound progress. The original theme line, "It's a great time in Detroit," has been retained and a number of programs established to increase tourism. Alexander also formed a planning council, composed of representatives from a variety of community and business groups from Detroit and its surrounding communities. It has developed a strategic vision for the area's future and has committed itself to implementing that vision. A four-color document outlines what the "region must do over the next 10 years to become a first-rate travel destination." The strategic plan addresses six areas of concern that require short-term and long-term action to accomplish the goal of increasing tourism. The plan recognizes metro Detroit's shortcomings and provides strategies for improvement. These six major points of the strategic vision can serve as a model for other communities planning on making major changes:

1. *Improve the appearance of the area* through beautification efforts along major interstate highway corridors, including significant landscape and architectural improvements in these areas supported through public and private funding.

2. *Provide a safe and secure experience to visitors* with improvements in street lighting, enhanced police presence in tourism areas, and increased public communications about these safety improvements.

3. *Provide an increased level of service excellence* by sponsoring educational programs for tourism industry employees, sponsoring college credit programs with state universities along with a new tourism extension program.

4. *Create regional collaboration* by enhancing recreational areas, pedestrian walkways and bikeways, and landscape and architectural improvements along interstate corridors in multicounty settings.

5. *Develop new attractions*, including attracting major convention class hotels, developing the Great Lakes Aquarium on the riverfront (done), and investing in the Detroit Science Center and Henry Ford Museum and Greenfield Village.

6. *Market metropolitan Detroit as a distinct destination that communicates the diversity and high quality of the brand* with signature events (Super Bowl XL in 2006) and world-class art exhibits and entertainment.

These goals clearly point out what was said earlier: Good tourism development makes a destination a better place for visitors and those who live in the community. Metropolitan Detroit will be cleaner, with new attractions and facilities and a renewed sense of purpose and spirit. Those benefits accrue to residents and tourists alike. Detroit has also accomplished another task that runs counter to what I believe usually happens: Bring in casinos and they will almost always dominate the branding of a destination. However, the strategic vision plan lays a clear framework for a metro Detroit, with its own unique identity and opportunities for visitors. Casinos (three at present) are just one of the attractions promoted as available for tourists and residents. And, in a smart move, casino representatives sit in on the planning council but do not dominate its agenda. With foresight, Detroit hopefully can escape the curse of gaming—that a destination becomes known for its gambling opportunities and little else.

Object Lesson Learned   In any positioning assignment, factors beyond the control of the CVB or the outside consultant can influence the outcome.

In this case, a new CVB leader (Alexander) was able to unify the community to develop a strategic vision and common sense of purpose. Quick results are usually expected, but not always easy to deliver, especially if a destination must first overcome negative impressions that outsiders hold about a place. Impatience by political leaders to see public coffers swell from tourism growth and hotel owners and managers, who want to fill beds quickly can often short circuit good efforts at preparing for a more positive long-term future. The Metro Detroit CVB has worked to counter that pressure and to keep casinos from dominating the image of the city.

SPECIAL SITUATIONS

Not all destinations require dramatic repositioning efforts. Sometimes tweaking an already positive image slightly can increase both the number of tourists that arrive and the amount they spend during the visit. Several examples of special cases demonstrate that sometimes a minimal repositioning effort can achieve desired results.

Beverly Hills and the Five Dollar Ice Cream Cone

Who would think that Beverly Hills, California would need help to increase tourism? Surprisingly, it had a special problem that deserved attention. This small but world renowned city squeezed between Los Angeles and West Hollywood overflows with wealth and extravagance. Modest-sized homes go for over a million dollars. Estates sell for tens of millions. But for those who can afford its housing costs, it provides a lot: clean streets, manicured lawns, and well-maintained public areas. It has low crime (even though high-crime areas surround it), no door-to-door solicitors (banned), shopping that can't be matched anywhere, and a school district envied by communities around the country. Movie stars and celebrities live everywhere. But you can't take a bus tour to see their homes because the city doesn't allow commercial use of its streets. The tear-down craze started here in which an older home is purchased and immediately demolished to make way for a newer and grander estate. The value of the land often exceeds the worth of a smaller home that sits on it.

Beverly Hills didn't have a tourism problem. People come from all over the U.S. and the world to see this quaint place often pictured in movies and TV series and written about in newspapers and magazines. Local residents will tell you that they have too many tourists. Visitors take up the precious few parking spots available, crowd the sidewalks during shopping hours, and generally make the city more congested and less like a community that exists for its residents. But the city faced a different, largely unrecognized problem. Visitors might come in droves, but didn't buy much while they there. Too often they opted for a double-dip ice cream cone and licked it slowly as they meandered around town. They visited streets and settings made famous in *Pretty*

Woman, Down and Out in Beverly Hills, Beverly Hills Cop I and *II, Beverly Hills 90210,* and the many other movies and media stories that have focused on this rich and famous city. They window-shopped, but didn't buy. Merchants wanted something done. The lookie-loos diverted attention of salespeople from wealthy local clients, who demanded exclusivity and lots of personal attention. Hoteliers and restaurateurs also complained. Those who came to the city most often didn't stay there and didn't eat there. A five-dollar cone was about all they bought. The Chamber of Commerce that controlled the Beverly Hills CVB wanted to find out why visitors didn't spend much in their fair city. And they wanted a marketing plan that would encourage tourists to open their wallets.

I developed a study design that intercepted visitors on the streets and in hotels and allowed me to handle several concurrent requirements. Beverly Hills doesn't allow interviewing, whether door to door or on street corners, and it almost took an act of the City Council to get permission. But I needed to determine a true ratio of how many people on the streets came from Beverly Hills itself, from surrounding communities in the Los Angeles area, from other states in the U.S., and from other countries. The questionnaire asked why they decided to come to Beverly Hills, what other places in Southern California they would visit, where they would do most of their shopping, and their images of Beverly Hills.

The results of the study proved very interesting—and actionable! Most tourists, whether from the U.S. or other countries, had similar reasons for visiting and similar preconceived images about Beverly Hills. They had seen and read so much about the place that they wanted to see it for themselves as part of their Southern California experience. Then they could return home and tell others about the famous places they visited in glamorous Beverly Hills. They didn't get around the city very much. They focused on Rodeo Drive, the Beverly Wilshire Hotel, and some high-end retail stores with big names like Gucci, Bulgari, and Versace. They might also drive around residential areas and gawk at expensive homes, most of which were hidden behind big walls and dense rows of hedges and trees. Based on impressions gathered from movies and TV shows, tourists assumed that the city had lots of glitz and glamour, but little else. They believed that people lived make-believe kinds of lives and were snobbish and not very friendly.

Visitors also assumed that shops and stores in Beverly Hills inflated their prices greatly, since these catered only to the very rich and famous. Thus, tourists generally just looked in the windows, walked in a few stores, and did their shopping elsewhere. Many planned to visit large malls dotted around Southern California, including nearby Beverly Center or the South Coast Plaza and Fashion Island malls in Orange County. So, prior to visiting Beverly Hills, they had already determined they would keep their hands over their wallets closed and just sightsee. For the most part, they also assumed that its hotels or restaurants were beyond their reach. All in all, tourists didn't help the city financially to the same degree they contribute to most areas. Little had been done by the Chamber of Commerce to counter the image created by Hollywood through movies and TV. Preconceived images determine the type of experience visitors will have at a destination, reinforce preconceived notions during the visit, and spread those views further after the trip through word-of-mouth advertising.

The images of the city, as indicated in the study, surprised members of the Chamber of Commerce and the CVB. They believed that Beverly Hills doesn't fit these common perceptions, a statement I can support. Its people, for the most part, go to work every day and have concerns similar to people in almost any town. They may have higher incomes and can afford better lifestyles, but they also go to church and attend PTA meetings in numbers that equal or exceed national averages. And, unknown to most, the city has its share of discount retail stores used by residents (and outsiders) and reasonably priced restaurants that often have prix fixe lunches and dinners that fit in most budgets. Also, moderately priced small hotels are scattered around, most of which are not part of major chains. You can enjoy the best of Beverly Hills on an average budget, but visitors generally didn't know this.

My presentation to CVB Directors and the Chamber of Commerce drew understanding chuckles when I reviewed some of the findings about tourist views of the city, but caused consternation among a few retailers when I gave my recommendations. Beverly Hills, I said, was a victim of an image created by Hollywood, and it needed to take steps to create its own identity. It should tone down the feeling of glitz, glamour, and gaudiness and replace it with a somewhat more conventional and conservative face that it presents to the public. Most important, if the city wanted visitors to spend more, it needed to get out the message that Beverly Hills doesn't cater only to the very wealthy. That message should emphasize some of the more reasonably priced stores, restaurants, and hotels and also include that the most elegant boutiques also sell items that most people can afford to buy. I met some strong resistance, primarily from high-end retailers. Why should Beverly Hills change an image that makes it the envy of the world? Everyone wants to see the place and most people are jealous that they can't afford to live here, I was told. But Bill Boyd, Executive Director of the CVB, who had worked with me on the Waikoloa project in Hawaii and used my ideas for the planning of Branson, Missouri, accepted my message. He directed the ad agency to develop a campaign along this line and to try it overseas first to avoid offending Board members at the start.

The first ads hit Germany, followed up by England, with a great branding statement—*It's cheaper in Beverly Hills*. This theme challenges all assumptions about the city. It fit the need for the moment because Beverly Hills didn't see more visitors. It already had more than it really wanted. It simply wished they would contribute to the public coffers while there. The ads gave some examples of bargains available and how even the most upscale stores sold items that many people wanted and could afford. In effect, the branding statement asked potential visitors to examine their long-held beliefs and drop their defenses against spending as they window-shopped. More important, the results confirmed the strategy. Local hotels, including the five-star Beverly

Hilton owned by Merv Griffin, reported that their European business had picked up. And Bill Boyd relayed an incident to me about one of the Board members who was one of the more vocal critics of the new campaign. He, along with his wife, had started an expensive and successful perfume and notions shop. After a divorce, he opened a high-end fashion boutique. He believed that the new campaign would lower the prestige of Beverly Hills (I had said that was almost impossible), and fewer people would be willing to hand over the amount of money required to buy his dresses. But, in a single week about a month after the campaign began, he sold four dresses to visitors from Europe. Each cost more than $1500. He was ecstatic and no longer complained about the direction of the campaign.

Beverly Hills obviously is a special place. Few destinations can match its panache or automatically attract so many tourists from around the world. But this case demonstrates that even the best places can let their image get out of control if not monitored properly, to their own detriment. Tourists will buy more readily when on vacation trips because they feel relaxed and drop many of their normal defenses against spending needlessly. But, consistent with the message of wanting value for their money, they have a fear of being gouged, especially in a place known for its wealth. In this case, a simple fix, rather than an image overhaul, did the trick. Consideration of the psychographics of the travelers only served as a backdrop to the project because the city already attracted a broad spectrum of visitors.

Sea Pines Plantation—Nature and Solitude Preserved

My invitation to consult with the team developing Sea Pines Plantation on Hilton Head Island in South Carolina came during its early stages of development. The group wanted to know if they had the right marketing approach and if they were developing the type of resort that could compete successfully in the marketplace. Although homes had already been constructed, golf courses and tennis courts put in place, and the area's master plan laid out, they could still change a number of features, if necessary. I explained my psychographic concepts, concentrating on the needs and characteristics of near-venturers that they would have to attract. They described their overall vision for the resort and even showed me detailed drawings of homes under construction. Then I took a tour. What I saw impressed me immensely. They had put together the type of resort that I would recommend to clients, and they had done it without my consultation. But they were aware of my concepts.

Charles Fraser, the founder, inherited the land from his grandfather. Locals called it scrub land because its tall, skinny pine trees didn't produce enough lumber to make a suitable harvest. But it was picturesque. Small rolling hills gently sloped into the Atlantic Ocean, and abundant wildlife made it a nature preserve. Reeds poked through beach sands, creating a feeling much like beaches in Maine. Shallow pools and ponds dotted the property. Fraser had a vision. He believed that he could develop the area as a very special kind of resort community appealing to the high end of the market. Because of the newness of development on Hilton Head Island, few travelers would know much about it. And, its out-of-the-way location would mean that most guests would have to fly to Savannah, Georgia, rent a car, and drive 45 minutes to Sea Pines. It would have to be something special to overcome these obstacles.

Fraser's vision mirrored closely what I had recommended to other clients, and the assignment became a test of whether my approach truly would work on a new resort project. In a variety of ways, he planned a community that offered a sense of isolation, serenity, and exclusiveness that near-venturers desire when they consider a new location for a leisure trip or for investing in a second home. A third of all land was set aside as nature preserves, and local bird and animal populations remained protected, even the alligators. All new homes required approval from an architectural committee to ensure that the design fit with the quiet and subdued ambience of the resort. The committee also allowed only earth tones for exterior colors, again to help the houses fade from view into their surroundings. And to add to that sense, most had extensive setbacks from the front road and were hidden by a row of scrub pines between the house and road. Though too thin for a lumberyard, the pines worked perfectly in a landscape design. These subtly filtered the magnificent estates from view, creating a sense that little residential development had occurred at Sea Pines Plantation. Commercial areas followed the same pattern—low-rise buildings, subtle color tones, and setbacks that kept them partially hidden from view. Strict standards required retail signage of designated size, shape, and background colors. Professionally designed golf courses along the waterfront and inlets enhanced the overall beauty. The Harbor Course, with its quaint lighthouse, has received television coverage during various PGA-sponsored championship matches. A tennis center also included a stadium court for professional tournament play. Condominiums and apartments received more attention to design than other resorts with which I had worked to ensure that rooms flowed together nicely. Kitchen and bath appliances and countertops conformed to the height of an average person. A manned guard gate kept out unauthorized persons to provide a degree of security and protection and to limit the amount of traffic.

Through an onsite survey, I determined the level of satisfaction with Sea Pines Plantation and how to increase revenue from visitors. The results reflected my suspicions. Satisfaction levels ranked high, and very few comments came from owners and guests about any perceived need for change. I provided suggestions on the kinds of facilities and services owners and visitors normally like that they would pay for. And I also offered comments on how to develop effective advertising to attract near-venturer types as buyers. But I generally told Fraser and his staff that they were on the right track. I encouraged them not to lose sight of their original vision. Maintain the development's subdued, natural setting, continue to limit density, and foster a distinct identity from the other projects that would soon dot Hilton Head Island, I suggested.

Sea Pines Plantation provides a case example of how a good beginning can ensure a long-term future by holding fast to the original concept. Resorts with less planning and fewer controls now surround it (Sea Pines is on the tip of Hilton Head), and these have not enjoyed the same level of success. And, unfortunately, a string of discount golf warehouse stores with garish signs line the major road to leading to all resorts. But Sea Pines continues to maintain its ambience of serenity and isolation behind its guarded gates, in spite of excessive nearby commercial development. The American Traveler Survey of Plog Research points to its continued success. Among eight golfing-focused destinations reviewed in the study, Sea Pines generally ranks only behind the Monterey Peninsula in California, with its world-famous Pebble Beach golf course, in the annual household income of its visitors. But Sea Pines also leads all destinations in the number of rounds of golf played annually by those who travel to its shores.

One unfortunate change happened: Charles Fraser lost control of the property during the unsettling economic times of the mid-1980s. He continued to sell lots at a rapid pace, but offered them at fixed, long-term, low interest rates while he borrowed short-term money at a time when interest rates rose unexpectedly. The banks took over and, in the end, profited handsomely. He recovered financially to some degree at a later date. But the point still remains: A good project seldom requires a major repositioning effort.

The Places that Dependables Love

Thus far, I have focused on how to position destinations to increase their appeal to venturers. They have many positive qualities that generally make them the best target market. They travel more, take trips further away from home, use air travel more, spend more on travel, and influence friends and associates to go to the places they have visited. That winning combination makes them an obvious choice in most situations. But not all places have qualities that appeal to this select group of travelers. Nor should all places try to cast a relatively similar image. Dependables also travel and there are a lot of them. And, they have one important advantage: They like to select the same place over and over again. That nice habit can lower marketing costs since, once captured, they don't need to be reminded repeatedly of where to take their next trips. And, because they don't demand novelty in their lives, little needs to be done to freshen a resort or destination from year to year. The same kind of entertainment appeals to them time and again, and they even like the familiar feel and decor of a hotel they have visited multiple times in the past.

Several kinds of destinations have a strong appeal to this group. And these places make money with these visitors. Highest on the list are warm and sunny spots where they can sit on the sand, have a beer or soda, and occasionally get their feet wet in the water or a pool. At night their entertainment might consist of a movie (they like the comforts of home wherever they travel) and an ice cream cone or a drink after the show. In the daytime, they'll window-shop at the touristy places and buy shirts with the names of the town or resort and the trinkets that remind them of their travels. It's easy to name the spots that they seek—Miami and other Florida beach cities (especially on the west coast), Palm Springs and some of the nearby desert communities, and Hawaii. But Hawaii presents an example of a destination that not only dependables like, but all other psychographic groups do too. Dependables can stroll up and down the streets of Waikiki or Wailea, while more venturesome types can tour the backsides of various islands or participate in adventure sports from scuba diving to hang gliding and surfing.

Golf resorts also capture a high percent of dependables. Most of these resorts sit in warm locales to allow year round play. As pointed out, dependables especially like the camaraderie of the game and 19th hole fellowship. You can find countless numbers at modestly priced golf resorts. Palm Springs not only has sunshine and warmth, but it also offers a lot of golf. But the prize in this category has to be Myrtle Beach, South Carolina. As of this writing, it has over 130 golf courses. The acreage devoted to golf equals the land that sits under many good-sized cities. With this many courses, competition becomes fierce to capture visitors. Thus package vacation prices fall to unbelievably low levels for airfare and hotel. It would be difficult to turn Myrtle Beach into a venturer-type of destination.

Gambling spots also rank high on their lists of favorite places. Slot machines and the tables not only offer a chance to hit it big, something vacationers can talk to their friends about if they score, but it's also a form of entertainment. They don't have to move around a lot—just sit on a chair or stool to play most of the games. Gambling establishments have learned that dependables like noise and lights. When a one-armed bandit hits, the sound of coins dropping into metal trays reverberates throughout the casino gaming areas. Brightly lit machines offer constant movement, even when not being played. And nighttime also offers a good selection of entertainment choices. Las Vegas, Nevada and Atlantic City, New Jersey capture a high percentage of dependables. Some venturers also drop by Las Vegas, fascinated by this most unreal of all cities, and want to check out the newest casino that has come online. They may play a few hands at one of the tables, but they tend to limit their wagers. They seek better odds. Few visit Indian casinos sprouting up rapidly around the country. These places, although colorful and noisy, don't have the impressive ambience of Las Vegas resorts. Thus, Indian casinos primarily attract true dependables. Cheap meals, noisy entertainment (often featuring Elvis Presley look-alikes), and free-flowing drinks add to a feeling of well-being and encourage gamblers to bet more at the tables. Casinos on reservations near major population centers in a number of states operate with little state or federal supervision—they can even take the visitors' dollars and not pay taxes on the profits.

One destination began from scratch with a focus on attracting dependables—Branson, Missouri. William Boyd, who understood my psychographic concepts quite well, was Director of Economic Planning for the state of Missouri during the time that plans for Branson were formulated. As was mentioned, we had worked together on the repositioning efforts for Waikoloa, Hawaii and Beverly Hills. He guided Branson's developers to establish a destination that appeals to dependables (called psychocentrics at that time). Branson has qualities dependables like. It features well-known country music stars, a favorite of this group, especially some of the stars of yesterday. Theaters in town are named after some of these big names who appear regularly in person. Knowing that Branson would attract a heavy proportion of drive visitors, Boyd convinced planners to include lots of parking space for cars and big motor homes. But even with forethought, the success of Branson has surprised many. Traffic delays getting in and out of town on weekends can almost spoil any trip. But a good dependable will put up with that problem more than most people, especially venturers.

In the final analysis, a destination has the best chance of success if it attracts the widest audience possible. But only a few places can fulfill that kind of a promise. Hawaii, as was mentioned, offers much for everyone. In the U.K., venturers can strike out on their own to discover overlooked villages and largely unknown castles, while dependables can enjoy a fully escorted tour to the better known spots. But this review points out that successful places can run the gamut in the types of crowds they attract, from the very venturesome to those placing at the dependable side of the scale. To ensure success, the positioning strategy and the reasons for that strategy must be carefully thought about in advance. Otherwise destinations can age ungracefully, an undesirable outcome for local citizens and visitors.

USING FESTIVALS TO JUMP-START TOURISM

Because turning around a destination takes time, especially if it currently has a negative image, I often recommend one surefire strategy to boost tourism quickly: Initiate a festival or big event program. It can take less than a year, from start to finish, to get a festival going and, from that point on, it builds every year in the number of visitors it attracts as word gets out. These also help to pull a community together and make local citizens feel proud about where they live and the many opportunities available for recreation and entertainment.

An event that targets a good niche can draw its audience from great distances. People follow their passions and will pay to be informed, entertained, or enjoy experiences different from their daily routines. These are win/win situations for just about everyone. Examples abound of successful events that attract thousands of visitors and millions of dollars in revenue. Edinburgh, Scotland hosts the largest arts festival in the world. Begun in 1947, and with an emphasis on classical music, opera, theater, dance and books (since 1983), it produces over 16,000 performances in August. Tanglewood in the Berkshires of Massachusetts continues to grow each year in popularity. The long-running Santa Fe (New Mexico) Opera, begun in 1957, has achieved wide recognition. The Stratford Festival of Canada (Province of Ontario), formed in 1953, sells over 600,000 tickets for its long season running from late April until late November.[6] Presenting only the works of Shakespeare, it has turned a working-class town into a center of culture, in addition to providing tax dollars and supporting local businesses. California offers many festivals featuring classical music, from small towns like Ojai (the Berkley classical music festival) to the big cities of Los Angeles, San Francisco, and San Diego (opera events). These help turn California into a constant event state. But it's not just the arts that draw audiences. Reno, Nevada is probably the festival capital of the world in terms of the variety of events it hosts. It fills hotels for two weeks in September, beginning with the Great Reno Balloon Race and ending with the National Championship Air Races. It precedes this with the Hot August Nights classic car show (over 200,000 visitors) and the Artown festivities and the Best in the West Nugget Rib Cook-Off.[7] Throw in the national bowling championships at the National Bowling Stadium, a Basque festival, jazz, classical music, and ballet festivals and Reno has probably covered more weeks of the year with special events than any other destination. Reno recognizes that it can't compete with the glitz of Las Vegas or its enormous marketing budget, so it chose the festival route to fill the town. Although not planned with these concepts in mind, Oktoberfest in Germany provides a month-long reason to visit the country to sample its hundreds of local beers and enjoy the entertainment. Other cities have cook-offs, frog jumping contests, avocado festivals, decorative gourd festivals, dog and horse shows, concerts on the green—the list goes on and on. And these all draw lots of visitors. In fact, a growing list of Web sites track different kinds of festivals and events, from jazz to classical to the frivolous (FestivalFinder.com; WhatsOnWhen.com; FestivalNet.com; JazzOnJazz.com; WorldwideBlues.com).

But developing a successful festival that will stand out among the many offerings and bring lots of tourists to town requires careful thought and planning. A few rules will clarify some of the issues to consider before moving forward:

Build on Local Strengths   Success comes more easily when local resources can be tapped to develop the event. If the community has some semi-known artists, a fledgling theater district, jazz groups, or whatever, it has the basis for creating a worthwhile event. A local museum may focus on a special period in history (World War II memorabilia) or the town has an interesting venue (like the Corn Palace in Mitchell, South Dakota) that can serve as the basis for a new idea. Tapping local talent and resources can help to jump-start an event, especially since knowledgeable enthusiasts live in the community

---

[6]Article by Barbara D. Phillips, *The Wall Street Journal*, July 18, 2002, p. D10.
[7]Article by Tom Gorman in the *Los Angeles Times*, August 5, 2001, p. A20.

who can provide much of the artistic talent, dedicated staff, and professional expertise to plan, promote, and run the event. And a community already attuned to the idea will willingly get behind all efforts to ensure its success, including inviting friends and relatives to town to share in the joys of the events. Ideas are limitless for the types of festivals—the arts, classic cars, jazz or classical music, eel and herring festivals (Sweden), reggae music, and on and on.

Develop Strong Community Backing The more that a community gets behind an event, the greater its chances for success. Get the local Chamber of Commerce to contribute dollars and personnel, ensure support from the local political establishment, woo the media to provide coverage, and tap all organizations that have talent related to the planned event. Because of the up-front organizing costs and the fact that it takes time to get the word out to attract a large audience, it is usually necessary to secure multiple sources of financial backing.

Choose a Soft Time The purpose of a festival is to increase tourism—at a time when it's needed. Plan the events at times when tourism is soft, in the shoulder months or the true off seasons. Too many planners think only about putting on events during the heavy travel months of summer, arguing that it's easier to attract big crowds at that time. True, but it does little to help the local economy. Hotels and restaurants already are jam-packed. They need guests when regular visitors have left town.

Plan an Extended Time Period One-day or weekend festivals don't produce the impact of festivals that run for a week or two or, as is occasionally the case, for several months. Short events attract mainly local visitors—people who reach the event within an hour's drive or less. They return home at night because they don't need a hotel. Air travelers will seldom come for a short-term event, unless it has strong interest for them. Tourism dollars and tax revenues increase exponentially as festivals exceed a two-day time period.

Don't Gouge A successful event can utilize all the facilities of a town, especially its hotels, restaurants, and entertainment venues. Far too often local businesses will raise rates for just about everything. While it may provide a boost in short-term revenue, it hurts in the long run. Visitors leave with a feeling that they were gouged, and they may never return. Too few seem willing to work for long-term goodwill that will create good word-of-mouth advertising for the community.

Consider Niche Markets Successful festival programs run the gamut, from festivals that appeal to large numbers of people to those that target small niches. Most planners assume they can only achieve success if they go after large audiences, such jazz or rock concerts and big sporting events. But consider one fact: Those who have uncommon interests have fewer opportunities to satisfy their curiosity by associating with like-minded people. They will travel farther and stay longer to enjoy their favorite activities. Hobbyists who assemble specialized train sets, or remote control scale model airplanes, or build small model ships have few opportunities to see the creations and skill levels of others like themselves. Some plan vacations around visits to places with events that focus on their interests and hobbies.

The flexibility of festivals in terms of what kind, when, and how long provide multiple opportunities for destinations to control their own destinies. And they can provide temporary relief until longer-term plans for a full repositioning effort can achieve maximum impact.

CHAPTER ELEVEN

Positioning Travel Suppliers—A Case Example: The Airlines

Destinations generally have an easier time developing effective positioning strategies than travel suppliers because destinations offer a greater variety of choices to their clientele: beaches or mountains, warm weather or cold, ancient castles or contemporary art museums, availability of golf and other sports, interesting local people, unique arts and crafts, domestic or international location, reasonably priced or expensive, quiet countryside or hectic city. The list of how destinations vary from each other seems endless. Only wine connoisseurs describing a favorite vintage can match the rich array of adjectives that travel writers use to describe the new places they have discovered to their readers. Travel suppliers, in contrast, generally don't have the same degrees of freedom as they attempt to create unique images for their products or services. Major airlines fly the same airplanes, now primarily manufactured by two companies—Boeing and Airbus. Rental car companies may feature one manufacturer over another, but all offer similar sized cars, along with a couple of specialty vehicles such as SUVs or convertibles. Hotel chains compete on quality and price, but brands with similar ambience and room rates exist in most cities. The frequency with which hotels are reflagged with different chain names points out that hotel chains competing in the same niche offer very similar products. Only cruise lines differentiate themselves more clearly, and they have maintained their sense of uniqueness for a couple of decades. In general, travel suppliers face the same dilemma as food processors like Procter & Gamble. With similar products and prices, they must hunt for a single dimension—the Unique Selling Proposition (USP)—to set them apart from their competitors. Many travel companies have given up the battle to distinguish their products from competitors. They primarily promote price, a strategy that undercuts the value of a brand, or they only remind travelers which destinations they serve.

A thorough review of potential positioning strategies for various travel suppliers could fill another volume—too much for inclusion here. But it is useful to take a look at airlines because, for the most part, they have been their own worst enemies. At one time, each carrier had a unique identity based on its colorful history and the personalities of the aviators who risked their fortunes and their lives during the early history of the industry. During the early decades, through the 1960s, flying created a sense of romance and excitement. Loyalty by fliers to one carrier or another often ran deep and grew out of their colorful backgrounds or the level of service provided inflight. Today, few people exhibit such dedication to any particular airline. Local residents may even attack a carrier that dominates a city with its hub and spoke system, viewing it as uncaring, arrogant, and too expensive. Frequent fliers often try to concentrate their flights on a single carrier to build up frequent flyer points and gain special privileges, but few try to convince friends to switch to their airline because of presumed better service. What a change from the days when airlines worked at differentiating themselves from each other to gain customer loyalty. But strategies exist that can help airlines carve out unique positions and create customer loyalty.

THE DIMENSIONS OF AIRLINE POSITIONING STRATEGIES

Few tasks can equal the excitement of creating a new positioning strategy for an airline because of the difficulties that must be overcome in order to ensure success. Startup carriers offer the easiest challenge. Lacking a previous history or identity, greater freedom exists to create a sense of uniqueness. But they must attract passengers quickly to generate revenue and create loyalty before a major carrier decides to mount a counterattack. Without the dead weight of restrictive union contracts that define work conditions and require highly paid senior pilots and mechanics, they have a built-in advantage: They can offer low fares and make money. But they still need an identity—a unique quality that sets them apart from all others to make them memorable. What will first-time fliers remember after their first trips? Will it be only low price, or will the carrier convey a sense of its personality that its passengers will talk about with friends and neighbors? And what story will the press tell after it gets started? Low fares alone don't guarantee success. Several dozen budget airlines have failed within two to three years of launch. If they had only known that a number of ideas that don't cost much could have established an identity that would have created attention in the marketplace and a more loyal following. Put in leather seats. Installation costs are double that for cloth seats, but leather also lasts more than twice as long. Paint the planes with a unique, standout logo. Don't put galleys onboard, even if management wants to serve food on longer flights. Expensive to install and maintain, galleys also take up a row or two of seats that can be sold for additional revenue. Instead, let passengers pick up a complimentary well-prepared deli lunch or dinner just before entering the cabin. Add multichannel entertainment at every seat. Advertising on the channels will pay for the installation and turn a profit. Give the airline a unique name—something a bit quirky so that people will talk about it and wonder how anyone came up with such an idea. And, if the airline has a management staff that can pull it off, give the airline a personality. That will definitely make it memorable. In each case, these suggestions are low cost or no cost to ensure that creeping expenses don't threaten an airline's financial future. But the major challenge continues to be how to turn around a struggling major carrier that has a long history of relationships with passengers. As pointed out earlier, it takes a lot of new information to change someone's mind about an airline (or any product or service).

Until airline deregulation in the U.S. in 1978, most commercial carriers had distinct images. Their positioning strategies set them apart from each other, and the tag lines in their ads constantly reminded fliers about the benefits of choosing one airline over another. They spent millions to enhance onboard service or to launch a new advertising campaign. A number of these strategies exist today, but usually in a watered-down and almost unrecognizable form. An airline might include more than one dimension in its positioning strategy but emphasize one characteristic over another. One point needs to be remembered: Airlines serve broad markets. Thus, only a few have successful strategies that appeal to a more venturesome audience. But that option does exist in select cases.

Several potential airline positioning strategies will be reviewed:

- Onboard service
- Hi-tech leadership
- Passenger comfort/care
- Unique personality
- Service to the world
- Safety
- Low price

Onboard Service

Onboard service can define differences between airlines but seldom is used as an effective positioning strategy today. Prior to 1978, government regulations required that all airlines operating within the U.S. or landing from foreign shores must charge the same price for flights between identical city pairs. In those regulated days, airlines primarily fought for passengers on the basis of inflight service. And they fought hard. Advertising campaigns frequently centered on first class service, assuming that the image created would spill over to economy class. Famous restaurants and chefs lent their names to inflight menus. TWA distinguished itself by installing the only inflight ovens to cook, not preheat, its choice chateaubriands. United had chefs flying on some flights to emphasize its New York class meals. American played off of a theme of being the airline that professionals fly and bragging about its gourmet meals served at 30,000 feet. A broad offering of drinks ensured that passengers got the brand of scotch or vodka that they desired.

International airlines generally provided the highest levels of onboard service for both meal quality and courteous, helpful inflight crews. But Pan Am was not to be outdone. With the most routes worldwide, it emphasized its international character. When it introduced the Boeing 747 to international service, it reserved the upstairs deck for a bar and a place to invite its first-class passengers to enjoy a sit-down meal at tables for four.

Coach passengers ultimately got the benefits of a spillover effect. Early in the history of commercial aviation, economy-class passengers bought airport lunches to bring onboard (that's true again, for JetBlue). Then airlines added a meal service, and finally offered a selection of three entrees, chosen from a handout printed menu. And United, on wide-bodied flights between Los Angeles and New York City, put on a great spread—a standup New York style deli lunch served throughout most of the flight. Continental Airlines installed a piano lounge on its DC10s for its Chicago to L.A. run. That, however, proved to be a disaster. Without a paid professional musician, the piano served as a place for passengers to bang out their renditions of "Chopsticks" or a terrible boogie-woogie version of "Heart and Soul". Gradually, after deregulation, service to passengers declined. No meals on flights under three hours for most airlines, or after 7:00 P.M., and reduced legroom. And, ultimately, cutbacks on even the little amenities such as snacks and upgrades for frequent fliers. For a time, first class and business class on international flights became the battleground for increasing amenities because high ticket prices from this small group of passengers provided half the profit that an airline could make on an international flight.

Does high service make a difference in loyalty? Yes! For several decades, Alaska Airlines offered one inch more legroom in coach and generally provided upgraded meals. Although it didn't promote its extra room heavily in ads, it always got higher marks for onboard comfort in Plog Research's airline surveys. And these ratings created a halo effect with passengers giving higher ratings for the other services offered by Alaska—reservations, check-in, inflight crew helpfulness, and baggage delivery. Throughout the turmoil and downgrading of services that has occurred since deregulation, one international carrier has refused to follow the downward trend—Singapore Airlines. They have established a worldwide reputation based on the "Singapore girl"—

young, attractive inflight attendants who smother even economy passengers with care and attention. It continues to steal passengers from other airlines where it competes, even when those passengers lose frequent flier points by not sticking with the carrier they use most often. Its branding theme, "It's a great way to fly," printed in small type in ads that it almost can't be read, is not even remembered by fliers. But its reputation from high levels of inflight service creates such a strong positive image that it almost does not need to advertise. Commitment by Singapore to running the top airline in the world is not skin deep. In a study on passenger preference for different airplanes conducted by Plog Research, Boeing obtained cooperation from a number of international airlines. Each carrier was to distribute and collect back questionnaires on twenty-five flights. The overall success rate was a bit above 50 percent (inflight crews distributed, collected, and returned questionnaires to our offices), with one carrier falling to 25 percent. Singapore, however, completed distribution and return of questionnaires on all but one flight. I was so amazed that I wrote a letter of congratulations to the Chairman of Singapore. When I got a return letter, I assumed it would be a polite note thanking me for my compliments. No! The Chairman wanted to know which flight was missed so that he could take corrective action. Amazing! No mistakes were allowed. Truly a six-sigma approach to customer service! Commitment to passengers running the best airline begins at the top.

High levels of onboard service can still win the loyalty of passengers today. But fliers are now a jaded group. They have seen so many changes come and go that they no longer believe that any carrier will make a long-term commitment to stand alone among all competitors. Too bad. An era of commitment to quality has been lost in the past, probably forever.

Hi-Tech

As a positioning strategy, this dimension includes a couple of characteristics that passengers can recognize—on-time performance, having a new and modern fleet of airplanes, and an emphasis on good maintenance procedures. In the late 1980s and into the early 1990s, Lufthansa wanted to be known as the hi-tech and hi-touch airline. It made it on the first count. It had a very young fleet, serviced it well, and enjoyed an above-average on-time record. It had more difficulty with the hi-touch part of the equation—excellent passenger care and comfort. The formal nature of the German inflight crew could not relate to passengers in the comforting manner of Singapore girls. Hi-tech by itself will only produce a small amount of customer loyalty.

An airline that is consistently behind schedule will lose passengers, but few recognize that true differences exist between carriers in on-time performance. Until it began expanding its routes across the U.S. in the late 1990s, Southwest Airlines had won more monthly on-time performance awards than any other carrier. Frequent fliers recognized that they would get to their destinations on time more often if they chose Southwest. It had a couple of advantages that helped it maintain on-time performance. As a short-haul airline (most flights are around an hour), passengers check fewer bags, helping it to turn its planes around more quickly. And, until recently, it has flown primarily in the Southern tier of the country, where weather delays occur less often. But, as Southwest expanded its routes into colder climates, it no longer consistently wins the monthly on-time performance awards. Today, the lack of a consistent winner confuses the message of which carrier can claim that label. On-time performance can only serve as a secondary, supporting positioning message. More important, unless a carrier can be certain it will continue to measure above competitors, it is a risky strategy to follow. A competitor may be able to make the claim next month, or the month after.

Passenger Comfort

Quite a few airlines have developed strategies around this dimension. But, most often, the message has centered on first or business class. Across the North Atlantic, between Europe and the U.S., the battle to gain premium paying passengers heated up in the 1990s. British Airways upped the ante when it offered full 180-degree sleepers in first class, bringing back a service that Pan Am introduced on its long-haul Clipper airplanes decades before. Others, like Continental, followed with nearly full reclining seats in business class. Ultimately, the 180-degree sleeper even migrated to business class. And meal upgrades and other amenities for the front-end passengers also followed, such as chauffeured limousine pickup in the departure city (Virgin Atlantic). But airlines have largely ignored coach passengers and their needs. As they have taken away legroom (declining from a standard 34-inch seat pitch to 31 or 32 inches) and put eight rows across in some Boeing 757s that were designed for seven rows, the folks flying "steerage" have had to endure increasing levels of discomfort. Airline executives argue that coach passengers want the cheapest fares possible, and they can only remain competitive by cramming in more people per flight. Passenger comfort ranks as a high priority among fliers but will likely get less attention in the future because of the concentration by airlines on reducing operating expenses at all levels. But the topic is so important that it is covered in greater depth in an upcoming section that describes an interesting chapter in the history of TWA.

Personality

This positioning strategy can offer great rewards—recognition in the marketplace, customer loyalty, and self-generating PR. But few airlines have the capability to develop a personality and carry it forth over time. Interestingly, personality shines forth most often among low-cost carriers. These seem willing to take the chance on being different. The big boys—traditional airlines—believe that they must maintain a more formal image in keeping with what they consider to be their higher standards of service. This approach makes onboard service more uniform and predictable, and often more boring. The best personality by far, and it set the standard for all others, was created by Pacific Southwest Airlines (PSA). Based in San Diego, California, it dominated the San Francisco/Los Angeles corridor and flew to some nearby states. It picked its inflight hostesses for looks and liveliness and dressed them in attention-grabbing mini-skirts. They carried on constant banter with passengers, many of whom they saw frequently as they commuted between the two cities. The hostesses would pull tricks on passengers. The story is told that one attendant hid in an overhead storage bin, startling the first person that opened it. On one late-night flight from San Francisco to Los Angeles, I witnessed a water gun fight between several passengers and the inflight crew. In turn, passengers developed a strong loyalty to PSA. Many remembered the names of the crew and even brought decorated cakes on board and sang "Happy Birthday" to a favorite inflight attendant. The front of the airplane featured a Kilroy-type smile painted on the nose, with the cockpit windows serving as the eyes. It stood out as the plane pulled up to the gate. PSA killed all competition. No major carrier was able to compete with its friendly onboard spirit. But, alas, all was lost when US Air (now US Airways) acquired it. I tried to convince executives at US Air to retain the spirit and feeling of PSA, including dedicating airplanes to specific routes so that the smile could remain on the airplanes. Their answer was that US Air, after taking over PSA, had become a coast-to-coast airline and they wanted passengers to recognize that fact. Management took off the airplane smiles, changed the snappy PSA uniforms to the more drab US Air standard, and sent the zippy girls on their way to all the destinations that the airline served. The impact began immediately. Its market share in the West went into free fall, and it failed to establish the national reputation it sought. Ultimately, it gave up all of the routes it acquired from PSA, thereby forfeiting its entire investment.

A small number of other airlines have also created a quirky personality to stand out in the crowd. Southwest allows its inflight attendants to personalize safety and other onboard announcements, adding humor to routine procedures ("Now that we've landed, we need someone to clean the lavatories. To volunteer, just stand up before the plane comes to a stop at the gate."). Its advertising also follows a different path. "After 30 years, it's still just peanuts." (Southwest doesn't serve meals; only peanuts.) And, in a TV commercial that shows a plane in the sky and stresses its low fares, an inflight attention bell is heard and a pilot announces, "You are now free to move about the country." The airline's personality reflects the much talked about antics of the president who guided it for years, Herb Kelleher, who received considerable press for constantly doing the unexpected. But Kelleher is a more buttoned down and focused executive than most people believe. He understands that his inflight crews have terribly boring jobs. With the short hop schedules of the airline, they give the same preflight safety announcements five or six times every day they fly. He wants them to have a constant sense of freshness as they approach their jobs. Virgin Atlantic Airways, the upstart transatlantic carrier from England, also reflects the spirit of its founder, Richard Branson, who made his fortune when he formed Virgin Records. He spoofs conventional designation for business class and coach, calling these "upper class" and "lower class." Although it's a discount airline, service levels in both classes remain above competitors, with coach passengers getting upgraded meals and more entertainment choices.

Emphasizing personality is a great way to position a new airline. But it is difficult for a long-established carrier to change its stripes and relate to its passengers in new and more offbeat ways. Customer contact personnel, long trained in doing everything by the book, would have difficulty adapting. Only when you start from scratch can a company consistently recruit the types of people who fit in with a different model of customer contact and service. Passengers themselves also expect certain kinds of behaviors and actions from the crew of airlines they fly regularly, and a dramatic turnabout could be traumatic.

Service to the World

So many carriers fly worldwide at present that this positioning strategy has limited ability to make one airline stand out from another. Mergers and acquisitions in the industry, along with governments allowing more flights from various countries, have reduced the industry to a smaller number of big and powerful companies. At one time, Pan Am could claim the leadership role internationally, but it lacked U.S. domestic routes (but later acquired some when it swallowed up National Airlines). The airline positioned itself as America's ambassadors to the world, almost an arm of the State Department. Its clipper fleet was famous in the Pacific and various parts of Asia. Its flights 1 and 2 started from New York and went around the world in opposite directions. TWA did not have the same international presence, but it could feed passengers to its international flights from a relatively strong domestic route structure. And it had panache of its own. Neither carrier exists today, but remnants of this strategy remain. Most major airlines fly both international and domestic routes and consistently promote their ability to carry passengers from their home cities to the destinations they serve. But no single airline can claim overall superiority.

Safety

Except in developing countries and small nations where travelers don't trust the national airline, a positioning strategy based on safety no longer carries the impact it once did. As recently as the late 1970s, it still had meaning. The public did not trust flying. Lots of PR and advertising helped overcome some of this concern, as was discussed earlier. When safety is emphasized, the message can only be approached indirectly to ensure success. In a series of radio commercials for Pacific Air Lines (PAL) in the 1970s, a well-known standup comic addressed the issue by announcing that PAL would provide security blankets and silly putty for the nervous fliers. The campaign backfired. It drove away large numbers of passengers and helped contribute to the airline's downfall and ultimate acquisition by another carrier. American Airlines put on some of the best—and the worst—ads on safety. Its claim as the airline that professionals fly carried the dual positive messages of high professional standards in serving passengers and great attention to issues of safety. The appropriate ads in print and TV showed gray-haired pilots with scrambled eggs on their hats and lots of service stripes on their sleeves inspecting their airplanes before takeoff. The inappropriate ads pictured the landing of an airplane, as seen from a camera mounted on the underbelly of an airplane. It's not a very exciting viewpoint but, worse yet, the dominant visual image came from the black tire skid marks created from earlier planes touching down. That brought a sense to nervous fliers that airplanes face a dangerous situation when they land. Most people don't recognize that the landing wheels are not spinning when they hit the ground, causing skid marks when the tires hit the pavement.

Pan Am unquestionably had the best branding theme based on safety and used it effectively for decades. "The world's most experienced airline" conveyed two messages: An experienced airline knows how to treat passengers well. And, experience also means that it knows how to fly safely in all situations. In spite of four accidents in 1973 that killed over 400 passengers (Papeete, Pago Pago, Denpasar, and Boston), people continued to fly Pan Am, even in the countries where these accidents happened. They believed it was a safe airline, based on its record and its advertising theme. I conducted focus groups around the world for Pan Am at the time to verify that the airline did not face a problem. But a woman in a group in Auckland, New Zealand summarized the feelings of many when she stated, "Pan Am has more planes in the air than any other airline, so it is going to have more accidents." But a series of new branding strategies confused the public about the benefits that Pan Am offered. When Pan Am Flight 103 exploded over Lockerbie, Scotland on December 21, 1988, the flying public ultimately blamed Pan Am for poor screening procedures at its Heathrow Airport facilities rather than the Libyan terrorists who planted the bomb. The airline went into a revenue tailspin from that point on that ultimately led to its demise.

The general point, however, is that safety has dropped to such a low priority among fliers that even startup carriers don't promote their safety standards. The assumption of most passengers is that if the Federal Aviation Authority, or the governments of other large nations, charter and oversee airlines, then they must be safe to fly.

Low Price

This message will get increased attention in the coming years. By necessity, startups must be low-budget operators to capture an audience. Low-priced airlines have a powerful positioning message. They will grab significant market share of both leisure and business fliers from competitors. And, in today's competitive environment, they can worry less about major airlines driving them out of business. The majors don't have the financial reserves, even in profitable years, to handle continuing losses to get rid of a competitor. More important, the major airlines can't seem to come up with an operating plan that includes low cost, high efficiency, and a quick turnaround of airplanes at the gate. Only reorganization through bankruptcy can lower the operating costs of some of these airlines to the point that they may be able to compete.

BRINGING TWA BACK TO LIFE: A Story of What Could Have Been

A great name in commercial aviation no longer exists—TWA. Its demise came after years of neglect by the wrong people. But it had a chance not only at survival, but to regain much of its past glory. But those in charge once again made shortsighted decisions that helped push it to its grave.

Background

Working with an established airline to turn it around represents a bigger challenge than helping to position a startup carrier, but also a greater sense of accomplishment when things go right. Without a prior history, a startup can choose any personality it wants to present to the public. But an airline with a history often carries a lot of negative baggage from its past problems related to how it has treated passengers. TWA presented that challenge. And the results proved highly successful, only to be undone by a musical chairs game that continued at senior levels of management in the company. The story is worth telling because it indicates how a proper positioning strategy, along with an exceptionally good branding effort, can turn a major airline around very quickly. And it also demonstrates how a major advantage can also be lost quickly—and forever.

TWA was one of my favorite clients. One of its directors, Rouvim Feguine, had assembled the industry group of 16 sponsors in 1966 that led to the New Markets for Air Travel project that my first company conducted (see Chapter 3). I continued to work with TWA since that time. The airline had an interesting but tortuous history. Howard Hughes, its founder, had set a pattern of always doing things differently. When most airlines bought the reliable but plain-Jane Douglas DC 4s after World War II (and later the DC 6s), Hughes opted for the most beautiful commercial airplane to grace the skies, the tri-tailed Lockheed Constellation. But its good looks didn't hide its higher operating costs and more frequent delays because of mechanical problems. The airline led the way in introducing inflight entertainment, upgraded meals, and establishing a consumer marketing section focused on monitoring passenger satisfaction. In the 1950s and 1960s, it consistently topped passenger ratings surveys. Hollywood celebrities flew it regularly on its Los Angeles to New York run, and it was heavily featured in Hollywood movies. It also gained notoriety several times when it spirited famous Russian ballet dancers to sanctuary in the U.S., all orchestrated by Rouvim Feiguine, who had escaped communist Russia as a young man. Its colorful history could easily fill an intriguing book or make a great plot for a movie. It helped shape commercial aviation as we know it today, and it deserved better treatment than it ultimately received.

The Problem

Howard Hughes ultimately lost interest and got rid of the airline. In the decades from the 1960s and 1970s, it provided top inflight service. By the early 1980s, however, it began a series of senior management changes that altered its character. Each new group wanted to put its own stamp on the airline, with the result that the carrier dropped continuously in service ratings and passenger preference from that point on. Carl Icahn, the arbitrageur, took over in 1985. After a bitter employee strike and a series of cutbacks in service and staff that he engineered, passenger ratings and load factors fell dramatically. He sold off landing rights to the most valuable international airport (Heathrow, London), and delayed orders for new airplanes. By 1992, he had to take the airline into bankruptcy. The airline was at death's door—out of money and with little passenger goodwill to help pull itself up by its bootstraps. The courts approved a reorganization plan that gave 45 percent of the airline to employees, who would also be represented on the Board of Directors. In turn, employees agreed to pay cuts, making them the largest owners of a now humbled TWA. But they had to wonder how long an airline could survive that was losing nearly $200 million every calendar quarter.

By the end of 1992, TWA had only $10 million in cash reserves. Even with delaying payments to suppliers, it could operate for only 60 days. For several years, it lost money even while competitors prospered. Poor employee morale, from a decade of management turnover and changing ownership, and reductions in inflight service levels greatly depressed passenger loyalty. Business fliers opted for other airlines. Leisure travelers selected TWA primarily when it offered the lowest fares, not a good way to make money. Its large and successful Getaway Vacations tour unit had dwindled dramatically and was on its last legs. It was forced to give away triple mileage points on all routes in a desperate effort to retain its base of business fliers who paid the highest fares. It offered more legroom in business class than most other competitors, but lowly coach passengers suffered through a series of cutbacks in the services they received. New management, operating under court supervision while in bankruptcy, looked for ways to cut costs. But service-level reductions would only further reduce preference for the carrier. A new approach had to be found. The common consensus among senior management at the time was to upgrade service levels above the competition and become the airline of choice for most travelers.

Situation Summary   An airline with a grand history now facing extinction. Falling revenue, extremely low cash reserves, and declining passenger loyalty paint a bleak future. Few on Wall Street expected the airline to survive very long after it emerged from its bankruptcy filing.

Approach to the Problem

I received a call from Robert Cozzi, Senior Vice President of Marketing and Planning at TWA, in late November of 1992. Could I please make a presentation to the senior management of TWA and its newly selected ad agency in mid-December in New York City? He wanted them to hear my assessment of the current competitive position of the airline and to offer recommendations about how to turn the airline around. I gave a quick yes.

Cozzi was a different sort of marketing guy. I had some contact when he was Vice President of Marketing at Eastern Airlines, but we worked more closely after he joined TWA in January 1986. An enthusiastic and bright individual who sought less personal glory than most marketing types, he developed high morale and loyalty among his staff. Although he had worked with Icahn earlier at TWA, he left the airline in January 1991 because he disagreed with Icahn's strategy of selling assets and cutting as many costs as possible. Cozzi believed, rightly, that TWA had to establish itself as an airline that people wanted to fly. In spite of Cozzi's quiet demeanor, he always demonstrated integrity and resolve, even more so when he left Icahn because he quit a job he truly liked. He was called back to the airline in October, 1992 by Glenn Zander and Robin Wilson, the new co-chairmen while it operated under the protection of bankruptcy laws.

The meeting took place in the Chrysler building in New York City at the corporate offices of the advertising agency, Backer Spielvogel Bates. It had just been given the assignment a month earlier. A highly respected large agency, Carl Spielvogel himself agreed to supervise the account. Cozzi convinced Spielvogel to take the account at a loss with the hope that a turnaround would lead to worldwide recognition and future profits when TWA became profitable again. With a couple of dozen people in attendance, the air was tense. Whatever decision was made would determine the future of an airline that everyone in the room truly loved and wanted to protect. At the time, most people at TWA and the ad agency believed that the airline had to change its penny-pinching ways and become a carrier with service standards above all industry competitors. An ad campaign had been planned to announce the new TWA and the benefits it now offered passengers. They would also continue their very generous frequent flier program to attract travelers, who would now notice the improvements and decide to choose TWA for future flights. The logic seemed right, but the conclusion was wrong.

I began my presentation by summarizing data charts from multiple studies that demonstrated TWA's current competitive position. The airline that once topped most lists on customer service dimensions now was last among competitors—American, United, Delta, and all foreign flag carriers. Food quality, helpfulness of inflight attendants, seat comfort and roominess, check-in, baggage delivery, inflight entertainment—just about everything imaginable had sunk below par. I presented a chart on "retained preference," an indicator of passenger loyalty that I had developed for our TravelTrak study that monitored airline competitiveness. It had fallen to dangerous levels (see Figure 11.1). Retained preference measures the percent of passengers who would choose to fly the same airline on the same route again, if they were given a chance to select any airline they wished. By the second quarter of 1992, only 37 percent of TWA's passengers on domestic routes would opt for TWA again, vs. about double that number (two-thirds to three-fourths) of those flying on its three largest competitors (American, Delta, and United). Internationally, the situation was the same. Data I presented showed that, although its seat pitch matched competitors, TWA was rated below all other airlines on seat comfort and roominess. A negative halo effect had taken over. If you don't like an airline, you don't like anything about it.

But they faced a much bigger problem than they had imagined. I hit hard on the fact that improvements in service levels win customers back very slowly. The first few times that passengers experience good flights on an airline with a poor image, they walk away saying to themselves, "Well, even the bad guys can do it right once in a while." It takes quite a few times of consistently

Figure 11.1   Domestic Retained Preference

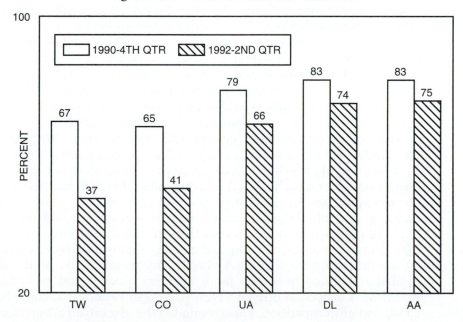

Source: NFO/PLOG Research, TravelTrak.

good flights to get rid of negative opinions to the point that passengers now believe that the improvements are real, not a fluke. And, even more time is required until positive word of mouth gets out. They would have a difficult time getting large numbers of fliers to take multiple flights so that opinion change could take place. I explained that the two quickest turnaround efforts I had seen that had achieved their stated goals were SAS and British Airways. SAS accomplished its goal in about two years at a cost of $400 to 500 million. British Airways did it faster, in about 18 months but at an expenditure of around $800 million. TWA had neither the time nor the money. They had only 60 days before they ran out of cash and would have to shut their doors. A different solution was necessary.

I suggested an approach that wouldn't cost much money, would have an immediate impact, and could potentially save the airline: Don't change business class. TWA was sufficiently competitive in that part of the cabin. Instead, concentrate on coach class. Although 80 percent of passengers fly coach, it produces only about half of the revenue on most flights. For this reason, most airlines devote little attention to service levels in coach. But TWA had an opportunity to stand out above the crowd and increase both revenue and profits. Why not give coach passengers the benefit they want most? The biggest and most frequent complaint in all surveys I have completed centers on lack of legroom. And, as flight length increases, the chorus of bitching rises. With a large international route structure, passenger discomfort becomes an even bigger issue. I added that Alaska Airlines provided one inch extra legroom on all flights and it got the highest marks for overall service of all major carriers. The one inch creates a positive halo effect for Alaska's meals, inflight crew service, and airport check-in. And, to drive the point home, I mentioned that the best remembered airline ad campaign that I had ever measured ran for only three months. Yet fliers spontaneously recalled it years later. Produced by Western Airlines (later acquired by Delta), it announced, "We give you three feet for your two legs," humorously pointing out that Western now offered 36-inch seat pitch—a couple of inches above the industry standard. I offered the conclusion that TWA, more than any other airline, could provide a benefit that ranked highest on passenger desires with very little cost. With low load factors, taking out a few seats in every airplane would not lead to lost revenue. That move would result in it carrying more passengers than before, producing greater revenue on each flight. I recommended that they increase seat pitch by one to two inches. Either change would be noticeable by passengers, but two inches would allow them to claim industry leadership. And they would not likely be matched by other carriers that did not want to lose capacity during high demand on early morning and evening flights used by business fliers, or during the peak summer period when leisure travelers take up the slack. TWA needed something to attract more travelers quickly, and no other strategy would work as well. It offered a clear passenger benefit that could be promoted against all competition. I also reminded the assembled group of my continuing belief: If you offer a benefit, brand it, and continually remind customers and prospects of that benefit in multiple ways. Otherwise your message can get lost in the clutter of too many competing ads.

With special support and encouragement from co-chairman Glenn Zander, Cozzi acted quickly and decisively. He accepted my recommendations and convinced the rest of senior management to stake TWA's future on offering more legroom. He put together a business plan that detailed both the benefits and costs of this change. His numbers accounted for the times when TWA would probably fly at full capacity and, therefore, would lose some revenue from the missing seats. But to make up for that shortfall, the airline would have to increase the number of passengers it carried by 0.5 percent not to lose ground. Any increase over that amount represented a gain. How many passengers was that? Only one extra person per flight! Cozzi also pointed out that reducing ticket prices provides no advantage in the marketplace. It would reduce TWA's revenue, and only provide a one- or two-day advantage over competitors that inevitably always match its fares after each new announcement.

After deciding to implement the idea, Cozzi enacted changes at lightning speed. He invited me back to the Chrysler Building headquarters of Backer Spielvogel Bates on January 11, 1993, less than a month after my first presentation. My task was to review, comment, and pass approval on the print ads prepared for the launch campaign and to look at the storyboards that outlined the television commercials that would be shot in a couple of weeks. This time, the conference room was packed—double rows on each side—with senior account executives for the agency from around the world and more TWA management levels than before. Although put together quickly, the campaign had all of the elements for success. Like good advertising, the message presented a clear benefit to passengers with good visuals to illustrate that TWA would remove seats from all airplanes in its fleet over the next 90 days to give passengers more room than on any other airline. And, in one brain storming session, Cozzi came up with one of the best branding identity tags that I have ever encountered. The new coach class service would be called *Comfort Class*. Those two words set it apart from all others. Easy to remember, it immediately conveyed the purpose of the new positioning strategy. The ad agency stole a page from Western Airlines' old theme line, "The only way to fly," and used a tag line that read, "The most comfortable way to fly," further reminding fliers that extra legroom means more comfort. My only comments focused on the need to take out some excess words in the copy to keep the message as simple as possible, and don't lose sight of the fact that people need to be reminded of the change over and over again. In other words, don't change or drop the campaign prematurely. But my biggest surprise came when I learned how much seat pitch would be added—an extra three to four inches, depending on the airplane model and the specific row in the airplane! I had hoped for two, but felt that even an inch would provide a benefit. If this much legroom didn't help in the marketplace, then my ideas were off track by 180 degrees!

Bob Cozzi rolled the dice on this change, betting TWA's future on a single concept. He used one million to take out the seats. He committed the remaining nine million of cash reserves to cover the ad campaign for the next 90 days, betting that revenue would pick up quickly if the campaign proved a success. TWA emerged from bankruptcy protection two days later (January 13). Cozzi worked at lightning speed. On January 15, the new ads broke in newspapers around the world. By mid-February, the television commercials came out. All ads, both print and TV, showed passengers enjoying greater roominess, enough to cross their legs comfortably while seated. And, the agency and TWA did a fabulous job in reminding fliers of the benefit they were now receiving. Boarding gate areas had signs promoting comfort class, and enplaning passengers saw a similar sign when they entered the cabin. Announcements by the inflight crew mentioned the new legroom and called it by name, and TWA's *Ambassador Magazine* followed the theme. TWA even added foot rests on routes to Europe and the Mideast from a supplier that offered them at low cost, a useful benefit on long-haul flights and a good visual reminder that the airline offered more legroom. Seldom had I seen a large client move so quickly and with such a sense of purpose. Everyone believed that this was the last chance to save a venerable old name in the aviation industry.

The Outcome

The results came in quickly and decisively. The popular press picked up on the change immediately with feature articles in major newspapers around the country. *Consumer Reports* writer Ed Perkins selected TWA as a preferred airline for the magazine and touted the advantages of Comfort Class in a series of syndicated columns in major newspapers around the country. *USA Today* devoted a four-column article with a large headline that began as follows:

> At the new Trans World Airlines, even its 6-foot-4 former owner will be able to cross his legs in coach class. A week after financier Carl Icahn turned TWA's control over to employees and creditors, the new management is pulling 10 to 40 seats from each of its 166 jets to give business class and coach fliers more room. . . . In an industry where most of the major players look pretty much alike, TWA will "provide a real difference in choice for consumers," says Salomon Bros. airline analyst Julius Maldutis.[1]

More important, passengers returned to TWA. Frequent flier gold and platinum card members began choosing the airline again because, if they couldn't get a hoped-for free upgrade on TWA, at least they would enjoy the comfort of greater room in Comfort Class. Other airlines couldn't match that benefit. Data from the ongoing TravelTrak study of Plog Research that monitors passenger reactions to airline services also reflected the improvement. Ratings on almost all items exceeded that of competitors—even in areas where

---

[1]Doug Carroll article in *USA Today*, January 15, 1993.

Figure 11.2   TWA Retained Preference (Percent of TWA Fliers Who Would Choose TWA Again)

Year	Retained Preference Percentage
1992	40%
1993	56
1994	63
1995	57
1996	51

no change had been made. The halo effect of greater seat comfort made the meals taste better, the inflight entertainment seem improved, airport check-in better, and baggage delivery more timely. The one dimension that did truly improve was friendliness/helpfulness of inflight attendants. Reacting to the rising chorus of passenger compliments, morale of inflight personnel shot up. The all important retained preference score jumped, as seen in Figure 11.2, which summarizes yearly averages for TWA over a five-year period. It points out that, starting from a low in 1992, the year of the second bankruptcy, retained preference improved significantly over the next two years. The reasons for the drop after that point coincide with other changes in the airline that will be reviewed shortly. This chart also hints at another point that was made earlier. Measures of customer loyalty never increase as fast as ratings of specific services since loyalties change more slowly. As pointed out previously, people often wonder if what they just experienced represent a true change or just a lucky happenstance.

Figure 11.3, also taken from TravelTrak, shows the striking change in legroom ratings of TWA vs. some of its select competitors. Starting at average ratings for legroom in 1992, it jumped nearly 30 points in 1993 and had triple the number of excellent marks of other carriers. On most dimensions, TWA had jumped from last to first place in passenger evaluations and loyalty, and only within a period of two calendar quarters. I had never seen that kind of a jump in ratings before in my research and consulting career.

Less important, but nice anyway, TWA gained recognition from a variety of sources. It received the Effie award for the most effective airline advertising

Figure 11.3   Percent Rating Excellent for Legroom in Coach

Year	TWA	Northwest	United	US Air
1992	15%	17%	13%	15%
1993	44	15	13	15
1994	46	14	12	14
1995	37	16	15	16
1996	27	16	13	17

in 1993 from the American Marketing Association and was written up as a case study in how to improve a company in the *Harvard Business Review*.[2] The authors followed that article with more detail in a book.[3]

Awards and recognition don't count for much unless revenues rise. As mentioned, that also happened—beyond expectations. Passenger loads increased quickly and the all important revenue per passenger mile shot up. Cozzi projected an extra $80 million in revenue for the year. Instead, it picked up more than $400 million. The airline increased its revenue by 10 percent in 1993, vs. 3 percent for the rest of the industry. Not only did more people select TWA, but revenue per passenger mile (RPMs in airline parlance) also increased. The carrier didn't have to sell as many deeply discounted seats to attract leisure travelers. An added surprise to most observers, it also picked up many more full-fare business fliers. In a July 21, 1997 letter to the president of another struggling carrier, Cozzi laid out a strong case that it should increase leg room to attract fliers. Cozzi attached a chart that showed the dramatic impact of increased legroom on yield. That chart, Figure 11.4, points out that yield for TWA increased above industry averages very quickly. The Western U.S. region director for SwissAir also told me at the time that TWA was stealing twenty-five or more passengers away from his airline on flights to Zurich, forcing the carrier to offer last minute discounts through travel agencies to fill space. This change surprised him because SwissAir maintained very high service standards in coach but offered the same tight seat pitch as all other competitors. My own research calculations indicated that TWA could charge $50 more per comfort class seat to Europe each way than competitors and still retain market share. Even economy passengers will pay more for comfort on long flights.

Unfortunately, comfort class became a victim of its own success. By mid-1994, TWA's high load factors convinced another new management team that the airline could gain additional revenue by stuffing seats back into airplanes on high-demand routes. They installed more seats on flights to Europe and the Mideast, where demand was exceptionally high, but planned to leave the space available on other routes. But their shortsightedness overlooked the fact that TWA no longer could promote its advantage. A "sometimes it's here and sometimes it's not" service undercuts all efforts at repositioning. The airline dropped references to comfort class in ads and other collateral materials, and inflight attendants no longer gave announcements pointing out the advantage on those flights that still had extra room. TWA now had no advantage in the marketplace. Worse yet, it had made a promise to fliers that it would provide more comfort and failed to live up to that promise. A bond of trust had been broken. Inflight attendants who had suffered through years of inferior service

---

[2]Adam M. Brandenburger and Barry J. Nalebuff, "The Right Game: Use Game Theory to Shape Strategy," *Harvard Business Review*, July–August 1995, pp. 57–73.
[3]Brandenburger and Nalebuff, *Co-opetition*, Doubleday, 1997.

Figure 11.4   Differences in TWA Yield Growth vs. Industry

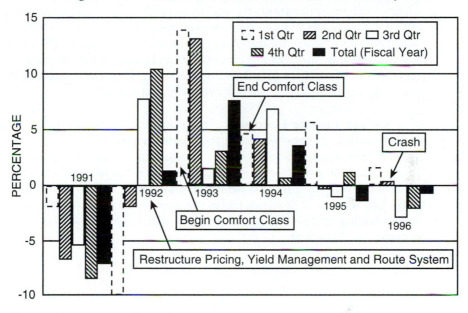

Gains or losses in TWA's yield are measured versus the industry's performance (i.e., TWA ± the difference from the industry).
Results: TWA's growth in yield, which translated into revenue, was dramatic during *Comfort Class,* and higher-yielding business traffic quickly dissipated with the end of the program.
Source: Robert Cozzi.

in the eyes of passengers flooded the headquarters offices of TWA with hundreds faxes from around the world to protest the change. The true count can never be known because the fax machines ran out of paper. But the damage had been done and the airline soon had to resort again to promoting its low fares, rather than its comfort advantage. Figure 11.4 also shows the decline after adding the seats into the fleet. Cozzi resigned again in protest over the change, recognizing that the airline had lost the basis of trust it had established with its customers. The service could not be reintroduced because fliers would not know when it might disappear once more. The crash of Flight 800 near Shirley, New York on July 17, 1996 was the final straw leading to the ultimate disappearance of a once great name. If TWA had continued with comfort class for the more than three years leading up to the crash, it might have developed sufficient goodwill with passengers to survive a horrible accident, as have American, United, Delta, and other major carriers.

The story has an epilogue. In 2000, American Airlines decided it would try to attract more passengers and garner greater loyalty by providing more legroom in coach. However, it never positioned the airline with a theme, such as TWA's "The most comfortable way to fly," nor did it brand the product, again like TWA's "Comfort Class." It simply announced in ads that American Airlines offers "more room throughout coach." Each ad seemed to have a different message about arriving more relaxed and refreshed or that "Your knees will thank you." Even though American took over a failing TWA in 2001, it did not use the opportunity to latch onto TWA's branding theme. As a result, American never came close to achieving the success of TWA, and cut back on the program in 2003. A good idea is probably lost forever.

Object Lesson Learned   An important customer benefit, positioned and branded properly—and promoted clearly in advertising—can turn around even a major company very quickly. In this situation, just about everything was done properly. But a "bean counter" mentality can kill a good idea by looking only at numbers on a piece of paper and forgetting that no company can survive if it doesn't provide a reason for customers to use its services. Adding extra seats on 15 percent of the fleet killed the concept for the remaining 85 percent.

CHAPTER TWELVE

A Delicate Balance for the Future of Travel

Ashleigh Brilliant, in one of his epigrams, wrote,

*My biggest problem is what to do about
All the things I can't do anything about.*[1]

Considering the ups and downs of travel during the past several decades, many may wonder why they became part of the industry and whether they should continue in their current jobs or choose a new field. Just when things seem to go right, something can happen to upset the equilibrium. But most will stay in their jobs for a variety of reasons. Inertia or lack of other applicable skills keeps some in place. The bigger reason, as pointed out in Chapter 1, is that it continues to be an exciting field that seduces many to remain even when the going gets tough.

Developing good marketing plans requires an understanding of some of the unfolding trends that will play out over the next decade or beyond. Opportunity and problems exist side by side and both will continue for the foreseeable future. Favorable demographic trends will push travel toward new heights. But, in a mature and highly competitive industry, it will be more difficult to find new ways to serve the market and to convince investors to back

---

[1]Ashleigh Brilliant, *I Have Abandoned My Search for Truth, and Am Now Looking for a Good Fantasy*, Woodbridge Publishing Company, Santa Barbara, CA: 1994.

novel and innovative business plans. This final section of the book looks at both good and the bad, the yin and yang, of what will impact the future of leisure travel. And it offers some suggestions about what is needed to make the travel experience more satisfying to encourage the growth of travel.

FAVORABLE UNFOLDING DEMOGRAPHICS—FOR NOW!

By now, practically everyone knows that demographic trends helped kick along the travel boom that occurred during the last half of the 1990s. As the population ages, increasing numbers of people have entered the empty nest stage or have retired. When children leave home, their parents enjoy new freedoms from responsibility that allow them to pursue long-ignored interests and take to the highways and skyways. Leisure travel has increased its ranking on the list of personal priorities for millions of people. Favorable demographic trends will continue for a while and then, gradually, the tide will turn. Figure 12.1 presents U.S. Census Bureau projections from the beginning of the 21st century through the first couple of decades. It points out the following:

- Population demographics work in favor of leisure travel during the first decade. The numbers of persons who fall into what I call the New Freedoms Group, labeled Mid-Late Careers by the Census Bureau, continue to expand dramatically. That group will grow by 28 percent. The Mature Explorers segment (a.k.a. Retirees) increases considerably (13 percent) for a combined total more than 119 million adults who are in their active travel years. These statistics point to an expanding future for travel during this time, barring other problems that will be discussed shortly.

- During the next decade, 2010 to 2020, the boomer bulge continues to alter the curve. Note that the Mature Explorer segment (45 to 64 years)

Figure 12.1   Population Shift by Age (in millions)

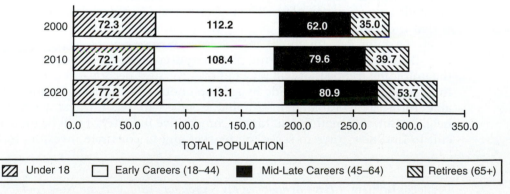

Source: U.S. Statistical Abstract, 2001.

increases by only 1.3 million during that decade while the Mature Explorers group jumps by 14 million.

- What happens next has received little notice from those who make long-term business decisions. What the Census Bureau calls the Early Careers group (18 to 44 years) remains relatively flat during this period. Its numbers increase by only one million between 2000 and 2020. As a result, travel could face a slowdown in growth by about the middle of the third decade (2025) as fewer younger people enter the empty nest stage. Travel will have to compete more ferociously to ensure that it stays on a growth path.

An aging population, in the U.S. and elsewhere in the world, will also impact travel in other ways. Some destinations will benefit, while others face declining markets. Older people have different interests than young people and, as the group of seniors grows, it will begin to influence the market in subtle ways. Figure 12.2 presents a list of items selected from a longer list in which travelers indicated the activities they pursued on their last vacation, separated by age groups. Several findings are apparent in these data. Specifically,

Destinations/venues that will benefit from an aging population:

- Destinations with cultural attractions (historic sites/churches; art museums/galleries; old homes/mansions)
- Cruises, tour programs, inclusive package vacations
- Gambling cities and casino locations
- Upscale restaurants and entertainment
- Family gatherings/events/reunions

Figure 12.2 Activities on Leisure Trips, Past Year (by Age Groups)

	Under 35	35–44 Yrs.	45–54 Yrs.	55–64 Yrs.	65+
Shopping	61%	60%	61%	61%	54%
Attending family event	51	49	48	55	59
Visited historic sites/churches	26	33	40	44	37
Fine dining	29	33	36	41	38
Visited theme park	36	37	24	17	11
Visited art museums/galleries	21	26	28	31	27
Visited casino/gambled	20	20	25	30	29
Night clubs/stage shows	19	16	15	17	12
Camping	18	19	16	11	8
Hiking/backpacking	12	11	11	6	3
Visited old homes/mansions	11	15	20	23	19

Source: NFO/PLOG Research, American Traveler Survey.

These results suggest that places of great historic interest can expect more visitors as the population continues to age. Thus, Europe (especially the United Kingdom), New England, and parts of the Old South in the U.S. should benefit from a rise in tourism. Similarly, Las Vegas, Atlantic City, and Indian casinos also show a potential for considerable growth. Cruise lines, tour companies, and other travel programs that provide more cocoon experiences will grow as travelers seek to cut down on hassles and to relax more completely wherever they go. And, as people get older, they place a greater emphasis on staying in close contact with family and friends and there will be more VFR trips. Finally, major cities that have great restaurants and outstanding entertainment will attract more travelers.

Destinations/activities that will suffer from an aging population:

- Theme parks
- Hard adventure travel
- Nighttime entertainment that focuses on young audiences
- Touristy places

The message is clear that theme parks must reinvent themselves in some manner to serve an aging population because of a lack of growth in the number of young persons, especially those with families. And, obviously, more rigorous kinds of adventure travel will take a hit. Older groups take less active vacations. And, youth-oriented nighttime entertainment will suffer from the fact that entertainment choices tend to change after the age of 35 and become somewhat more conventional in form. Finally, places that have grown old and tired (touristy) and crowded will have a difficult time increasing their tourism base. As travelers continue to become more experienced, they also become more sophisticated in their choices.

Shopping, the most common activity for all groups, will hold up well. It will benefit from the fact that older travelers who are at the peak of their earnings careers and have built up good equity can afford to spend more. They also shop for more people—themselves, children, grandchildren, and other relatives.

Demographics will subtly create another set of winners and losers. Figure 12.3 presents information on future plans of travelers for their next trip, again separated by age groups. It indicates that, as people age, they tend to

Figure 12.3   Type of Future Trips Will Take (by Age Groups)

	Under 35	35–44 Yrs.	45–54 Yrs.	55–64 Yrs.	65+
Go back to same destination	47%	47%	45%	52%	55%
Go to similar destination	3	2	2	2	2
Go to new/different destination	50	51	53	46	43

Source: NFO/PLOG Research, American Traveler Survey.

select *fewer new destinations*. More often they plan to return to the same place they visited on their last leisure trip. The implication of this finding is straightforward: There will be less brand switching in the future (changing of locations selected for future trips). Therefore, *destinations that deliver the most satisfying travel experiences will have the best opportunity to grow. Those that deliver marginal experiences will suffer declines*. Although this statement may seem obvious, it emphasizes a point made earlier. Too many destinations are currently in a state of decline. They don't deliver high levels of satisfaction to their visitors, who, in turn, could provide favorable word-of-mouth advertising. Those places that control the travel experience to a greater degree will not have to allocate the same amount of marketing and sales dollars in order to stay competitive. Achieving that goal should begin now or the consequences will become painfully evident sooner than most destinations might imagine. The ten to one rule (Chapter 7) points out the difficulties of turning around a destination that has allowed a negative image to develop over time.

THE BEST MARKETS TO TARGET FOR GROWTH

Destinations that want to increase tourism need to consider the growth potential of markets throughout the world. Data presented thus far indicate that leisure travel within and outbound from the United States will continue on a growth path for at least the first couple of decades of the 21st century. The U.S. is the largest travel market in the world and will retain that status for the foreseeable future. However, other countries show stronger growth potential. This conclusion comes from a detailed analysis of data from the World Tourism Organization (WTO) in Madrid, Spain by Dr. Douglas Frechtling. A respected researcher and professor at George Washington University, he analyzed 20 countries in terms of their long haul growth potential. He took into account past travel trends, population demographics, income growth, and a number of other factors to develop the information contained in Figure 12.4. The analysis, completed in 1998, is still current at the time of this writing, he indicates. Several conclusions stand out in this chart:

- The United Kingdom, Germany, France, and Japan, in that order, show the greatest potential for growth in percentage increase and the number of new tourists they will contribute to world markets in the first decade of the 21st century.

- Canada, Brazil, Spain, and Taiwan also show high percentage increases. The biggest jump appears for South Korea, but its smaller population base makes it a lesser player in this chart.

- No country shows a decrease, but the differences are dramatic. Venezuela provides few tourists and dim prospects for contributing to world tourism. Sweden follows the same path to some degree.

Figure 12.4   Long-Haul Tourist Volumes Generated by 20 Countries

Countries	1998 # Long-Haul Visitors (millions)	1989–1998 Annual Growth Rate	1998–2010 # Long-Haul Visitors (millions)	Total Growth of Long-Haul Visitors (millions)	1998–2010 % Total Growth
United States	32.3	6%	56.0	24.0	74%
Japan	12.4	5	20.0	7.8	63
United Kingdom	10.9	2	29.0	19.0	174
Germany	7.7	10	17.0	9.2	120
France	6.8	8	16.0	8.7	113
Canada	4.8	7	8.3	3.5	73
Italy	3.4	7	4.9	1.5	44
Australia	3.1	7	5.4	2.3	74
Brazil	2.1	6	4.3	2.2	105
Netherlands	2.1	7	3.9	1.9	91
Isreal	2.0	10	3.2	1.2	60
Spain	1.8	6	3.6	1.8	100
Switzerland	1.6	4	2.2	0.7	47
Taiwan	1.4	24	3.2	1.8	129
Argentina	1.2	4	1.8	0.6	50
Mexico	1.1	6	2.1	1.0	91
Sweden	0.9	7	1.1	0.2	22
Belgium	0.9	3	1.2	0.4	44
South Korea	0.7	8	2.3	1.5	214
Venezuela	0.7	3	0.8	0.1	14

Source: Projections by Dr. Douglass Frechtling.

Other factors should also be considered by destinations wanting to attract tourists from other countries. First, the number of vacation days available determines the degree to which tourists can take extended vacation trips that make long-haul travel possible. Of the major industrialized nations, according to WTO data,[2] U.S. workers have the fewest days available, about 12. Contrast that with the more than 40 days given to workers in Italy, 36 in France, 35 in Germany, and about 28 in Great Britain. Brazil provides 34 days vacation for its workers, on average, and Canada 25. The lowest number on the list of major countries, other than the U.S., is Japan at 25.

Another factor also comes into play in deciding which countries contribute the best tourists. Specifically, the amount of spending on trips by visitors. From various studies I have conducted over the years, I have developed a rank ordering of those that spend freely vs. those that spend less:

---

[2]World Tourism Organization, summarized in *BusinessWeek,* August 26, 2002, p. 142.

Above Average Spenders

Germans

Italians

Brazilians

Average or Slightly Above Average Spenders

English

Americans

Japanese

Below Average Spenders

Australians

French

Canadians

This list may seem surprising, but it has a basis in fact. Germans, Italians, and tourists from Brazil generally choose a better class of hotel and buy more entertainment and other add-ons to their trips. Although Brazil has considerable poverty, those who can afford to travel often do it in style. They like to purchase expensive electronic equipment not available in Brazil when they visit other countries. It may seem surprising that the Japanese do not belong in the top category of this list, but most still travel on packaged trips. Even their shopping tends to be controlled to some degree by interrelated Japanese firms. Australians are very smart travelers. Savvy about how to get travel good travel bargains, they make their money go farther at destinations. In contrast, Canadians have suffered for years from a weak Canadian dollar, making travel an expensive proposition when they leave home. Thus, they have less to spend.

Combining information from several sources suggests that tourists from Germany, Italy, and Brazil should measure high on the lists of those tourism bureaus that want to attract more international visitors. Residents in each country have an abundance of vacation days available and show strong potential for tourism growth. Germans have high incomes, and Italians and Brazilians who can afford international travel spend more willingly than most groups. The English should be considered because of the very high potential for growth exhibited and the fact that they spend at relatively good (average) levels. Contrary to the recommendations of many, the Japanese do not place high on the prospect list. Although they demonstrate relatively good growth potential and their spending habits measure at least at average, cultural issues can make this a difficult market. They change their habits slowly, and the courting process can take years and require a sizeable marketing investment before satisfactory results appear. And, as the number of visitors grows, ethnic operators may take over and direct them to Japanese owned hotels and shops.

Also important to consider, if political or economic instability appears, they stop traveling to that particular region more quickly than tourists from most countries. Hawaii faced that problem during the Gulf War in 1991, and Asian nations experienced a similar dramatic dropoff in arrivals during the Asian economic crisis of the mid-1990s. The main point of this brief section, however, is to provide background information for tourism officials to do their own planning and target the best international tourists for their locales.

TERRORISM, POLITICAL INSTABILITY, AND DISEASE OUTBREAKS

The horrendous terrorist attacks on New York City and Washington, D.C. on September 11, 2001, the Gulf War in 2003, and the outbreak of severe acute respiratory syndrome (SARS), also in 2003, demonstrate dramatically how these kinds of events can devastate the travel market. Close to 10 million tourism related jobs were lost worldwide, some airlines went into bankruptcy or required government help to survive, and the travel patterns of people changed significantly. Events throughout the world impact the ebb and flow of tourism dramatically, and these are always unpredictable. When an unfortunate event occurs, tourists vote with their feet. They cancel travel plans. Airplanes have been bombed by terrorists and tourists executed in far away lands. These events had a short-term impact, primarily in the region where they occurred. But 9-11 has had long-term implications.

Countering this trend, fortunately for those in the industry, leisure travel continues to rank high on the list of priorities in people's lives. Travel by Americans did not decrease in 2001 after 9-11. It increased. But people got into the family car, camper, or SUV and drove rather than taking to the skies. And they went to closer destinations and emphasized visits to friends and relatives more than in the past. This fact is confirmed by data from NFO/Plog Research's annual American Traveler Survey and U.S. government statistics, which indicate that gasoline sales increased in the latter part of 2001 and into 2002. People were driving to more destinations and taking more trips but of shorter duration. The important point, however, is that this finding demonstrates that *leisure travel is now considered an essential part of most people's lives and will continue that role for the foreseeable future!* But the fortunes of various travel providers and destinations will wax and wane depending on these unforeseen circumstances.

The future success of leisure travel ultimately depends on a healthy airline industry. That possibility will remain problematic for some time. From the beginning of commercial aviation in the 1920s until the turn of this century, the airline industry has suffered so many ups and downs that it made only meager profits. Since the 9-11 attacks, it has lost close to 30 billion dollars. It could take a couple of decades of profitable operations to recover those losses. Low-cost airlines, especially new startups, will continue to put revenue and profit pressures on major carriers that are locked into high-cost labor contracts for years to come. Bankruptcy filings typically reduce labor expenses by

10 to 15 percent, not the 30 to 40 percent that is required to stay competitive. But the biggest impediment to air travel continues to be the hassles associated with taking an air trip. The difficulties of getting through airport security, the discomforts of cramped flights, and the impersonal nature of air travel combine to reduce the felt need to go to places that only can be reached by air. Unless some of these problems can be ameliorated, every segment of the industry that depends on air travel will suffer. The beneficiaries will be nearby destinations and the hotels, restaurants, and attractions located at those places that can be reached easily by auto from major population centers. The challenges loom large. It will take innovative marketing ideas and thinking to ensure a great future for the industry.

TRAVEL AGENTS: MUCH MALIGNED AND MUCH NEEDED!

Travel agencies grew up in concert with airlines. For decades the two worked together to form an effective distribution system. Each needed the other. Agencies earned most of their revenue from commissions on airline tickets, selling about two-thirds of the total, with the remainder mostly accounted for by airline ticket offices and 800 reservations numbers of airlines. In turn, airlines recognized that travel agencies were an effective way to sell tickets because their own city ticket offices lost money. But the relationship also had its ups and downs. Beginning in the 1970s, travel agency owners began a concerted effort to get the commissions above five percent level offered at the time. They succeeded, with levels going to 10 percent and sometimes higher with commission overrides (incentives for increasing volume with an airline or other travel supplier). But two dramatic events during the decade of the 1990s changed the travel distribution system in ways that will continue to unfold for years to come. The first came like a bombshell out of the night—the setting of commission cuts, followed closely by commission caps. The second was the more gradual, but its impact ultimately will be even greater—the growth of the Internet as a source for travel information and to book trips. Each changed travel distribution forever. This topic is important because every marketing director must make a decision as to whether or not to commit promotional dollars to target travel agencies.

In February 1995, Delta Air Lines took the first step, a bold and drastic move to lower its costs of doing business. It capped domestic commissions paid to travel agents at $25 one way, $50 roundtrip on all flights within the U.S. It came to the conclusion that travel agents mostly took orders from customers who had already made up their minds about the choice of carriers for their upcoming trips. If travel agents have little influence over airline choice, Delta reasoned, why reward them with high commissions? The outcry from travel agents was instantaneous and loud. Many industry observers predicted that Delta would suffer an immediate downturn in passenger bookings as agents stopped recommending the airline. But that didn't happen. Business

travelers continued to choose Delta because it met their schedule requirements or from a loyalty to its frequent flier program. Leisure travelers have little loyalty, however. Most often they buy the lowest-priced tickets. Noting that
Delta didn't suffer as predicted, other carriers quickly followed its lead. United
Airlines took the next step, cutting base commission levels on U.S. and international flights to eight percent in September 1997. Following a series of
sequential reductions by major U.S. and international carriers, domestic and
international base pay to travel agencies fell to zero percent by March 2002.

The second shoe to drop has been more gradual—the growth of the Internet. As a useful tool for planning and booking trips, it came together in the
early 1990s. Some forecasters at the time predicted that it would command up
to 40 percent of all bookings by 1995. It didn't come close. Near the end of the
decade, airlines typically reported that about 4 percent of their revenue came
from the Internet, with hotels and rental cars around 2 percent. But its pene-
tration has accelerated since then. At the time of this writing, about half of
leisure travelers use the Internet to plan some of their trips, with about one
out of five booking air travel, hotels, and/or rental cars. The Internet accounts
for 7 percent of hotel revenues[3] and about 10 percent of airline bookings.
Leisure travelers look to it for help more than business travelers, contrary to
early predictions, but growth in usage has also slowed down. The Internet, like
much else in travel, is showing signs of maturity. It will continue its uphill
march, but at a slower rate than in the past. The Internet has stolen revenue
from travel agencies as more people go to discount sites, such as Expedia and
Travelocity, to buy tickets, hotel rooms, and rental cars. And the airlines have
jumped into the fray, establishing their own sites and aggressively courting
travelers with deals available only through their own Web sites or on the
airline-owned Orbitz site.

This double whammy forced a large number of travel agencies to close
their doors. With no commissions and a dwindling number of customers, they
could not support their costs even when they charge clients fees for their services. The high point in the number of full-service travel agency locations in
the U.S. came in September 1997, when the total reached 33,775, according to
the Airlines Reporting Corporation.[4] By January 2003, that number had
shrunk to around 25,000. It could ultimately drop to around 22,000, about the
same number as car dealers in the U.S. But, contrary to many predictions,
travel agencies will not disappear from the scene. Smart and battle-hardened
owners are learning how to survive in a tough environment and, surprisingly,
a few report that they now make more money than the ever did in the past.
And, some have started to grow again. They will survive for a very important
reason: Travelers need their services—some travelers most of the time and

---

[3]Article by Ted C. Fishman in *Worth Magazine*, July/August 2002, pp. 23–24.
[4]Confirmed in telephone conversation November 19, 2002 with Allan Muten, Director
of Corporate Communications, Airlines Reporting Corporation (ARC).

most travelers some of the time. The limitations of the Internet become apparent to anyone who uses it regularly to plan trips or purchase tickets. Planning a leisure trip through the Internet poses special problems. Since almost every site is sponsored by a destination, the information provided tends to be biased, presenting all the glories of a destination and its travel partners (hotels, tour and package companies). The prospective leisure traveler must sort out the wheat from the chaff, truth from hype, and try to determine what information represents a fair and accurate picture of the destination and its facilities. Comparing destinations requires searching multiple sites, a time-consuming process. Searching for the best air fares and hotel room rates presents a similar challenge. Surprisingly, the major travel sites (Expedia, Travelocity, Orbitz, etc.) offer different deals on air fares and hotel rates for the same products. To get the best price, a traveler must wade through the various sites and search multiple options about departure times, dates, and airlines. In contrast, a good travel agency has the tools to handle these tasks quickly, easily, and efficiently. They have more powerful search engines tied into bigger databases that can come up with the most competitive fares and hotel rates very quickly. That's worth a fee to a large number of people, especially since travel agencies seldom lose contests with the Web about which can locate the best airfares.

   To predict the end of the travel agency business ignores a couple of historic facts. First, larger agencies have recognized the opportunity provided by the depressed values to acquire smaller agencies that serve geographic areas or niche markets they don't currently cover. As their volumes expand, they can achieve greater economies of scale to increase their profits and give them more staying power when they face difficult times. They can also negotiate hidden commissions with airlines if they increase their volume of bookings on a preferred carrier. This often unreported event has increased in spite of the publicly stated airline zero commission policies. The strong will survive and prosper; the weak will go away and make the market more productive for those still around. Second, most forecasters forget the simple fact that new technology often works side by side with old technology, rather than replacing it. Consider faxing. When businesses universally placed fax machines in their offices, I thought Federal Express (FedEx) would face a difficult fight for survival. Instead, FedEx has grown, even as every business and many homes now possess fax machines. Next, the Internet appeared with its very handy e-mail capabilities. Cheaper, faster, and more convenient than faxing, I wondered if this was the day that faxing would disappear. Wrong again. All three forms of communication exist side by side—faxing, FedEx, and e-mail. And, add video-conferencing to this array since the technology is now relatively cheap, easy to use, and reliable. Each serves a purpose. The number of travel agencies may continue to decline slightly for several years, but they will not disappear. To survive, they must become smarter. More knowledgeable agents, bigger and better databases of travel information on destinations (such as the Weissmann Reports), and continually improving search engines that can access all sites quickly are some of the keys to a healthier future. And agencies have also learned to push products better. Most have learned to change their product mix and sell a greater portion of high-commission items like cruises, tours, and packages. Surprisingly, travel agencies can handle the future better than the companies that tried to put them out of business—the airlines. Nonunionized and with greater freedom to change their business models, agencies have not incurred the huge losses of major airlines in the years following September 11, 2001.

The question still needs to be addressed as to whether or not travel agents can move business or are they just order takers for people who have already made up their minds. The answer is yes and no. In many situations, clients direct them to book a preferred airline or hotel or give a departure schedule or hotel location near to appointments that limit choice. In these situations, they simply fulfill orders. But, especially for leisure travel, situations frequently exist where their advice is welcomed and their recommendations followed. I have conducted numerous focus groups with travel agents and multiple quantitative studies that address this question. The results usually come out the same. Travel agents exert the greatest influence early and late in the trip planning process. When travelers begin to think about where to go next or what kind of a trip to take, they seek advice and help. And, when they have made those decisions, they now want help about how to get there, where to stay, and what to do while there. They may use a variety of sources, including friends and relatives to help make those decisions, but travel agents often become a critical part of the mix. A simple little example of the power of agents sticks in my mind. Gary Marshall, who was Vice President of Marketing, North America for Jet Set Vacations, told me a story of how he moved a considerable amount of excess inventory in a short period of time. Jet Set sells a variety of vacation packages and excess airline inventory through travel agencies, with a focus on the South Pacific. Air New Zealand had called because they hadn't sold a sufficient amount of inventory deposited with Jet Set and they were concerned that some empty seats would go unused on upcoming flights. Gary put out a fax to a targeted group of travel agencies, offering Air New Zealand flights at a discount price. The seats sold out quickly. But, unrecognized by the agents, those seats were already available in the promotion book given to them earlier by Jet Set, and at a lower price! That may sound like a "for shame" on agents for not selling these seats with the deeper discount, but it points to a central problem in dealing with the travel agency community. Each day they receive more offers through the mail, faxes, e-mails, and sales calls than they can possibly review. A book of offers, as Jet Set had presented, probably received only a casual review in most travel agencies because it arrived in the overloaded daily mail. It did not require immediate attention. In contrast, the special fax met the criteria of a good advertising approach presented earlier. The message was relevant, presented clearly and simply, and it invited immediate action. The evolutionary-based sensory scanning mechanisms contributed to the fact that agents recognized the offer in the midst of all the other materials they received daily. The moral of this story is simple: Airlines, and most hotel chains, have failed to make their messages stand out in the minds of travel agents. Selling basically the same product at the same price, airlines have given little reason for travel agents to make recommendations. But when a more viable product is presented, whether based on superior service and quality or lower price, agents will take notice and move market share. The travel agency community will not disappear, regardless of the words of doomsayers. Destinations, hotels, cruise lines, tour operators, and even airlines should always consider that they need effective distribution systems. And, every distribution method costs dollars to maintain, even airline-sponsored Internet sites. Travel agents can control a meaningful amount of market share under the right conditions. Pity the poor airlines that could have turned to travel agents to help pull them out of their tailspin of falling revenues after the 9-11 disaster. However, the soured relationship means that they have to find a way to right themselves on their own with little sympathy from their former partners.

CHAPTER THIRTEEN

Leisure Travel—Now More Important Than Ever

The relationship between business and leisure travel has changed over time. After World War II, travel providers focused heavily on the leisure market, recognizing that it offered the greatest chance for growth since the majority of the adult population had never taken a trip by air. In time, however, the corporate market began to receive more attention because of the frequent number of trips taken by business travelers and the loyalty they demonstrated to suppliers after the introduction of loyalty programs. Now the emphasis has swung back again. For many companies, the leisure market represents the greatest potential for future growth opportunities.

BUSINESS TRAVEL: NO LONGER THE BIG KID ON THE BLOCK!

It seems that a lot of people love the 80-20 rule. They build business plans on the formula. They confidently predict the future because previous history indicates that the rule has withstood the test of time. Investors ante up billions of dollars to help companies take advantage of growth opportunities that seem almost certain, based on assumptions from the rule. Travel, like other industries, has also believed in the far-reaching conclusions of this idea. Since it has implications for the future of many aspects of travel, it is worthwhile to digress briefly to review the changing relationship between business travel and the leisure market.

In brief, the rule states that 80 percent of a company's revenues come from 20 percent of its clients. The clear implication, then, is to identify this important segment, capture it, and treat its members well to make certain they become loyal customers. For travel, the obvious choice is frequent business fliers (i.e., those who take five or more business trips a year). To gain their loyalty, airlines and hotels have designed rich frequent flier programs that not only earn points for miles flown (or nights at hotels) but also extra perks. These include early boarding at airports, upgrades to the business class cabin or concierge floors (at hotels) depending on space availability, double or triple mileage points, special call-in numbers for reservations, and much more. But it comes with a catch. Business travelers have traditionally paid a premium, especially for their airline seats. Air fares for business travelers typically were two to three times the cost of a leisure ticket, and up to six times higher than the lowest discounted ticket within months after September 11, 2001. Airlines justified this differential on the basis that they built their airlines around the needs of business travelers. Inventory is held to accommodate last-minute bookings by business travelers, flight schedules conform to business requirements (a heavy loading of early morning and evening departures), and most flights operate seven days a week when demand would only justify five- or six-day schedules. The complex hub and spoke system that allows fliers to get to most places with minimum layover time when connecting flights are required also serves their needs. For these privileges, business fliers should pay a premium, the airlines suggest. Save the pricey seats for business fliers and fill in the rest with discount leisure travelers. Airlines viewed this as a win-win situation. Business travelers got what they wanted most—an airline built to serve their needs. And leisure travelers got what they wanted most—cheap seats to destinations around the world. Sophisticated software programs helped the airlines determine times of peak demand to control their pricing. For the most part, individual business fliers complied. Many complained about the differential in pricing between leisure and business fares, but they continued to fly whenever the demands of business took them out of town. They showed strong loyalty to airline frequent flier programs. To protect their gold or platinum card status and the many perquisites that this provides, they flew preferred carriers whenever possible, even if the schedules were less convenient. They would even pay higher prices for specific flight segments or endure multiple stopovers when double or triple mileage points were offered on certain routes, including driving to more distant airports to take advantage of double and triple mileage bonus offers. That surprising behavior occurred at all levels in companies. I can remember one senior executive in a focus group I conducted who lived in the San Fernando Valley and commuted daily between the Valley and San Francisco. His salary was well over $300,000 and the point totals in his preferred airline program would already take him, his family, and friends around the world first class. But he added an hour and a half to his schedule every day (45 minutes each way) by driving to Los Angeles International Airport, rather than flying out of nearby Burbank/Hollywood Airport, to gain the extra mileage points available on a special promotion at that time.

But a funny thing happened on the way to the twenty-first century. As the economy softened toward the latter part of the 1990s, CEOs and CFOs began to look more closely at new ways to control costs and contribute more to the bottom line to continue on a growth curve and keep stockholders happy. Many companies had already cut back on spending for information technology, reduced the size of annual salary increases, and cut payrolls dramatically. But one area escaped a close review throughout most of this period—business travel. In the past, CEOs and CFOs complained the most about what they viewed as excessively high travel costs. In their view, air travel was the only industry in which high-volume users (large companies) paid more than low-volume users (individual leisure travelers). In all other relationships, they received substantial discounts for volume purchases. In fact, big companies did get preferential treatment—negotiated discounts for guaranteed volumes of business, but not to the degree they desired. The complaints of senior executives largely fell on the deaf ears of two inattentive audiences. The airlines, with history on their side, believed that business travel was such an integral part of everyday business operations that companies would not be able to cut back on travel. And, when companies tried to clamp down to control costs, business fliers themselves would often violate the rules and fly when they wanted to and on the airlines of their choice to build up their frequent flier mileage totals. They simply stated that the cheaper (not desired) flights were booked, or didn't allow them to reach their destinations on time. And what lowly travel manager, buried deep in the bowels of a company, could stand up to a senior vice president of marketing or one of the corporate division heads to enforce a new rule that required flying coach instead of business class? Large companies would negotiate reduced rates with major airlines, hotel chains, and rental car companies in return for guaranteed volumes of revenue, but companies sometimes had difficulty meeting their commitments because of the number of people who worked outside the rules.

Advancing technology, however, ultimately gave CEOs and CFOs new tools to control travel costs. Beginning in the 1970s, I conducted studies for the airlines and related travel suppliers about every five years, looking at the potential impact of new technologies on travel demand. The primary questions were generally similar: Would new forms of communication through technology reduce business travel? For a couple of decades, the answer always came out the same. No, the need for in-person meetings had not diminished and advancing technologies had not proved useful as a travel substitute. Video conferencing during this period was expensive, difficult to operate, and seemed stilted and impersonal. Talk of videophones popped up from time to time, but the technology never reached a level of low cost, reliability, and universal acceptance. Then important changes were noted in the 1995 Plog Research study, which looked at the market five years into the future (i.e., to the year 2000). Videoconferencing now had achieved critical mass. With dramatically lowered costs for installation and an ease of operation that allowed novices to operate it rather than dedicated technicians, many large companies were implementing plans to reduce the need for on-site technical reviews of their own operations.

And the rapid growth of the Internet, which began to expand exponentially around that time, provided a means for sales personnel to keep in touch with clients more frequently without having to schedule as many in-person visits.

The biggest benefit from technology, however, came from an unanticipated source: New travel management software allowed companies to control travel expenses in a way not possible in the past. Individual travelers, based on their own personal choices, could no longer bypass company policies. The new software required all corporate travelers to book through an Intranet system that ensured that they chose airlines and hotels where corporate discounts had been negotiated. It became virtually impossible to get around the system, even for senior executives. To choose something not recommended required approval of someone more senior in the organization, and lots of paperwork. And the number of trips authorized declined, again because the advanced software programs made it more difficult to justify sudden trips. With these control procedures, a lot of companies discovered that they could make a 10 percent pretax contribution to profits by enforcing and controlling travel costs, and without impairing the company's competitive position in the marketplace. How? The math is rather straightforward. Travel costs in a well-managed program can be reduced by about a third over a program that had previously received only loose oversight. Consider a company with annual revenues of $100 million. Travel expenses typically consume 2 to 4 percent of corporate revenues. Using an average of 3 percent in travel costs, a one-third reduction would produce savings of $1 million. Considering the fact that most companies feel comfortable if they can make a 10 percent profit ($10 million), that additional $1 million adds 10 percent profit to the bottom line. And that contribution will continue in the future, year after year. It's difficult for any company to grow a business by 10 percent in any single year, in terms of new profits. The savings come from negotiating deep discounts with travel suppliers, and then ensuring that corporate travelers conform to new booking and travel policies by using the new software to control how they make reservations. And what was once a powerless and relatively ineffective group of people, corporate travel managers, has now achieved a new level of importance and status in companies. Top management, recognizing their potential contribution to profits, has elevated them to a higher level of responsibility and given them greater power and authority to do their jobs. In a few companies, they even have direct access to the CEO. Earl Foster left travel management at Hewlett Packard to take over the travel department at Seagram's (liquor, Universal Studios, and theme parks) with the assurance of direct line of communication to CEO, Edgar Bronfman, Jr.

THE FUTURE WILL BE DIFFERENT

Having found a new way to reduce travel expenses through travel management software, companies don't plan to let up in the future. Corporate travelers have learned that they must adapt or face the wrath of senior management. CEOs and CFOs will continue to push hard for profits in good times and bad. Airlines, hotels, rental car companies, and others that hope for a return to the good old days will have a long wait. Corporate travel will increase, but at more modest rates than in the past. And business fliers will not offer the lucrative returns that they once did. Not only will more travel conform to the negotiated rates offered by travel suppliers, but also discount airlines have become a larger part of the mix. In late 2002, Delta Airlines decided to face the music and dance. It stated that discount carriers accounted for 22 percent of corporate travel in the U.S. and projected it to grow to 30 to 40 percent by 2010.[1] As a result, in 2003 it started a separate low cost "airline within an airline," called *Song*, to compete with Southwest, JetBlue, and Air-Tran Airways.[2] (Note: On some important routes in Great Britain, low-cost carriers already have achieved 40 percent share.) Delta, and other major carriers, had already tried this route in the past (Delta Express—still flying, but at a reduced level; Continental Lite, etc.). However, the majors can't lower their costs to those of discount airlines or simplify their operations in the same way. But pilots for the new Delta continue to get higher wages than pilots on discount carriers. And, when major carriers attempt to operate low-cost carriers with a lower wage structure, the experiments typically lead to organizational problems because of the disparity in wages between two similar operations within the same company. Labor unions fear the expansion of the low-wage carrier at the expense of its higher-priced sister airline. And the obvious status problems resulting from different salary structures lead to friction up and down the ranks of employees of both lines. Also, all negotiated wage reductions always "snap-back" provisions (i.e., salaries will return to previous levels when an airline moves into profitability again in the future). That clause greatly reduces the possibility of developing a long-term plan for stability and growth.

Airlines have also experimented a number of times in the past with new fare structures designed to protect revenue and yield while giving the appearance of a more rational relationship between business and leisure fares. American's Value Pricing approach, rolled out in 1992, reduced the number of fares available but was quickly dropped because it cost the carrier market share as competitors matched or undercut these fares. American led the way again on November 14, 2002, when it slashed walk-up coach seats by up to 40 percent on some routes and raised restricted leisure fares in an experiment to lure back business travelers. That approach was also duplicated by other large airlines. But most of these attempts at salvation do not address the more pressing need to lower operating costs dramatically in order to gain parity with discount carriers. The airlines have such a poor record of profitability that they have been unable to create a reserve of funds to help them through difficult times. The Air Transport Association (ATA) has kept records on profitability since 1947. It

---

[1]Article by Martha Brannigan and Nicole Harris, *Wall Street Journal*, November 15, 2002, p. B6.
[2]Article by Nicole Harris, *Wall Street Journal*, November 21, 2002, p. D3.

points out that U.S. scheduled airlines have made only 0.1 percent profits during that entire time.[3] Although the heaviest losses were in 2001, 2002, and 2003, the industry recorded red ink of $2.5 billion from 1947 to 1995. The profitable years from 1995 to 2000 were wiped out dramatically in the wake of 9-11. Overall, the airlines are more cyclical and sensitive to economic downturns than most other industries. Carriers will face continued problems as they try to adapt to the new realities of a market that has become more price sensitive than ever.

The clear message from this review is that leisure travel will grow in importance in the future. It's a more stable market, not dropping to the same degree as business travel during soft economic times, and recovering more quickly even if the economy is slow in turning around (see Chapter 2). Following the September 11th terrorist attacks in New York City and Washington, D.C., as was pointed out, the amount of travel increased rather than declined. The industry as a whole failed to benefit because the family car substituted for air travel as more vacationers avoided the hassles of negotiating new airport security procedures. *Major travel providers—airlines, hotels, and rental car companies—must learn how to make good money from leisure travelers if they want to prosper in the future.* The leisure traveler is king again! New strategies must take into account that the two markets now look more similar than in the past. Both groups are now very price sensitive and will continue to be in the future. The 80-20 rule no longer applies as it did in the past. It will be more like 65-35, or even more equal. A larger portion of airline revenue will continue to derive from those who fly more frequently (business travelers), but they will buy fewer high-priced tickets, regardless of the condition of the economy. Leisure travelers take about three-fourths of all trips (most of these by family auto) and fill half of airline seats, but their dominance will grow in the future. Airlines especially must change their formulas to get more profitable revenue from the leisure market because it will contribute a greater portion of their total revenue. Leisure travelers no longer can be looked on as a group that simply fills excess seats. Those carriers that fail to recognize this fact will face increasing difficulties over time. Hotels can adapt more easily. Historically they operated on a different formula—larger discounts to the corporate market and small reductions to vacationers. Thus, they have not conditioned leisure guests to expect deep discounts. And, operating mostly with a nonunion work force, they can restructure more easily, downsizing or changing job definitions when convenient. Rental car companies face the fewest difficulties. They quickly adjust fleet size to demand when needed, and corporate travelers already get bigger discounts through negotiated rates than the leisure market. No need for further discounts. Hail to the new conquering hero, leisure travelers! Their importance will be felt far and wide in the travel arena.

---

[3]Data provided by e-mail and telephone conversation with David Swierenga, Chief Economist, ATA, on November 25, 2002.

CHAPTER FOURTEEN

Ensuring a Future for Leisure Travel

Looking into the crystal ball for leisure travel points to good news and bad news, opportunities and problems. Assuming world stability, the good news is that travel will continue to grow at least until the middle of the third decade of this century, as discussed in Chapter 12. Travel has become a psychological necessity. And aging populations in developed countries will produce an increasing number of empty nesters who have the freedom and the financial equity that allows them to take trips when they want to throughout the world. The bad news is that the travel product continues to decline in the quality of the experience it provides to travelers, reducing travel demand to some degree. Other products now offer serious competition for household discretionary income. New cars cost less, on an inflationary adjusted basis, than they did a decade or two ago. These cars drive better, have more amenities, offer better styling, and provide better gas mileage than a decade ago. That's serious competition for discretionary dollars. Technology has also done the same for home and auto sound systems, home theaters, and much more. But, while all of this has happened, too many destinations around the world have become more crowded, more expensive, noisier, less friendly, and generally not as comfortable a place to be as in the past. As a result, leisure travel's potential for future growth has probably been reduced by about half, as mentioned earlier. Only the cruise lines seem to have it right. Each year new ships come online that offer new delights, cleanliness that can only be matched by top-end resorts, and food quality that can rival some of the best restaurants of Europe. And all of this at a comparative travel bargain, a surefire formula for future success.

THE NECESSITY OF GOOD TOURISM PLANNING

Land-based destinations will continue to dominate the travel scene for the foreseeable future. They offer unmatched variety, historic sites, significant cultural opportunities, a chance to buy unique goods, magnificent scenery, the opportunity to meet peoples of the world, and a broad variety of outdoor and indoor activities. But any destination that wants to continue on a strong growth curve must recognize that it faces a competitive marketplace. Travelers can choose from tens of thousands of places to visit. To stand out in the crowd, effective tourism planning must begin before the destination has declined to a point of no return. A poor reputation, along with an infrastructure that has deteriorated over the years, may present a situation from which recovery is almost impossible. My advice to those who control the future of each destination is to avoid letting that happen by concentrating early on effective tourism planning. Obviously, destinations differ in what they need to ensure a successful future. A newly developing area must not allow excessive commercial development to dominate the landscape. A major city like Paris or London should not allow the decline or destruction of areas and historic buildings that attract tourists. As mentioned, people turn up their noses at dirt—dirty streets and buildings, dirty hotel rooms, and litter and clutter everywhere. Destinations all face a similar task. They must determine what it is that makes them unique so that they can enhance those qualities over time. And they must decide which psychographic segment they will target and ensure that the place retains the qualities that this segment most desires.

PLANNING FOR A BETTER FUTURE

Over the years, I have developed a set of ten guiding principles to help tourism planners focus on the tasks that confront them—to benefit both tourists and local populations. These concepts apply to developing areas and long-established destinations, big cities and small. If these guidelines are followed, a destination has a better chance at growing its tourism base over the long term. The principles deserve repeating in an effort to remind tourism planners of the constant need to monitor and improve the quality of the product offered to the traveling public:

1. *Protect what is unique or natural* about an area for the benefit of local populations and tourists. Destinations that maintain a sense of uniqueness or preserve their natural beauty offer the best travel experiences and will prosper consistently over time. Local residents also will enjoy their communities to a greater degree. Good planning can help ensure that the twin goals are met.

2. *Reduce density*—don't overcrowd an area with too many hotels, low-grade tourist shops, fast food restaurants, game parlors, and so on.

Crowds and clutter diminish the travel experience greatly. This may seem counter to the needs of major cities, but the rule still applies. Those areas of a city that generate high volumes of tourists should convey a feeling that they have been protected from excessive commercial development and overcrowding.

3. *Enhance the feeling of seclusion and privacy* to contribute to the ambience that most travelers want (i.e., a retreat and escape from the cares of the world and the pressures they face back home). The more that a destination can create a feeling for each visitor that everyone has waited anxiously for his or her arrival, the greater the chance that the person will spread great word-of-mouth advertising and return for a future visit.

4. *Seek quality throughout.* Good planning will result in building codes that require new buildings to conform to the character and quality of a destination. Renovation of older buildings and new construction should fit the architectural style and ambience of the past. A destination that ensures high standards for new construction of hotels, office buildings, retail centers, and public spaces will attract a higher-quality audience that spends more, stays longer, returns more often, and spreads the good word about a marvelous vacation experience.

5. *Emphasize variety throughout.* The more activities available at a place, the greater the likelihood that something will be of interest to each visitor. The target market for that destination is larger. Sometimes new product must be developed, as museums, art galleries, festivals and events, and so on in order to ensure broad appeal across the psychographic spectrum.

6. *Restore the natural and historic to retain a sense of heritage, whenever possible.* Even new destinations need a sense of heritage. Restored historic sites bring back a clearer sense of past cultures, a quality that will increase in importance as the age of most travelers increases. Older folks have more interest in culture, the arts, and history. The crowds at the isolated city of Ephesus, Turkey after its great restoration effort attest to the importance of this task.

7. *Value local cultures and traditions.* Most travelers want uniqueness when they visit a destination. They especially enjoy the opportunity to experience a culture that differs from their own. Those differences can be dramatic, as in visiting places where an insular population does not speak the tourists' language, or subtle, as when someone from New York City travels to a Maine fishing village. Similarly, local populations feel better about themselves and support the efforts of tourism officials when they recognize that their traditions and customs are valued and appreciated by tourists and the planners in their communities. Parts of Hawaii and some islands in the South Pacific provide case examples on the wrong side of the equation. Unfettered

tourism development has obliterated local cultures and customs. From that point on, tourists often experience only staged presentations of previous local dances or practices, usually offered as entertainment rather than a true experience of original culture.

8. *Institute height limits on buildings* to protect vistas and scenic views. For developing areas with dramatic scenery, this rule generally means that buildings should be no taller than the trees, or about three stories. Far too many beach areas in the U.S., Mexico, and the Caribbean have huge commercial-sized hotels that block vista views for all but those in guest rooms facing the ocean or mountains. When that happens, natural beauty has disappeared. Major cities with a strong tourism base, like London, Paris, and New York, have a different challenge. Planning councils must focus on cleaning up run-down areas and preventing high-rise development that would change the character of areas with an historic or cultural heritage.

9. *Negotiate open areas* to provide the "breathing room" that enhances every section or area of a destination. Thus, newly developing locations should set aside open areas that protect natural habitat (as Sea Pines Plantation has) or allow room for public parks and picturesque areas, especially along beach front areas. Cities should concentrate on developing vista corridors where citizens and tourists can look down long streets toward more distant dramatic views. Many cities with tall buildings, like New York, now have space rights laws written into local building codes that require setbacks for all new buildings. These rights typically can be traded between development projects, but the effect is the same—to increase the feeling of openness and allow sunshine to penetrate down to street level. More openness can help remove a depressive feeling permeates too many center city areas.

10. *Gain community acceptance* so that local populations benefit the most from tourism development. Whether for tourism or in the course of normal growth and development, planning councils too often ignore the needs of their citizens. Because of conflicting demands and pressures in every community, especially those with an educated population, the task can sometimes be arduous and drawn out. In the end, however, it produces better planning and greater community acceptance. A good political leader knows how to listen carefully to the views of various factions and also when to cut off debate and move forward.

Collectively, the first letter of each primary word forms the acronym PRESERVING, to signify that the best progress is accomplished through concerted effort to develop a long-range plan that considers the interests of tourists and residents. *Preserve, protect,* and *plan*—these three P's will ensure a better future for leisure travel at all destinations. Preservation societies that designate historic buildings help to preserve the uniqueness of areas. Sometimes they can seem to get out of hand, as when a group wanted to protect a garish car wash of the 1950s in the San Fernando Valley section of Los Angeles during the late 1990s. However, most of their efforts have helped communities preserve traditions, interesting architecture, and the ambience of interesting or historic sections of communities.

Tourism, as the world's largest industry, continues to have the potential to provide multiple benefits to almost all involved. People will travel, even when local or national economies face mild recessions. Travelers help stimulate economies back to health by creating jobs in the communities where they live and the places they visit. Bringing people together of disparate backgrounds, tourists and locals, can also enhance efforts toward world peace as people from different cultures get to know each other and discover that, "After all, we're all pretty much alike." Effective planning that cleans up blighted areas and restores a sense of the community's past also makes it a better place to live. Travel can produce cross-cultural understanding that lasts a lifetime. Few industries can offer as many benefits, with so few drawbacks if properly managed, as tourism. But we must take steps to reduce travel's negative impact and emphasize its positive side. Hundreds of millions of more people will be traveling in the 21st century. If we don't take proper steps now to control how tourism unfolds, we will suffer the consequences of a good industry run amok. Awareness of the problems and the need for solutions will, it is hoped, lead to more positive actions over the long term.

Index